UK Biodiversity Group

Action Plan Volume 2

Vertebrates
Vascular plants

English Nature

THE RT HON JOHN PRESCOTT MP
DEPUTY PRIME MINISTER AND SECRETARY OF STATE FOR THE
ENVIRONMENT, TRANSPORT AND THE REGIONS

Dear Deputy Prime Minister,

BIODIVERSITY ACTION PLANS

I am writing to you in my capacity as Chairman of the United Kingdom Biodiversity Group about the latest group of biodiversity action plans for vertebrates and flowering plants.

The 1994 United Kingdom Biodiversity Action Plan set out a strategy for implementing the Convention on Biological Diversity which was signed by the United Kingdom at the Rio Earth Summit in 1992.

The present Government has endorsed the plan and the means for giving effect to it, under the supervision of the United Kingdom Biodiversity Group, comprising representatives of, amongst others, Government Departments, statutory agencies, non governmental organisations, local authorities and the private sector.

The plan emphasises policy integration and partnership between interested organisations. These interests were brought together in a steering group which reported in 1995 and identified the need for some 400 action plans for the United Kingdom's most threatened species and some 40 habitat plans for our most vulnerable areas.

Published with the 1995 report were 116 species and 14 habitat action plans.

This letter covers the second set of action plans - for 56 species. The plans represent the culmination of many months of work involving Government departments and their scientists, agencies, voluntary conservation groups, owners or managers of land and academic bodies to set challenging but achievable targets to conserve these species.

As with the first set of species and habitat action plans, each plan will have a lead partner to co-ordinate action.

Each plan is costed and we would hope, as with the already published plans, to be able to make substantial progress towards implementation by redirecting existing resources as well as by attracting some new funding. We are beginning to have some success in securing private sector support through encouraging companies to champion individual species, though further progress is needed here.

Over the remainder of 1998 further groups of action plans will be published so that by early next year we will have completed our objective of publishing action plans for some 400 priority species and around 40 key habitats. These will go a long way towards fulfilling the United Kingdom's domestic objectives under the Biodiversity Convention. Thereafter, the UK Biodiversity Group, supported by country groups in England, Scotland, Wales and Northern Ireland, will be focusing increasingly on implementation of the action plans. In many cases this will involve advising you and your ministerial colleagues on the policy changes which achievement of the plans requires. The challenge for lead partners to meet action plan targets should not be underestimated and will require commitment from all sectors, including a continuation of the strong support the Government is giving to this process.

On behalf of the United Kingdom Biodiversity Group, I commend the action plans set out in this attached report.

Yours Sincerely,

John Plowman.

John Plowman

Contents   Page

1. Introduction

1.1 This report by the UK Biodiversity Group builds on the 1995 UK Biodiversity Steering Group Report. It contains 56 action plans for priority vertebrate and vascular plants species. The format of these new plans follows closely the example set in the Steering Group Report. Each plan has been developed to set specific, measurable, achievable, realistic and time-bounded targets for the species concerned. Each plan has been costed and then finalised by consensus across the full range of statutory and non-statutory organisations represented on the UK Biodiversity Group.

1.2 To aid delivery of these new action plans, this report includes with each species action plan a UK distribution map so that both national organisations and local biodiversity initiatives are clear about the distribution of each species in relation to their operations.

1.3 To enable national level work to commence immediately, Lead Partners and Contact Points have been agreed by the UK Biodiversity Group to coordinate the implementation of each of the 56 species action plans (Lead Partners and Contact Points are listed at Annex 1).

1.4 The process of action planning and plan implementation is designed to focus conservation efforts towards the highest UK priorities. The number of species for which action plans have been/are being prepared as a proportion of the total number of UK species within each taxonomic group is set out in Table 1. This focus on priorities is essential to enable real progress to be made, however, work undertaken on these species and associated habitats will also benefit a much greater number of related species.

2. Progress with action plan implementation

2.1 Following the publication of the Steering Group Report, there has been much new action undertaken at both national and local levels to conserve the UK's biodiversity. Specialist steering groups have coordinated national work towards published habitat and species targets, whilst over 100 local biodiversity initiatives have been started. Work at all levels has seen much improved cooperation and communication between individuals and organisations, led by the example of collective preparation of national action plans and the voluntary commitment to action that underpins them. Implementation of these 56 new action plans should follow the practice that has been applied earlier.

2.2 The UK Biodiversity Information Group has been developing proposals, set out in the Steering Group Report, for a National Biodiversity Network, an electronically linked series of data sets including local record centre data and national recording scheme data (BRC, BTO, CS2000). Proposals for funding the development of this network are being considered by the National Heritage Lottery Fund.

2.3 A key area of future work relates to how we report progress towards species and habitat targets, and use these reports to direct effort and resources to where they are most needed. This reporting process will build links between country biodiversity groups, national level habitat and species steering groups, and local biodiversity groups, bringing greater coherence and synergy to our efforts. A pilot reporting process underwent trials in 1997/8, and will be modified and finalised over the next six months. The aim is for a full reporting process to be undertaken in 1999 in order to gather information about progress with action plan implementation. This will contribute to work on the Biodiversity Millennium Report.

3. Revision of species lists

3.1   The UK Steering Group Report included three lists of species, which became widely known as the 'short', 'middle' and 'long' lists. This terminology led to some confusion about the relative priority of species on the three lists and the assumption that the action planning process would address progressively all the listed species. The intention was always that action plans would be prepared for all 'short' and 'middle' list species, but not the species on the published 'long' list.

3.2   The lists published in the Steering Group Report result from the knowledge available in the Autumn of 1995. As more information becomes available, the species meeting qualification criteria continue to change. For this reason the UK Biodiversity Group commissioned a review of qualifying species in 1997, prior to undertaking further action plan preparation. This review of species qualifying against 'short/middle' list criteria resulted in about 100 further species being identified. In addition a few species were found to no longer meet qualification criteria.

3.3   For these reasons, the UK Biodiversity Group agreed to revise the list structure and terminology to ensure clarity, and to publish a revised list of species for which action plans have been or are being prepared. The revision takes the following form:

    3.3.1   all species which meet the published 'long' list criteria are classified as **'Species of Conservation Concern'**

    3.3.2   from within the list of Species of Conservation Concern, all species which qualify under the published 'short' and 'middle' list criteria[1] are classified as **'Priority Species'**

3.4   The UK Biodiversity Group has agreed that the following principles apply to each priority species:

    3.4.1   each species should be the subject of targeted action

    3.4.2   action for any species should be framed within either a dedicated action plan or a conservation statement

    3.4.3   species which have not been recorded for the last 10 years should have a conservation statement, making search for that species the key requirement. If found as a result of this search, the species will then be subject to an action plan

    3.3.4   species whose conservation needs may be delivered through existing habitat or species action plans, or those in preparation, should have a conservation statement, making the link to the related plan and setting biological targets for that species

3.5   The status of species will continue to change as a result of natural processes, improvements to our information base and the impact of conservation efforts directed towards priority species. We need to retain a flexibility to adjust our focus to meet these changes in priority. The new reporting process will be the key mechanism to enable such judgements and adjustments to be made.

---

[1] Qualification criteria for the list of Species of Conservation Concern, and for the list of Priority Species are at Annex 2.

4. Timetable for future publications

4.1 This report represents one step towards completion of the action planning process. A further 250 species action plans and 25 habitat action plans are currently being prepared, and will be finalised and published over the next 12 months. These plans will be made available in a similar form to this volume and distributed through the DETR Biodiversity Secretariat in Bristol.

4.2 The action planning process needs to be recognised as an essential first step in the conservation of the UK's biodiversity. Action plans provide the means of setting out a robust scientific case for conservation action and building consensus between the key bodies involved about the best means of achieving biological objectives. However, action planning is not an end in itself; the value of this work lies in providing a clear focus and platform for subsequent action.

Table 1. Number and proportion of terrestrial and freshwater species in the UK (excluding bacteria, viruses and algae) with Species Action Plans

Source - Biodiversity: The UK Action Plan/JNCC Annual Report '96/'97

Taxonomic group	No. of species in UK	No. of SAPs (published 1995)	No. of SAPs (second round)	Total SAPs	% of species with SAPs
Flowering plants and stoneworts	1,500	21	46	67	4.47
Lichens	1,500	7	25	32	2.13
Bryophytes	1,000	11	33	44	4.40
Ferns	80	2	2	4	5.00
Fungi	15,000	4	9	13	0.09
Insects	22,500	32	131	163	0.72
Arthropods other than insects	3,500	0	5	5	0.14
Non-arthropod invertebrates	4,000	12	3	15	0.38
Freshwater fish	38	4	1	5	13.16
Amphibians	6	2	1	3	50.00
Reptiles	6	1	0	1	16.67
Birds	390	9	17	26	6.67
Mammals	48	8	3	11	22.92
Total	**49,568**	**113**	**276**	**389**	**0.78**

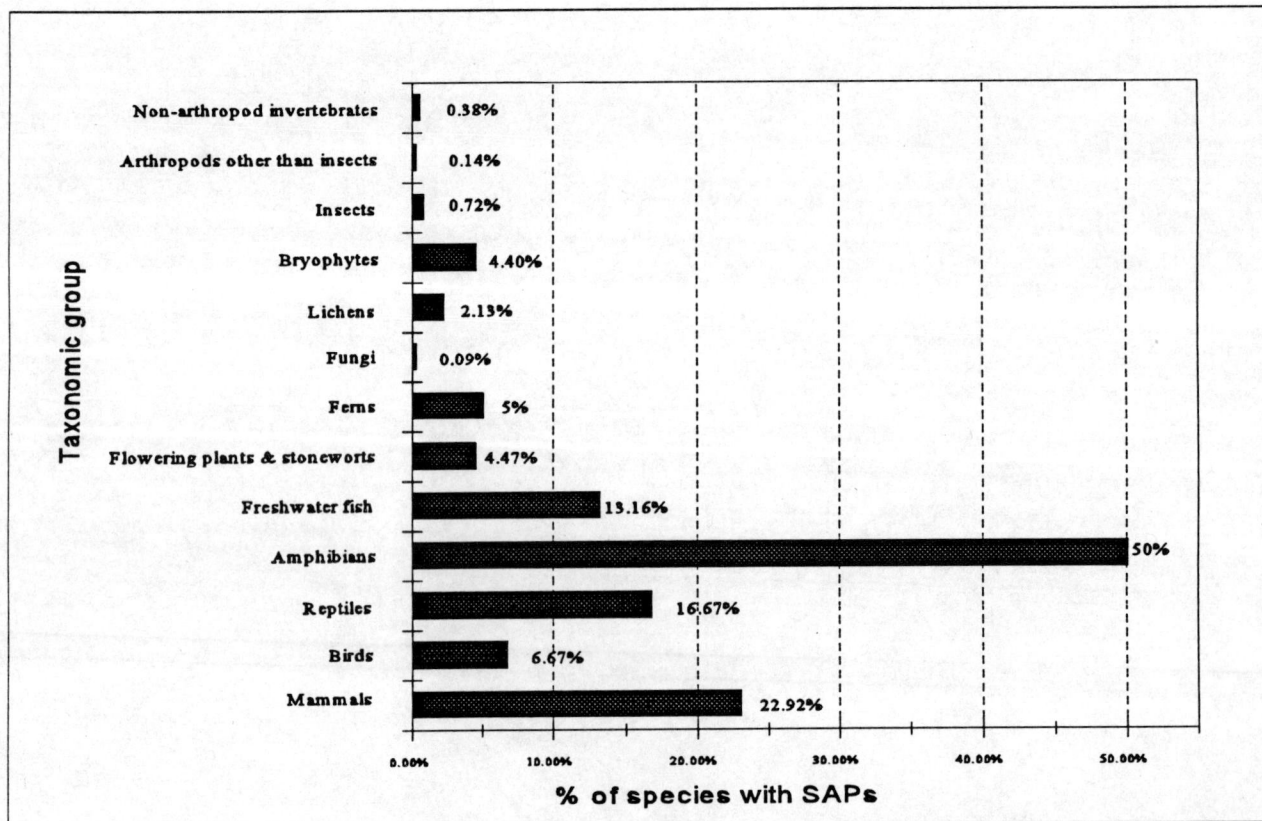

Annex 1.   Contact points and lead partners

	Contact Point	Lead Partner
Mammals		
Barbastelle bat *Barbastella barbastellus*	English Nature	Bat Conservation Trust
Bechstein's bat *Myotis bechsteinii*	English Nature	Bat Conservation Trust
lesser horseshoe bat *Rhinolophus hipposideros*	Countryside Council for Wales	Bat Conservation Trust
Birds		
marsh warbler *Acrocephalus palustris*	Environment Agency	Royal Society for the Protection of Birds/ Wildlife Trusts
nightjar *Caprimulgus europaeus*	Forestry Commission	Royal Society for the Protection of Birds
linnet *Carduelis cannabina*	Ministry of Agriculture Fisheries and Food	Royal Society for the Protection of Birds
cirl bunting *Emberiza cirlus*	Ministry of Agriculture Fisheries and Food	Royal Society for the Protection of Birds/ English Nature
reed bunting *Emberiza schoeniclus*	English Nature	Royal Society for the Protection of Birds
wryneck *Jynx torquilla*	Scottish Natural Heritage	Royal Society for the Protection of Birds
red-backed shrike *Lanius collurio*	Scottish Natural Heritage/ English Nature	Royal Society for the Protection of Birds
woodlark *Lullula arborea*	Forestry Commission	Royal Society for the Protection of Birds
common scoter *Melanitta nigra*	Scottish Natural Heritage	Royal Society for the Protection of Birds/Wildfowl and Wetlands Trust
corn bunting *Miliaria calandra*	Ministry of Agriculture Fisheries and Food	Royal Society for the Protection of Birds/ English Nature
spotted flycatcher *Muscicapa striata*	English Nature/Countryside Council for Wales	Royal Society for the Protection of Birds
tree sparrow *Passer montanus*	Ministry of Agriculture Fisheries and Food	Royal Society for the Protection of Birds
red-necked phalarope *Phalaropus lobatus*	Scottish Natural Heritage	Royal Society for the Protection of Birds
bullfinch *Pyrrhula pyrrhula*	Ministry of Agriculture Fisheries and Food	Royal Society for the Protection of Birds
roseate tern *Sterna dougallii*	English Nature/ Department of the Environment (Northern Ireland) -Environment and Heritage Service	Royal Society for the Protection of Birds
turtle dove *Streptopelia turtur*	Ministry of Agriculture Fisheries and Food	Royal Society for the Protection of Birds/ English Nature
Amphibian		
pool frog *Rana lessonae*	English Nature	English Nature

	Contact Point	Lead Partner
Vascular Plants		
an alchemilla *Alchemilla minima*	English Nature	English Nature
tower mustard *Arabis glabra*	English Nature	Plantlife
wild asparagus *Asparagus officianalis* ssp. prostratus	Countryside Council for Wales	The National Trust
interrupted brome *Bromus interruptus*	English Nature	Royal Botanic Garden Kew
scottish small-reed *Calamagrostis scotica*	Scottish Natural Heritage	Royal Botanic Garden Edinburgh
prickly sedge *Carex muricata ssp muricata*	English Nature	English Nature
true fox sedge *Carex vulpina*	English Nature	English Nature
cornflower *Centaurea cyanus*	Ministry of Agriculture Fisheries and Food	Plantlife
Shetland mouse-ear *Cerastium nigrescens*	Scottish Natural Heritage	Scottish Natural Heritage
stinking hawk's-beard *Crepis foetida*	English Nature	Royal Society for the Protection of Birds
deptford pink *Dianthus armeria*	English Nature/ Countryside Council for Wales	Plantlife
red-tipped cudweed *Filago lutescens*	Ministry of Agriculture Fisheries and Food	Plantlife/ English Nature
broad-leaved cudweed *Filago pyramidata*	Ministry of Agriculture Fisheries and Food	Plantlife/ English Nature
purple ramping-fumitory *Fumaria purpurea*	Ministry of Agriculture Fisheries and Food	English Nature
red hemp-nettle *Galeopsis angustifolia*	Ministry of Agriculture Fisheries and Food	Plantlife
corn cleavers *Galium tricornutum*	Ministry of Agriculture Fisheries and Food	Plantlife
dune gentian *Gentianella uliginosa*	Countryside Council for Wales	Countryside Council for Wales
hawkweeds (Shetland spp only) *Hieracium Sect.Alpestria*	Scottish Natural Heritage	Shetland Amenity Trust
pygmy rush *Juncus pygmaeus*	English Nature	English Nature
cut-grass *Leersia oryzoides*	English Nature	Environment Agency
sea lavender *Limonium (endemic taxa)*	Countryside Council for Wales/ English Nature	The National Trust/Botanical Society of the British Isles
marsh clubmoss *Lycopodiella inundata*	Countryside Council for Wales/ English Nature	Plantlife
pennyroyal *Mentha pulegium*	English Nature	English Nature
pillwort *Pilularia globulifera*	Scottish Natural Heritage	Countryside Council for Wales/ Plantlife
grass-wrack pondweed *Potamogeton compressus*	English Nature	British Waterways Board

	Contact Point	Lead Partner
woolly willow *Salix lanata*	Scottish Natural Heritage	National Trust for Scotland
shepherd's needle *Scandix pecten-veneris*	Ministry of Agriculture Fisheries and Food	Plantlife
triangular club-rush *Schoenoplectus triqueter*	English Nature	Environment Agency
perennial knawel *Scleranthus perennis* ssp *prostratus*	English Nature	Wildlife Trusts
small-flowerered catchfly *Silene gallica*	Ministry of Agriculture Fisheries and Food	Plantlife
greater water-parsnip *Sium latifolium*	English Nature	Environment Agency
Ley's whitebeam *Sorbus leyana*	Countryside Council for Wales	National Botanic Garden of Wales
Cotswold pennycress *Thlaspi perfoliatum*	English Nature	Plantlife
spreading hedge-parsley *Torilis arvensis*	Ministry of Agriculture Fisheries and Food	Plantlife
broad-fruited corn-salad *Valerianella rimosa*	Ministry of Agriculture Fisheries and Food	Plantlife
oblong woodsia *Woodsia ilvensis*	Scottish Natural Heritage	Royal Botanic Garden Edinburgh

Annex 2. Species selection criteria

Criteria for selecting 'species of conservation concern'

Species which qualify for one or more of the following categories should be considered as species of conservation concern:

- threatened endemic and other globally threatened species

- species where the UK has more that 25% of the world or appropriate biogeographical population

- species where numbers or range have declined by more than 25% in the last 25 years

- in some instances where the species is found in fewer than 15 ten km squares in the UK

- species which are listed in the EU Birds or Habitats Directives, the Bern, Bonn or CITES Conventions, or under the Wildlife and Countryside Act 1981 and the Wildlife Order (Northern Ireland) 1985

Criteria for selecting 'priority species'

Species which qualify for one or more of the following categories should be considered as priority species:

- species which are globally threatened

- species which are rapidly declining in the UK, ie by more than 50% in the last 25 years

Annex 3 Priority species list

List 1. Priority species with existing, or proposed for, action plan

MAMMAL	*Arvicola terrestris*	water vole
MAMMAL	*Barbastella barbastellus*	barbastelle
MAMMAL	*Lepus europaeus*	brown hare
MAMMAL	*Lutra lutra*	european otter
MAMMAL	*Muscardinus avellanarius*	dormouse
MAMMAL	*Myotis bechsteinii*	Bechstein's bat
MAMMAL	*Myotis myotis*	greater mouse-eared bat
MAMMAL	*Phocoena phocoena*	harbour porpoise
MAMMAL	*Pipistrellus pipistrellus*	pipistrelle bat
MAMMAL	*Rhinolophus ferrumequinum*	greater horseshoe bat
MAMMAL	*Rhinolophus hipposideros*	lesser horseshoe bat
MAMMAL	*Sciurus vulgaris*	red squirrel
MAMMAL	Single grouped plan for baleen whales	
MAMMAL	Single grouped plan for dolphins	
MAMMAL	Single grouped plan for toothed whales	
BIRD	*Acrocephalus paludicola*	aquatic warbler
BIRD	*Acrocephalus palustris*	marsh warbler
BIRD	*Alauda arvensis*	skylark
BIRD	*Botaurus stellaris*	bittern
BIRD	*Burhinus oedicnemus*	stone curlew
BIRD	*Caprimulgus europaeus*	nightjar
BIRD	*Carduelis cannabina*	linnet
BIRD	*Crex crex*	corncrake
BIRD	*Emberiza cirlus*	cirl bunting
BIRD	*Emberiza schoeniclus*	reed bunting
BIRD	*Jynx torquilla*	wryneck
BIRD	*Lanius collurio*	red-backed shrike
BIRD	*Loxia scotica*	scottish crossbill
BIRD	*Lullula arborea*	woodlark
BIRD	*Melanitta nigra*	common scoter
BIRD	*Miliaria calandra*	corn bunting
BIRD	*Muscicapa striata*	spotted flycatcher
BIRD	*Passer montanus*	tree sparrow
BIRD	*Perdix perdix*	grey partridge
BIRD	*Phalaropus lobatus*	red-necked phalarope
BIRD	*Pyrrhula pyrrhula*	bullfinch

BIRD	*Sterna dougallii*	roseate tern
BIRD	*Streptopelia turtur*	turtle dove
BIRD	*Tetrao tetrix*	black grouse
BIRD	*Tetrao urogallus*	capercaillie
BIRD	*Turdus philomelos*	song thrush
AMPHIBIAN	*Bufo calamita*	natterjack toad
AMPHIBIAN	*Rana lessonae*	pool frog
AMPHIBIAN	*Triturus cristatus*	great crested newt
REPTILE	*Lacerta agilis*	sand lizard
REPTILE	Single grouped plan for turtles	
FISH	*Alosa alosa*	allis shad
FISH	*Alosa fallax*	twaite shad
FISH	*Cetorhinus maximus*	basking shark
FISH	*Coregonus albula*	vendace
FISH	*Coregonus autumnalis*	pollan
FISH	*Lota lota*	burbot
FISH	*Raja batis*	common skate
FISH	Single grouped plan for selected commercial fish species	
FISH	Single grouped plan for selected deep water fish species	
ANT	*Anergates atratulus*	dark guest ant
ANT	*Formica aquilonia*	scottish wood ant
ANT	*Formica exsecta*	narrow-headed ant
ANT	*Formica nigricans*	black-backed meadow ant
ANT	*Formica rufa*	red wood ant
ANT	*Formica rufibarbis*	red-barbed ant
ANT	*Formica transkaucasica*	bog ant
ANT	*Formicoxenus nitidulus*	shining guest ant
BEE	*Andrena ferox*	mining bee
BEE	*Andrena gravida*	banded mining bee
BEE	*Andrena lathyri*	a mining bee
BEE	*Bombus distinguendus*	great yellow bumble bee
BEE	*Bombus humilis*	brown-banded carder bee
BEE	*Bombus ruderatus*	large garden bumble bee
BEE	*Bombus subterraneus*	short haired bumble bee
BEE	*Bombus sylvarum*	shrill carder bee
BEE	*Colletes floralis*	northern colletes
BEE	*Lasioglossum angusticeps*	a mining bee
BEE	*Nomada armata*	a nomad bee

BEE	*Nomada errans*	a nomad bee
BEE	*Nomada xanthosticta*	a nomad bee
BEE	*Osmia inermis*	a mason bee
BEE	*Osmia parietina*	a mason bee
BEE	*Osmia uncinata*	a mason bee
BEE	*Osmia xanthomelana*	a mason bee
BEETLE	*Agabus brunneus*	a water beetle
BEETLE	*Amara famelica*	a ground beetle
BEETLE	*Anisodactylus poeciloides*	a ground beetle
BEETLE	*Anostirus castaneus*	a click beetle
BEETLE	*Aphodius niger*	a scarab beetle
BEETLE	*Badister anomalus*	a ground beetle
BEETLE	*Bembidion argenteolum*	a ground beetle
BEETLE	*Bidessus minutissimus*	a water beetle
BEETLE	*Bidessus unistriatus*	a water beetle
BEETLE	*Byctiscus populi*	a leaf-rolling weevil
BEETLE	*Carabus intricatus*	blue ground beetle
BEETLE	*Cathormiocerus britannicus*	a weevil
BEETLE	*Chrysolina cerealis*	rainbow leaf beetle
BEETLE	*Cicindela germanica*	a tiger beetle
BEETLE	*Cicindela hybrida*	a ground beetle
BEETLE	*Cicindela sylvatica*	heath tiger beetle
BEETLE	*Cryptocephalus coryli*	a leaf beetle
BEETLE	*Cryptocephalus exiguus*	a leaf beetle
BEETLE	*Cryptocephalus nitidulus*	a leaf beetle
BEETLE	*Cryptocephalus primarius*	a leaf beetle
BEETLE	*Cryptocephalus sexpunctatus*	a leaf beetle
BEETLE	*Curimopsis nigrita*	mire pill beetle
BEETLE	*Donacia aquatica*	a reed beetle
BEETLE	*Donacia bicolora*	a reed beetle
BEETLE	*Dyschirius angustatus*	a ground beetle
BEETLE	*Ernoporus tiliae*	a bark beetle
BEETLE	*Gastrallus immarginatus*	a beetle
BEETLE	*Gnorimus nobilis*	a chafer
BEETLE	*Graphoderus zonatus*	spangled water beetle
BEETLE	*Harpalus dimidiatus*	a ground beetle
BEETLE	*Harpalus froelichi*	a ground beetle
BEETLE	*Harpalus obscurus*	a ground beetle
BEETLE	*Helophorus laticollis*	a water beetle

BEETLE	*Hydrochara caraboides*	lesser silver water beetle
BEETLE	*Hydroporus cantabricus*	a water beetle
BEETLE	*Hydroporus rufifrons*	a water beetle
BEETLE	*Laccophilus obsoletus*	a water beetle
BEETLE	*Limoniscus violaceus*	violet click beetle
BEETLE	*Lucanus cervus*	stag beetle
BEETLE	*Malachius aeneus*	scarlet malachite beetle
BEETLE	*Melanapion minimum*	a weevil
BEETLE	*Melanotus punctolineatus*	a click beetle
BEETLE	*Oberea oculata*	a longhorn beetle
BEETLE	*Pachytychius haematocephalus*	a weevil
BEETLE	*Panagaeus cruxmajor*	a ground beetle
BEETLE	*Paracymus aeneus*	a water beetle
BEETLE	*Procas granulicollis*	a weevil
BEETLE	*Psylliodes sophiae*	flixweed flea beetle
BEETLE	*Pterostichus aterrimus*	a ground beetle
BEETLE	*Pterostichus kugelanni*	a ground beetle
BEETLE	*Rhynchaenus testaceus*	a jumping weevil
BEETLE	Single grouped plan for *Bembidion testaceum, Lionychus quadrillium, Hydrochus nitidicollis, Meotica anglica, Perileptus areolatus* and *Thinobius newberyi*	beetles
BEETLE	Single grouped plan for *Harpalus cordatus* and *Harpalus parallelus*	ground beetles
BEETLE	*Stenus palposus*	a rove beetle
BEETLE	*Synaptus filiformis*	a click beetle
BEETLE	*Tachys edmondsi*	a ground beetle
BUTTERFLY	*Argynnis adippe*	high brown fritillary
BUTTERFLY	*Aricia artaxerxes*	northern brown argus
BUTTERFLY	*Boloria euphrosyne*	pearl-bordered fritillary
BUTTERFLY	*Carterocephalus palaemon*	chequered skipper
BUTTERFLY	*Eurodryas aurinia*	marsh fritillary
BUTTERFLY	*Hesperia comma*	silver-spotted skipper
BUTTERFLY	*Lycaena dispar*	large copper butterfly
BUTTERFLY	*Lysandra bellargus*	adonis blue
BUTTERFLY	*Maculinea arion*	large blue butterfly
BUTTERFLY	*Mellicta athalia*	heath fritillary
BUTTERFLY	*Plebejus argus*	silver-studded blue
CORAL	*Leptopsammia pruvoti*	cup coral
CRICKET/GRASSHOPPER	*Decticus verrucivorus*	wart-biter grasshopper
CRICKET/GRASSHOPPER	*Gryllotalpa gryllotalpa*	mole cricket

CRICKET/GRASSHOPPER	*Gryllus campestris*	field cricket
CRICKET/GRASSHOPPER	*Stethophyma grossum*	large marsh grasshopper
CRUSTACEAN	*Austropotamobius pallipes*	freshwater white-clawed crayfish
CRUSTACEAN	*Triops cancriformis*	freshwater tadpole shrimp
DAMSEL/DRAGONFLY	*Coenagrion mercuriale*	southern damselfly
FLY	*Asilus crabroniformis*	a robber fly
FLY	*Blera fallax*	a hoverfly
FLY	*Bombylius discolor*	a beefly
FLY	*Bombylius minor*	a beefly
FLY	*Callicera spinolae*	a hoverfly
FLY	*Chrysotoxum octomaculatum*	a hoverfly
FLY	*Doros conopseus*	a hoverfly
FLY	*Dorycera graminum*	a large otitid
FLY	*Eristalis cryptarum*	a hoverfly
FLY	*Hammerschmidtia ferruginea*	a hoverfly
FLY	*Lipsothrix ecucullata*	a cranefly
FLY	*Lipsothrix errans*	a cranefly
FLY	*Lipsothrix nervosa*	a cranefly
FLY	*Lipsothrix nigristigma*	a cranefly
FLY	*Myolepta potens*	a hoverfly
FLY	*Odontomyia hydroleon*	a soldier fly
FLY	*Psilocephala rustica*	a stiletto fly
FLY	*Rhabdomastix hilaris*	a cranefly
FLY	*Thereva lunulata*	a stiletto fly
FLY	*Thyridanthrax fenestratus*	a beefly
FLY	*Tipula serrulifera*	a cranefly
MOLLUSC	*Anisus vorticulus*	a snail
MOLLUSC	*Atrina fragilis*	fan mussel
MOLLUSC	*Catinella arenaria*	sandbowl snail
MOLLUSC	*Margaritifera margaritifera*	a freshwater pearl mussel
MOLLUSC	*Myxas glutinosa*	glutinous snail
MOLLUSC	*Ostrea edulis*	native oyster
MOLLUSC	*Pisidium tenuilineatum*	a freshwater bivalve
MOLLUSC	*Pseudanodonta complanata*	a freshwater mussel
MOLLUSC	*Segmentina nitida*	a freshwater snail
MOLLUSC	*Thyasira gouldi*	northern hatchet shell
MOLLUSC	*Vertigo angustior*	a snail
MOLLUSC	*Vertigo genesii*	a snail

MOLLUSC	*Vertigo geyeri*	a snail
MOLLUSC	*Vertigo moulinsiana*	a snail
MOTH	*Acosmetia caliginosa*	reddish buff
MOTH	*Aspitates gilvaria gilvaria*	straw belle
MOTH	*Athetis pallustris*	marsh
MOTH	*Bembecia chrysidiformis*	fiery clearwing
MOTH	*Calophasia lunula*	toadflax brocade
MOTH	*Catocala promissa*	light crimson underwing
MOTH	*Catocala sponsa*	dark crimson underwing
MOTH	*Coleophora tricolor*	a case-bearing moth
MOTH	*Coscinia cribraria bivittata*	speckled footman
MOTH	*Cosmia diffinis*	white-spotted pinion
MOTH	*Cucullia lychnitis*	striped lychnis
MOTH	*Cyclophora pendularia*	dingy mocha
MOTH	*Dicycla oo*	heart
MOTH	*Epione paralellaria*	dark bordered beauty
MOTH	*Eustroma reticulata*	netted carpet
MOTH	*Hadena albimacula*	white spot
MOTH	*Heliophobus reticulata*	bordered gothic
MOTH	*Hemaris tityus*	narrow-bordered bee hawk
MOTH	*Hydraecia osseola hucherardi*	marsh mallow
MOTH	*Hydrelia sylvata*	waved carpet
MOTH	*Hypena rostralis*	buttoned snout
MOTH	*Idaea dilutaria*	silky wave
MOTH	*Idaea ochrata cantiata*	bright wave
MOTH	*Jodia croceago*	orange upperwing
MOTH	*Lycia zonaria britannica*	belted beauty
MOTH	*Lygephila craccae*	scarce blackneck
MOTH	*Minoa murinata*	drab looper
MOTH	*Moma alpium*	scarce Merveille du Jour
MOTH	*Mythimna turca*	double line
MOTH	*Noctua orbona*	lunar yellow underwing
MOTH	*Oria musculosa*	brighton wainscot
MOTH	*Paracolax derivalis*	clay fan-foot
MOTH	*Paradiarsia sobrina*	cousin German
MOTH	*Pareulype berberata*	barberry carpet
MOTH	*Pechipogon strigilata*	common fan-foot
MOTH	*Phyllodesma ilicifolia*	small lappet
MOTH	*Polia bombycina*	pale shining brown

MOTH	*Polymixis xanthomista*	black-banded
MOTH	*Rheumaptera hastata*	argent and sable
MOTH	*Schrankia taenialis*	white-line snout
MOTH	*Semiothisa carbonaria*	netted mountain
MOTH	*Siona lineata*	black-veined
MOTH	*Trichopteryx polycommata*	barred toothed stripe
MOTH	*Trisateles emortualis*	olive crescent
MOTH	*Tyta luctuosa*	four-spotted
MOTH	*Xestia alpicola alpina*	northern dart
MOTH	*Xestia ashworthii*	Ashworth's rustic
MOTH	*Xestia rhomboidea*	square-spotted clay
MOTH	*Xylena exsoleta*	sword grass
MOTH	*Zygaena loti scotica*	slender Scotch burnet
MOTH	*Zygaena viciae argyllensis*	New Forest burnet moth
SEA ANEMONE GROUP	*Amphianthus dohrnii*	sea fan anemone
SEA ANEMONE GROUP	*Edwardsia ivelli*	Ivell's sea anemone
SEA ANEMONE GROUP	*Eunicella verrucosa*	broad sea fan
SEA ANEMONE GROUP	*Nematostella vectensis*	starlet sea anemone
SEA MAT	*Lophopus crystallinus*	a freshwater bryozoan
SPIDER	*Clubiona rosserae*	a spider
SPIDER	*Clubiona subsultans*	a spider
SPIDER	*Dolomedes plantarius*	fen raft spider
SPIDER	*Eresus cinnaberinus*	ladybird spider
SPIDER	*Uloborus walckenaerius*	a spider
STONE FLY	*Brachyptera putata*	a stonefly
TRUE BUG	*Cicadetta montana*	New Forest cicada
TRUE BUG	*Hydrometra gracilenta*	the lesser water measurer
WASP	*Cerceris quadricincta*	a solitary wasp
WASP	*Cerceris quinquefasciata*	a solitary wasp
WASP	*Chrysis fulgida*	a ruby-tailed wasp
WASP	*Chrysura hirsuta*	a ruby-tailed wasp
WASP	*Evagetes pectinipes*	a spider wasp
WASP	*Homonotus sanguinolentus*	a spider wasp
WASP	*Pseudepipona herrichii*	a mason wasp
WORM	*Hirudo medicinalis*	medicinal leech
WORM	Prostoma jenningsi	a nemertean
ALGA	Anotrichium barbatum	red alga
FUNGUS	Armillaria ectypa	an agaric
FUNGUS	*Battarraea phalloides*	a phalloid

23

FUNGUS	*Boletus regius*	the royal bolete
FUNGUS	*Boletus satanas*	devil's bolete
FUNGUS	*Buglossoporus pulvinus*	oak polypore
FUNGUS	*Hericium erinaceum*	hedgehog fungus
FUNGUS	*Hygrocybe calyptraeformis*	waxcap
FUNGUS	*Hygrocybe spadicea*	a wax cap
FUNGUS	*Hypocreopsis rhododendri*	an ascomycete
FUNGUS	*Microglossum olivaceum*	an earth tongue
FUNGUS	*Poronia punctata*	nail fungus
FUNGUS	Single grouped plan for *Bankera fuligineoalba, Hydnellum aurantiacum, Hydnellum caeruleum, Hydnellum concrescens, Hydnellum ferrugineum, Hydnellum mirabile, Hydnellum peckii, Hydnellum scrobiculatum, Hydnellum spongiosipes, Phellodon confluens, Phellodon melaleucus, Phellodon tomentosus, Sarcodon fuligineo-violaceus, Sarcodon imbricatus* and *Sarcodon scabrosus*	fungi
FUNGUS	*Tulostoma niveum*	a stalked puffball
LICHEN	*Alectoria ochroleuca*	alpine sulphur-tresses
LICHEN	*Arthothelium dictyosporum*	a lichen
LICHEN	*Arthothelium macounii*	a lichen
LICHEN	*Bacidia incompta*	a lichen
LICHEN	*Belonia calcicola*	a lichen
LICHEN	*Biatoridium monasteriense*	a lichen
LICHEN	*Bryoria smithii*	a lichen
LICHEN	*Buellia asterella*	starry Breck-lichen
LICHEN	*Calicium corynellum*	a lichen
LICHEN	*Caloplaca aractina*	a lichen
LICHEN	*Caloplaca luteoalba*	orange-fruited elm-lichen
LICHEN	*Catapyrenium psoromoides*	tree catapyrenium
LICHEN	*Catillaria aphana*	a lichen
LICHEN	*Catillaria subviridis*	a lichen
LICHEN	*Cladonia botrytes*	a lichen
LICHEN	*Cladonia mediterranea*	a lichen
LICHEN	*Cladonia peziziformis*	a lichen
LICHEN	*Collema dichotomum*	river jelly lichen
LICHEN	*Enterographa elaborata*	a lichen
LICHEN	*Enterographa sorediata*	a lichen
LICHEN	*Graphina pauciloculata*	a lichen
LICHEN	*Gyalecta ulmi*	Elm gyalecta
LICHEN	*Gyalideopsis scotica*	a lichen
LICHEN	*Halecania rhypodiza*	a lichen

LICHEN	*Heterodermia leucomelos*	ciliate strap-lichen
LICHEN	*Lecanactis hemisphaerica*	churchyard lecanactis
LICHEN	*Opegrapha fumosa*	a lichen
LICHEN	*Opegrapha paraxanthodes*	a lichen
LICHEN	*Peltigera lepidophora*	ear-lobed dog-lichen
LICHEN	*Pseudocyphellaria aurata*	a lichen
LICHEN	*Pseudocyphellaria norvegica*	a lichen
LICHEN	*Schismatomma graphidioides*	a lichen
LICHEN	*Squamarina lentigera*	scaly breck-lichen
LICHEN	*Teloschistes chrysophthalmus*	a lichen
LICHEN	*Thelenella modesta*	a lichen
LICHEN	*Zamenhofia rosei*	Francis' blue-green lichen
LIVERWORT	*Acrobolbus wilsonii*	a liverwort
LIVERWORT	*Adelanthus lindenbergianus*	Lindenberg's leafy liverwort
LIVERWORT	*Cephaloziella nicholsonii*	a liverwort
LIVERWORT	*Herbertus borealis*	a liverwort
LIVERWORT	*Jamesoniella undulifolia*	marsh earwort
LIVERWORT	*Lejeunea mandonii*	a liverwort
LIVERWORT	*Leiocolea rutheana*	Norfolk flapwort
LIVERWORT	*Marsupella profunda*	western rustwort
LIVERWORT	*Pallavicinia lyellii*	veilwort
LIVERWORT	*Petalophyllum ralfsii*	petalwort
LIVERWORT	*Riccia hueberneriana*	violet crystalwort
MOSS	*Acaulon triquetrum*	triangular pigmy moss
MOSS	*Andreaea frigida*	a moss
MOSS	*Barbula glauca*	glaucous beard-moss
MOSS	*Barbula mamillosa*	a moss
MOSS	*Barbula tomaculosa*	a moss
MOSS	*Bartramia stricta*	rigid apple moss
MOSS	*Brachythecium appleyardiae*	a moss
MOSS	*Bryoerythrophyllum caledonicum*	a moss
MOSS	*Bryum mamillatum*	dune thread moss
MOSS	*Bryum neodamense*	a moss
MOSS	*Bryum warneum*	a moss
MOSS	*Buxbaumia viridis*	green shield moss
MOSS	*Campylopus setifolius*	a moss
MOSS	*Cryphaea lamyana*	multi-fruited river moss
MOSS	*Desmatodon cernuus*	a moss
MOSS	*Ditrichum cornubicum*	Cornish path moss

MOSS	*Ditrichum plumbicola*	a moss
MOSS	*Drepanocladus vernicosus*	slender green feather-moss
MOSS	*Ephemerum stellatum*	a moss
MOSS	*Fissidens exiguus*	a moss
MOSS	*Leptodontium gemmascens*	thatch moss
MOSS	*Orthodontium gracile*	a moss
MOSS	*Orthotrichum obtusifolium*	blunt-leaved bristle-moss
MOSS	*Orthotrichum pallens*	a moss
MOSS	*Pohlia scotica*	a moss
MOSS	*Rhynchostegium rotundifolium*	round-leaved feather-moss
MOSS	*Seligeria carniolica*	a moss
MOSS	*Seligeria paucifolia*	a moss
MOSS	*Sematophyllum demissum*	a moss
MOSS	*Sphagnum balticum*	baltic bog moss
MOSS	*Thamnobryum angustifolium*	derbyshire feather-moss
MOSS	*Thamnobryum cataractarum*	a feather-moss
MOSS	*Tortula freibergii*	a moss
MOSS	*Weissia multicapsularis*	a moss
MOSS	*Weissia rostellata*	a moss
MOSS	*Zygodon forsteri*	knothole moss
MOSS	*Zygodon gracilis*	Nowell's limestone moss
STONEWORT	*Chara connivens*	convergent stonewort
STONEWORT	*Chara curta*	lesser bearded stonewort
STONEWORT	*Chara muscosa*	mossy stonewort
STONEWORT	*Nitella gracilis*	slender stonewort
STONEWORT	*Nitella tenuissima*	dwarf stonewort
STONEWORT	*Nitellopsis obtusa*	starry stonewort
STONEWORT	*Tolypella intricata*	tassel stonewort
STONEWORT	*Tolypella prolifera*	great tassel stonewort
VASCULAR PLANT	*Alchemilla minima*	an alchemilla
VASCULAR PLANT	*Alisma gramineum*	ribbon-leaved water-plantain
VASCULAR PLANT	*Apium repens*	creeping marshwort
VASCULAR PLANT	*Arabis glabra*	tower mustard
VASCULAR PLANT	*Artemisia norvegica*	Norwegian mugwort
VASCULAR PLANT	*Asparagus officinalis*	wild asparagus
VASCULAR PLANT	*Athyrium flexile*	Newman's lady-fern
VASCULAR PLANT	*Bromus interruptus*	interrupted brome
VASCULAR PLANT	*Calamagrostis scotica*	scottish small-reed
VASCULAR PLANT	*Carex muricata muricata*	prickly sedge

VASCULAR PLANT	*Carex vulpina*	true fox-sedge
VASCULAR PLANT	*Centaurea cyanus*	cornflower
VASCULAR PLANT	*Cerastium nigrescens*	shetland mouse-ear
VASCULAR PLANT	*Cochlearia micacea*	mountain scurvy-grass
VASCULAR PLANT	*Coincya wrightii*	lundy cabbage
VASCULAR PLANT	*Cotoneaster cambricus*	wild cotoneaster
VASCULAR PLANT	*Crepis foetida*	stinking hawk's-beard
VASCULAR PLANT	*Cypripedium calceolus*	lady's-slipper orchid
VASCULAR PLANT	*Damasonium alisma*	starfruit
VASCULAR PLANT	*Dianthus armeria*	deptford pink
VASCULAR PLANT	*Epipactis youngiana*	Young's helleborine
VASCULAR PLANT	*Filago lutescens*	red-tipped cudweed
VASCULAR PLANT	*Filago pyramidata*	broad-leaved cudweed
VASCULAR PLANT	*Fumaria occidentalis*	western ramping-fumitory
VASCULAR PLANT	*Fumaria purpurea*	purple ramping-fumitory
VASCULAR PLANT	*Galeopsis angustifolia*	red hemp-nettle
VASCULAR PLANT	*Galium tricornutum*	corn cleavers
VASCULAR PLANT	*Gentianella anglica*	early gentian
VASCULAR PLANT	*Gentianella uliginosa*	dune gentian
VASCULAR PLANT	*Juncus pygmaeus*	pygmy rush
VASCULAR PLANT	*Juniperus communis*	juniper
VASCULAR PLANT	*Leersia oryzoides*	cut-grass
VASCULAR PLANT	*Linnaea borealis*	twinflower
VASCULAR PLANT	*Liparis loeselii*	fen orchid
VASCULAR PLANT	*Luronium natans*	floating water plantain
VASCULAR PLANT	*Lycopodiella inundata*	marsh clubmoss
VASCULAR PLANT	*Melampyrum sylvaticum*	small cow-wheat
VASCULAR PLANT	*Mentha pulegium*	pennyroyal
VASCULAR PLANT	*Najas flexilis*	slender naiad
VASCULAR PLANT	*Najas marina*	holly-leaved naiad
VASCULAR PLANT	*Pilularia globulifera*	pillwort
VASCULAR PLANT	*Potamogeton compressus*	grass-wrack pondweed
VASCULAR PLANT	*Potamogeton rutilus*	shetland pondweed
VASCULAR PLANT	*Ranunculus tripartitus*	three-lobed water-crowfoot
VASCULAR PLANT	*Rumex rupestris*	shore dock
VASCULAR PLANT	*Salix lanata*	woolly willow
VASCULAR PLANT	*Saxifraga hirculus*	yellow marsh saxifrage
VASCULAR PLANT	*Scandix pecten-veneris*	shepherd's needle
VASCULAR PLANT	*Schoenoplectus triqueter*	triangular club-rush

VASCULAR PLANT	*Scleranthus perennis prostratus*	prostrate perennial knawel
VASCULAR PLANT	*Silene gallica*	small-flowered catchfly
VASCULAR PLANT	Single grouped plan for *Euphrasia cambrica, Euphrasia campbelliae, Euphrasia heslop-harrisonii, Euphrasia rivularis, Euphrasia rotundifolia* and *Euphrasia vigursii*	eyebrights
VASCULAR PLANT	Single grouped plan for *Hieracium* Sect. *Alpestria* (13 Shetland species only)	hawkweeds
VASCULAR PLANT	Single grouped plan for *Limonium* (endemic taxa)	sea lavender
VASCULAR PLANT	*Sium latifolium*	greater water-parsnip
VASCULAR PLANT	*Sorbus leyana*	a whitebeam
VASCULAR PLANT	*Spiranthes romanzoffiana*	Irish lady's tresses
VASCULAR PLANT	*Thlaspi perfoliatum*	perfoliate pennycress
VASCULAR PLANT	*Torilis arvensis*	spreading hedge-parsley
VASCULAR PLANT	*Trichomanes speciosum*	killarney fern
VASCULAR PLANT	*Valerianella rimosa*	broad-fruited corn salad
VASCULAR PLANT	*Woodsia ilvensis*	oblong woodsia

List 2. Priority species which may be addressed through a habitat or existing species action plan

ANT	*Formica lugubris*	northern wood ant
BEETLE	*Amara strenua*	a ground beetle
BEETLE	*Anisodactylus nemorivagus*	a ground beetle
BEETLE	*Bembidion humerale*	a ground beetle
BEETLE	*Bembidion nigropiceum*	a ground beetle
BEETLE	*Cicindela maritima*	a dune tiger beetle
BEETLE	*Cryptocephalus decemmaculatus*	leaf beetle
BEETLE	*Dromius sigma*	a ground beetle
BEETLE	*Harpalus punctatulus*	a ground beetle
BEETLE	*Octhebius poweri*	a water beetle
BEETLE	*Psylliodes luridipennis*	a flea beetle
BEETLE	*Tachys micros*	a ground beetle
CRUSTACEAN	*Gammarus insensibilis*	lagoon sand shrimp
CRUSTACEAN	*Palinurus elephas*	crawfish
MOTH	*Scotopteryx bipunctaria*	chalk carpet
SEA ANEMONE GROUP	*Clavopsella navis*	a brackish water hydroid
SEA ANEMONE GROUP	*Funiculina quadrangularis*	sea pen
SEA SLUG	*Tenellia adspersa*	lagoonal sea slug
SEA SQUIRT	*Styela gelatinosa*	sea squirt
SPIDER	*Euophrys browningi*	a spider

TRUE BUG	*Aphrodes duffieldi*	a leaf hopper
TRUE BUG	*Orthotylus rubidus*	a capsid bug
WORM	*Armandia cirrhosa*	lagoon sand worm
LICHEN	*Chaenotheca phaeocephala*	a lichen
LIVERWORT	*Marsupella stableri*	a liverwort
MOSS	*Micromitrium tenerum*	millimetre moss
MOSS	*Orthotrichum sprucei*	a moss
MOSS	*Plagiothecium piliferum*	hair silk moss
MOSS	*Weissia sterilis*	a moss
STONEWORT	*Chara baltica*	Baltic stonewort
STONEWORT	*Chara canescens*	bearded stonewort
STONEWORT	*Lamprothamniun papulosum*	foxtail stonewort
STONEWORT	*Tolypella nidifica*	bird's nest stonewort

List 3. Priority species not recorded in the last 10 years

FISH	*Acipenser sturio*	sturgeon
FISH	*Coregonus oxyrhynchus*	houting
BEETLE	*Badister peltatus*	a ground beetle
BEETLE	*Ceutorhynchus insularis*	a weevil
BEETLE	*Dromius quadrisignatus*	a ground beetle
BEETLE	*Protapion ryei*	a weevil
MAYFLY	*Heptagenia longicauda*	a mayfly
MOTH	*Thetidia smaragdaria maritima*	Essex emerald
FUNGUS	*Boletopsis leucomelaena*	a bracket fungus
LICHEN	*Bellemerea alpina*	a lichen
LICHEN	*Caloplaca nivalis*	snow caloplaca
LICHEN	*Hypogymnia intestiniformis*	a lichen
LICHEN	*Pertusaria bryontha*	alpine moss pertusaria
LIVERWORT	*Fossombronia crozalsii*	a liverwort
MOSS	*Atrichum angustatum*	lesser smoothcap
MOSS	*Bryum calophyllum*	a moss
MOSS	*Bryum turbinatum*	a moss
MOSS	*Bryum uliginosum*	a moss
MOSS	*Ephemerum cohaerens*	a moss
MOSS	*Orthotrichum gymnostomum*	a moss
MOSS	*Pictus scoticus*	a moss
MOSS	*Sphagnum skyense*	a bog moss
MOSS	*Tetrodontium repandum*	a moss

| MOSS | *Weissia squarrosa* | a moss |
| VASCULAR PLANT | *Cochlearia scotica* | Scottish scurvy-grass |

Annex 4

Action Plans for priority vertebrate and vascular plant species

Mammals

Barbastelle bat (*Barbastella barbastellus*)
Action Plan

1. Current status

1.1 The barbastelle bat is mainly a woodland species. It uses old buildings and trees as summer roosts and underground sites and other suitable places such as hollow trees for hibernation. Riparian woodland may form an important habitat in some areas. It feeds mainly on lepidoptera taken in flight, but may also glean insects and spiders from vegetation.

1.2 This species is widely distributed in England and Wales with centres of population in south-west and mid-west England, and Norfolk. It is believed to be rare in the UK, with only 340 records since 1802. Only one UK maternity roost and less than 30 hibernation sites are currently known. The most recent UK population estimate is approximately 5000 individuals but the overall population trend is not known. The barbastelle bat is widespread in continental Europe, but appears to be rare almost everywhere.

1.3 This species is listed on Appendix II of the Bonn Convention (and its Agreement on the Conservation of Bats in Europe, 1994), Appendix II of the Bern Convention (and its appropriate Recommendations) and Annexes II and IV of the EC Habitats and Species Directive. It is protected under Schedule 2 of the Conservation (Natural Habitats, etc.) Regulations, 1994 (Regulation 38) and Schedule 5 of the Wildlife and Countryside Act 1981. The 1996 IUCN Red List of Threatened Animals classifies this species as *Vulnerable*.

2. Current factors causing loss or decline

Threats to this species are poorly understood, but its low population density and slow population growth make it particularly vulnerable to factors such as:

2.1 Further loss and fragmentation of ancient deciduous woodland habitat.

2.2 Loss, destruction and disturbance of roosts or potential roosts in buildings, trees and underground sites.

2.3 A reduction in numbers of insect prey due to habitat simplification acting through factors such as fertiliser use and intensive grazing.

3. Current action

3.1 The barbastelle bat is the subject of a Species Recovery Programme Phase 1 project funded by English Nature. It is included in the DETR sponsored National Bat Monitoring Programme which aims to establish baseline data for the species and to propose a long-term monitoring protocol.

3.2 A network using local bat group volunteers working closely with SNCO staff is established and continues to develop. These people are routinely consulted over development proposals and other issues relating to Schedule 5 of the Wildlife and Countryside Act 1981.

3.3 Some of the known hibernation sites have been protected by grilling; some are within SSSIs.

3.4 Research is being carried out in Norfolk, Surrey and Devon with the aim of locating roosts and identifying habitat requirements of the barbastelle bat.

3.5 A pan-European meeting organised by the IUCN Coordinating Panel for the Conservation of Bats in Europe was held in 1997 and reviewed current knowledge of the barbastelle bat and its conservation requirements.

4. Action plan objectives and targets

This action plan is intended to promote the work recommended under English Nature's Species Recovery Programme and also to propose more general measures for the conservation of this species:

4.1 Maintain the known range and populations.

4.2 Increase the total population size of this species by improving woodland age structure, particularly in wooded river valleys, to increase roosting and foraging opportunities.

5. Proposed action with lead agencies

Successful action for the barbastelle bat will require a fuller understanding of its breeding biology and general foraging and roosting requirements. Research in known areas of occupation will be needed to identify these requirements. Meanwhile, practical action should focus on the protection of regularly used roost sites and habitat surrounding them.

5.1 Policy and legislation

5.1.1 Pursue the principles and requirements of the Agreement on the Conservation of Bats in Europe. (ACTION: CCW, DETR, EA, EN, FA, FE, LAs, MAFF, WOAD)

5.1.2 When next reviewed, consider targeting the Woodland Grant Scheme (Project 3), Forest Design Plans, Countryside Stewardship Schemes, ESAs, and other relevant agri-environment and forestry schemes to land in the vicinity of important roost sites, with the aim of enhancing terrestrial and aquatic habitats used by barbastelle bats.

Consideration should be given to the retention of hollow, veteran, dying and dead trees in hedgerows and woodlands. (ACTION: CCW, DETR, EN, FA, FE, MAFF, WOAD)

5.1.3 Ensure that consideration is given to habitat surrounding key bat sites when developing structure plans and assessing planning applications. (ACTION: CCW, EN, LAs)

5.1.4 Ensure that the requirements of the barbastelle bat are considered during the development of Local Environment Agency Plans in areas where this species occurs. (ACTION: EA)

5.2 Site safeguard and management

5.2.1 Ensure the long-term protection of maternity roosts, key hibernation roosts and, where appropriate, the habitat surrounding these sites. Consider notifying such areas as SSSIs where it is necessary to achieve this. (ACTION: CCW, EN, FA, FE)

5.3 Species management and protection

5.3.1 None proposed.

5.4 Advisory

5.4.1 When appropriate, advise relevant project officers for Countryside Stewardship, the Woodland Grant Scheme and other forestry and agri-environment schemes of the location of key roost sites, their importance and appropriate habitat management for the surrounding areas. (ACTION: CCW, EN, FA, FE, MAFF)

5.4.2 Establish links with organisations associated with the care and restoration of old buildings in the vicinity of barbastelle bat sites, in order to encourage provision for the requirements of the species within old buildings. (ACTION: CCW, EN, LAs)

5.4.3 Advise tree surgeons, tree wardens and foresters operating in the vicinity of barbastelle bat sites on tree management practices which will assist the conservation of this species. (ACTION: CCW, EN, FA, LAs)

5.4.4 Continue to support the current network providing bat conservation advice including the use of licensed bat workers/wardens for roost visits. (ACTION: CCW, EN)

5.5 Future research and monitoring

5.5.1 Continue to search for maternity roosts and hibernation sites. On locating such sites, undertake autecological research and monitoring into the roosting requirements and foraging habitats of this species, with a view to refining habitat protection and management practices. (ACTION: CCW, EN, FC, JNCC)

5.5.2 Research the food and feeding requirements of the species. (ACTION: CCW, EN, JNCC)

5.5.3 Develop and maintain a national database for bat records. (ACTION: JNCC)

5.5.4 Consider the recommendations of the National Bat Monitoring Programme once they are produced. (ACTION: DETR)

5.6 Communications and publicity

5.6.1 Raise awareness of bat conservation issues amongst owners of large country houses and farm buildings through relevant organisations and appropriate property and farming magazines. (ACTION: CADW, CCW, EH, EN)

5.6.2 Maintain discussions on the conservation of the species on a pan-European scale through the IUCN Coordinating Panel for the Conservation of Bats in Europe and the European Bat Agreement. (ACTION: CCW, DETR, EN)

5.6.3 Raise awareness of the importance of old trees as roost and hibernation sites. (ACTION: CCW, EN, FA)

5.7 Links with other action plans

5.7.1 It is likely that implementation of this action plan will benefit Bechstein's and lesser horseshoe bat.
5.7.2 The plan should be considered in conjunction with those for lowland beech, wet woodlands, lowland wood pastures and parkland, broadleaved and yew woodland, and chalk rivers.

Barbastelle Bat

Barbastella barbastellus

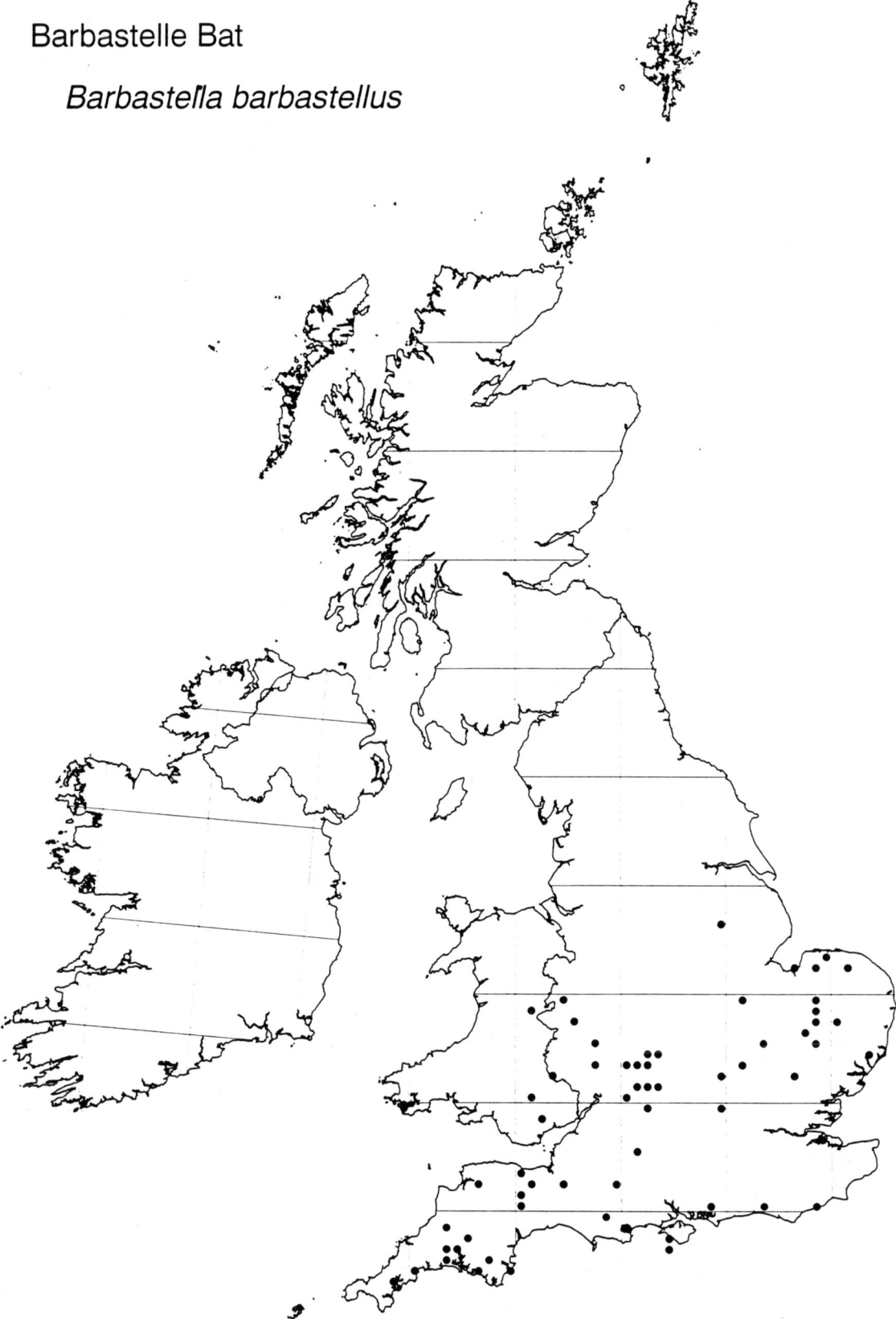

Distribution of Barbastelle bat in Britain and Ireland, 1970-1995 (by 10 Km square).
Source: Bat Conservation Trust, English Nature

Bechstein's bat (*Myotis bechsteinii*)
Action Plan

1. Current status

1.1 Bechstein's bat is a very rare tree-dwelling bat, mostly associated with old growth broadleaved woodland. A few individuals are found in underground sites during hibernation, but it is likely that most individuals roost in trees all year. The bat feeds on invertebrates including spiders and resting day-flying insects which are picked from branches and leaves. Maternity roosts are small, ranging from a few to about 30 individuals.

1.2 This species is considered to be rare in the UK with only 140 records since 1800. It occupies a restricted distribution across the south of England with population centres in Devon, Dorset, Gloucestershire, Isle of Wight, Somerset and Wiltshire. There have also been two recent records from Wales and the identification of several roosts in Surrey in 1997. Only one maternity roost and less than 20 hibernation roosts are currently known in the UK with almost all records being of isolated individuals. The most recent population estimates are of around 1500 individuals with overall population trends unknown. Bechstein's bat is widespread but rare throughout continental Europe.

1.3 This bat is listed on Appendix II of the Bonn Convention (and its Agreement on the Conservation of Bats in Europe, 1994), Appendix II of the Bern Convention (and its appropriate Recommendations) and Annexes II and IV of the EC Habitats and Species Directive. It is protected under Schedule 2 of the Conservation (Natural Habitats, etc.) Regulations, 1994 (Regulation 38) and Schedule 5 of the Wildlife and Countryside Act 1981. The 1996 IUCN Red List of Threatened Animals classifies this species as *Vulnerable* (VU A2c).

2. Current factors causing loss or decline

Threats to this species are poorly understood, but its low population density, exacting habitat requirements and low rates of reproduction make this species particularly vulnerable to factors such as:

2.1 Further loss and fragmentation of open ancient deciduous woodland habitat.

2.2 Loss, destruction and disturbance of roosts or potential roosts (particularly in old trees).

3. Current action

3.1 A recent assessment of all records has been made and used to help prepare an action plan as part of English Nature's Species Recovery Programme Phase 1 project for Bechstein's bat. It is included in the DETR sponsored National Bat Monitoring Programme which aims to establish baseline data for the species and to propose a long-term monitoring protocol.

3.2 A network using local bat group volunteers working closely with SNCO staff is established. These people are routinely consulted over development proposals and other issues relating to Schedule 5 of the Wildlife and Countryside Act 1981.

3.3 Some known hibernation sites have been physically protected against disturbance (eg grilling of underground sites) and some are within SSSIs. The one known maternity roost is within a proposed SAC.

3.4 English Nature's Species Recovery Programme includes an initiative to provide bat boxes for this species in Dorset and Wiltshire in woodlands where roost sites are limiting. These are also used for monitoring.

3.5 Research has been carried out in Surrey using radio-tracking to identify day roosts. The work was part-funded by the Vincent Wildlife Trust.

3.6 This species is proposed for an international programme of survey and monitoring under the European Bat Agreement.

4. Action plan objectives and targets

This action plan is intended to promote the work recommended under English Nature's Species Recovery Programme, and also to propose more general measures for the conservation of this species.

4.1 Maintain the known range and populations.

4.2 Increase the national population size of this species by improving woodland age structure to enhance roosting and foraging opportunities.

5. Proposed action with lead agencies

The retention of old trees and woodland around roost sites is essential to the survival of Bechstein's bat. Detailed population assessment and monitoring are currently difficult because little is known about the bat. More research into its ecology and behaviour is needed to refine the conservation action proposed in this plan. It will be important to find and protect further key (particularly maternity and hibernation) roosts.

5.1 Policy and legislation

5.1.1 Pursue the principles and requirements of the Agreement on the Conservation of Bats in Europe. (ACTION: CCW, DETR, EA, EN, FA, FE, LAs, MAFF)

5.1.2 When next reviewed, consider targeting the Woodland Grant Scheme (Project 3), Forest Design Plans, Countryside Stewardship Schemes, ESAs and other relevant agri-environment and forestry schemes towards land in the vicinity of important roost sites, with the aim of enhancing and extending habitat used by bats. Consideration should be given to the retention of hollow, veteran, dying and dead trees in hedgerows and woodlands. (ACTION: CCW, DETR, EN, FA, FE, MAFF, WOAD)

5.2 Site safeguard and management

5.2.1 Ensure the long-term protection of maternity roosts, key hibernation roosts and the habitat surrounding these sites. Consider notifying such areas as SSSIs where it is necessary to achieve this. (ACTION: CCW, EN)

5.3 Species management and protection

5.3.1 Continue to install bat boxes and expand their use from an initial focus in Dorset and Wiltshire to include other important population centres. (ACTION: CCW, EN, FA, FE, LAs)

5.4 Advisory

5.4.1 Advise relevant project officers for Countryside Stewardship, the Woodland Grant Scheme and other agri-environment and forestry schemes of the location of key roost sites, their importance and appropriate habitat management for the surrounding areas. (ACTION: CCW, EN, FA, FE, MAFF)

5.4.2 Advise tree surgeons, tree wardens and foresters operating in the vicinity of Bechstein's bat sites on tree management practices which will assist the conservation of this species. (ACTION: CCW, EN, LAs)

5.4.3 Continue to support the current network providing bat conservation advice including the use of licensed bat workers/wardens for roost visits. (ACTION: CCW, EN)

5.5 Future research and monitoring

5.5.1 Continue to search for maternity and cave roosting sites. On locating such sites, undertake autecological research and monitoring into the roosting requirements and foraging habitats of this species, with a view to refining habitat protection and management practices and producing guidelines on the construction and installation of artificial roosts. (ACTION: CCW, EN, JNCC, FC)

5.5.2 Research the food and feeding requirements of the species. (ACTION: CCW, EN, JNCC)

5.5.3 Develop and maintain a national database for bat records. (ACTION: JNCC)

5.5.4 Consider the recommendations of the National Bat Monitoring Programme once they are produced. (ACTION: DETR)

5.6 Communications and publicity

5.6.1 Maintain discussions on the conservation of the species on a pan-European scale through the IUCN Coordinating Panel for the Conservation of Bats in Europe and the European Bat Agreement. (ACTION: CCW, DETR, EN)

5.6.2 Use the conservation requirements of Bechstein's bat to illustrate the importance of native deciduous woodland. (ACTION: CCW, EN, FA, FE)

5.6.3 Raise awareness of the importance of old trees as roost and hibernation sites. (ACTION: CCW, EN, FA)

5.7 Links with other action plans

5.7.1 It is likely that implementation of this action plan will benefit barbastelle and lesser horseshoe bat.

5.7.2 The plan should be considered in conjunction with those for lowland beech, wet woodlands, lowland wood pastures and parkland, broadleaved and yew woodland, and chalk rivers.

Bechstein's bat

Myotis bechsteinii

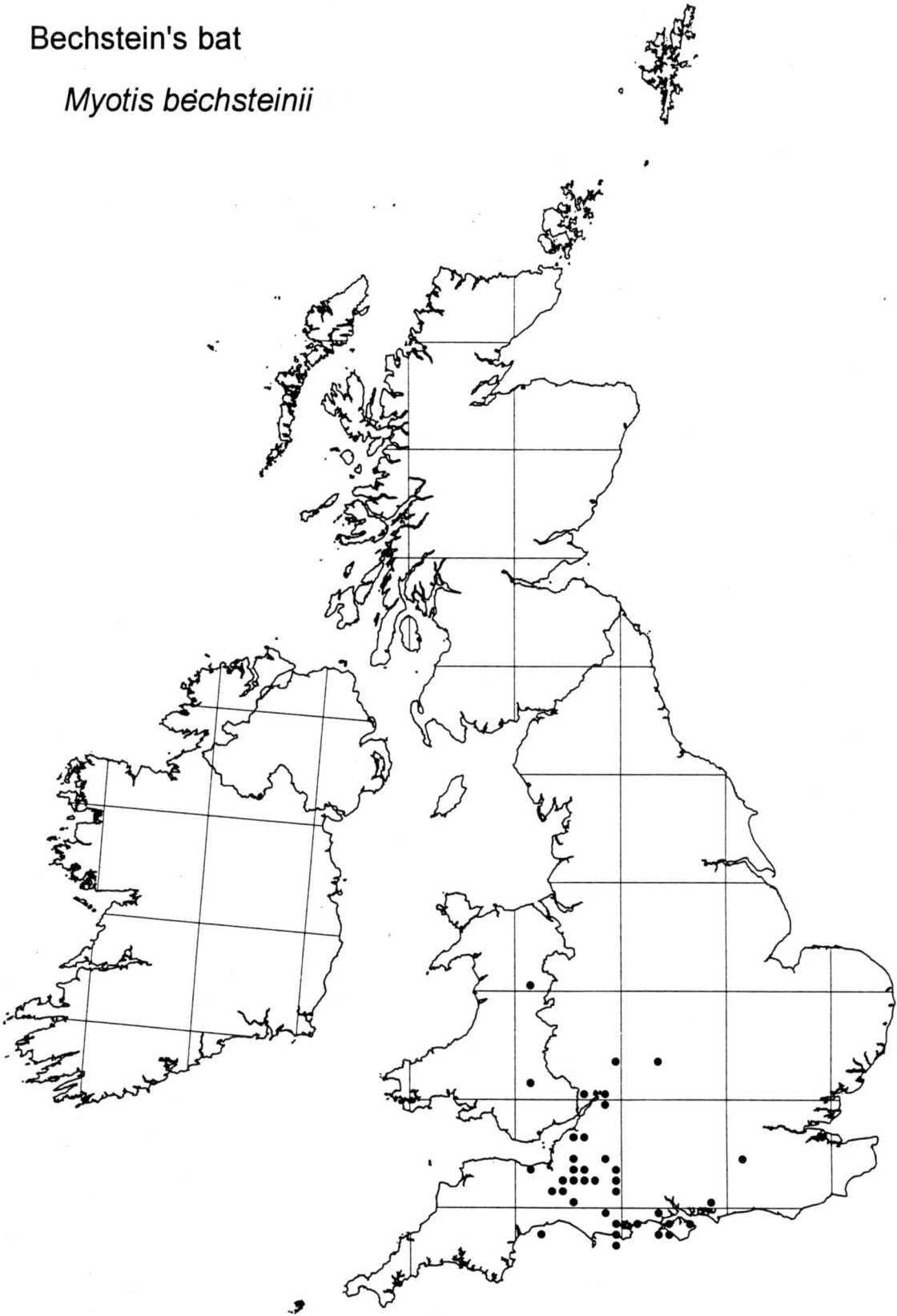

Distribution of Bechstein's bat in Britain and Ireland, 1970-1995 (by 10 Km square).
Source: Bat Conservation Trust, English Nature

Lesser horseshoe bat (*Rhinolophus hipposideros*) Action Plan

1. Current status

1.1 The lesser horseshoe bat was originally a cave-roosting bat, although most summer maternity colonies now use buildings, particularly old large houses and farm buildings. Most still hibernate in underground sites such as caves. Females forage within 2-3 km of the maternity roost, feeding on insects taken in flight in mixed woodland, hedgerows and treelines.

1.2 In Britain, the lesser horseshoe bat is now found only in south-west England and Wales. It was formerly present in south-east England and the Midlands. Current estimates suggest a UK population of 14,000 divided equally between Wales and England. About 230 summer (or all-year) roosts are known and about 480 hibernation roosts. Of the latter, only 20% are used by more than 10 bats. The lesser horseshoe bat is widespread throughout central and southern Europe, but has undergone severe decline in the northern part of its range.

1.3 This species is included in Appendix II of the Bonn Convention (and its Agreement on the Conservation of Bats in Europe) and Appendix II of the Bern Convention (and Recommendation 36 on the Conservation of Underground Habitats). It is also listed on Annexes II and IV of the EC Habitats and Species Directive. It is protected under Schedule 2 of the Conservation (Natural Habitats, etc.) Regulations 1994 (Regulation 38) and Schedule 5 of the Wildlife and Countryside Act 1981. The 1996 IUCN Red list of Threatened Animals classifies this species as *Vulnerable* (VU A2c).

2. Current factors causing loss or decline

2.1 Loss of, or damage to, summer maternity roost sites. This is mainly due to deterioration and unsympathetic renovation of old buildings and barns, although identifying small colonies can be problematic.

2.2 Loss of, or damage to, underground sites used mainly for hibernation, often through blocking of old mines or similar sites for safety purposes, and increased leisure or 'casual' use.

2.3 Further loss, damage and fragmentation of woodland foraging habitat, old hedgerows and tree lines, and other appropriate habitat.

3. Current action

3.1 Coordinated monitoring of summer roosts in Wales and England has taken place over the last five and three years respectively. Some monitoring of hibernation sites has been carried out over the past year. It is included in the DETR sponsored National Bat Monitoring Programme which aims to establish baseline data for the species and to propose a long-term monitoring protocol.

3.2 A network using local bat group volunteers working closely with SNCO staff is established and continues to develop. These people provide advice on development proposals and issues relating to Schedule 5 of the Wildlife and Countryside Act 1981.

3.3 An autecological project (commissioned by the Vincent Wildlife Trust) on distribution, roosting and foraging habitats has recently been completed.

3.4 At least 12 sites are notified as SSSIs for this species. Four of these have also been proposed as SACs for this species. Around 70 other sites are within SSSIs.

3.5 The species is selected for proposed international collaboration on population monitoring under the European Bat Agreement.

4. Action plan objectives and targets

4.1 Maintain the current range and populations.

4.2 In the long term, expand the current range through natural recolonisation and landscape enhancement, into areas where research shows that climatic and landscape features are suitable.

5. Proposed action with lead agencies

Existing measures to protect roosts should be maintained and improved and should incorporate the need to protect roosts other than maternity and hibernation roosts. Increased effort should be given to the identification and protection of foraging habitat around roosts.

5.1 Policy and legislation

5.1.1 Pursue the principles and requirements of the Agreement on the Conservation of Bats in Europe. (ACTION: CCW, DETR, EA, EN, FA, LAs, MAFF, WOAD)

5.1.2 When next reviewed, consider targeting the Woodland Grant Scheme (WGS) (Project 3), Forest Design Plans, Countryside Stewardship Schemes, ESAs and other relevant agri-environment and forestry schemes to land in the vicinity of important roost sites, with the aim of enhancing and extending habitat used by bats. (ACTION: CCW, DETR, EN, FA, FE, MAFF, WOAD)

5.1.3 Establish mechanisms to ensure routine survey of mines or other underground sites due for closure or change of use, or otherwise considered vulnerable, with a view to protecting any bat colonies identified. (ACTION: CCW, EN, FE, JNCC)

5.1.4 Ensure that consideration is given to key maternity roost sites and the surrounding habitat when developing structure plans and assessing planning applications, particularly those for redundant buildings. The provision of alternative roost sites should be considered to mitigate any loss, as should the need for survey on planning applications for old buildings in current (and any expanded) range. (ACTION: CCW, EN, LAs)

5.2 Site safeguard and management

5.2.1 Ensure that management agreements for all SSSIs where the lesser horseshoe bat is known to occur take account of the requirements of this species. (ACTION: CCW, EN)

5.2.2 Identify representative numbers of key maternity, hibernation and other roosts across the range of this species and ensure that they are notified to Local Authorities and fully protected from damaging developments. Ensure adequate representation in the SSSI series. (ACTION: CCW, EN, LAs)

5.2.3 Include the lesser horseshoe bat on the list of reasons for notification on those SSSIs which have been notified for other reasons (eg geology) but which also support important bat roosts. (ACTION: CCW, EN)

5.3 Species management and protection

5.3.1 None proposed.

5.4 Advisory

5.4.1 When appropriate, advise project officers for Countryside Stewardship, the WIG scheme and other forestry and agri-environment schemes of the location of key roost sites, their importance and appropriate habitat management for the surrounding areas. (ACTION: CCW, EN, FA, FE, MAFF, WOAD)

5.4.2 Establish links with organisations associated with the care and restoration of old buildings in the vicinity of lesser horseshoe bat sites, in order to encourage provision for the requirements of the species within old buildings. (ACTION: CADW, CCW, EH, EN, LAs)

5.4.3 Advise organisations engaged in underground research and recreation on the location and importance of lesser horseshoe bat roosts and the need to avoid causing disturbance to them. (ACTION: CCW, EN, LAs)

5.4.4 Advise key landowners, managers and other relevant organisations in the vicinity of important populations of this species on appropriate habitat management for the conservation of the lesser horseshoe bat. (ACTION: CCW, EN)

5.4.5 Continue to support and expand the current network providing bat conservation advice including the use of licensed bat workers/wardens for roost visits. (ACTION: CCW, EN)

5.5 Future research and monitoring

5.5.1 Maintain and enhance national monitoring, in relation to pan-European proposals under the Agreement on the Conservation of Bats in Europe. (ACTION: CCW, DETR, EN)

5.5.2 Undertake research to identify the habitat requirements of this species and the appropriate

management of feeding areas needed to maintain populations at a favourable conservation status. The findings should be used to inform development of guidelines and policies for habitat protection, creation and management around roost sites. (ACTION: CCW, EN, FA, JNCC)

5.5.3 Assess the importance of mating roosts, underground sites and satellite or minor summer sites used by small numbers of bats with a view to establishing protection for key sites. (ACTION: CCW, EN)

5.5.4 Develop and maintain a national database for bat records. (ACTION: JNCC)

5.5.5 Consider the recommendations of the National Bat Monitoring Programme once they are produced. (ACTION: DETR)

5.6 Communications and publicity

5.6.1 Raise awareness of bat conservation issues amongst the owners of large country houses and farm buildings through relevant organisations and appropriate property and farming magazines. (ACTION: CADW, CCW, EH, EN)

5.6.2 Raise awareness of this bat species among land managers and Local Authorities. (ACTION: CCW, EN)

5.6.3 Maintain discussions on the conservation of the species on a pan-European scale through the IUCN Coordinating Panel for the Conservation of Bats in Europe and the European Bat Agreement. (ACTION: CCW, DETR, EN)

5.7 Links with other action plans

5.7.1 It is likely that implementation of this action plan will benefit barbastelle and Bechstein's bat.

5.7.2 The plan should be considered in conjunction with those for lowland beech, wet woodlands, lowland wood pastures and parkland, broadleaved and yew woodland, and chalk rivers.

Lesser Horseshoe bat

Rhinolophus hipposideros

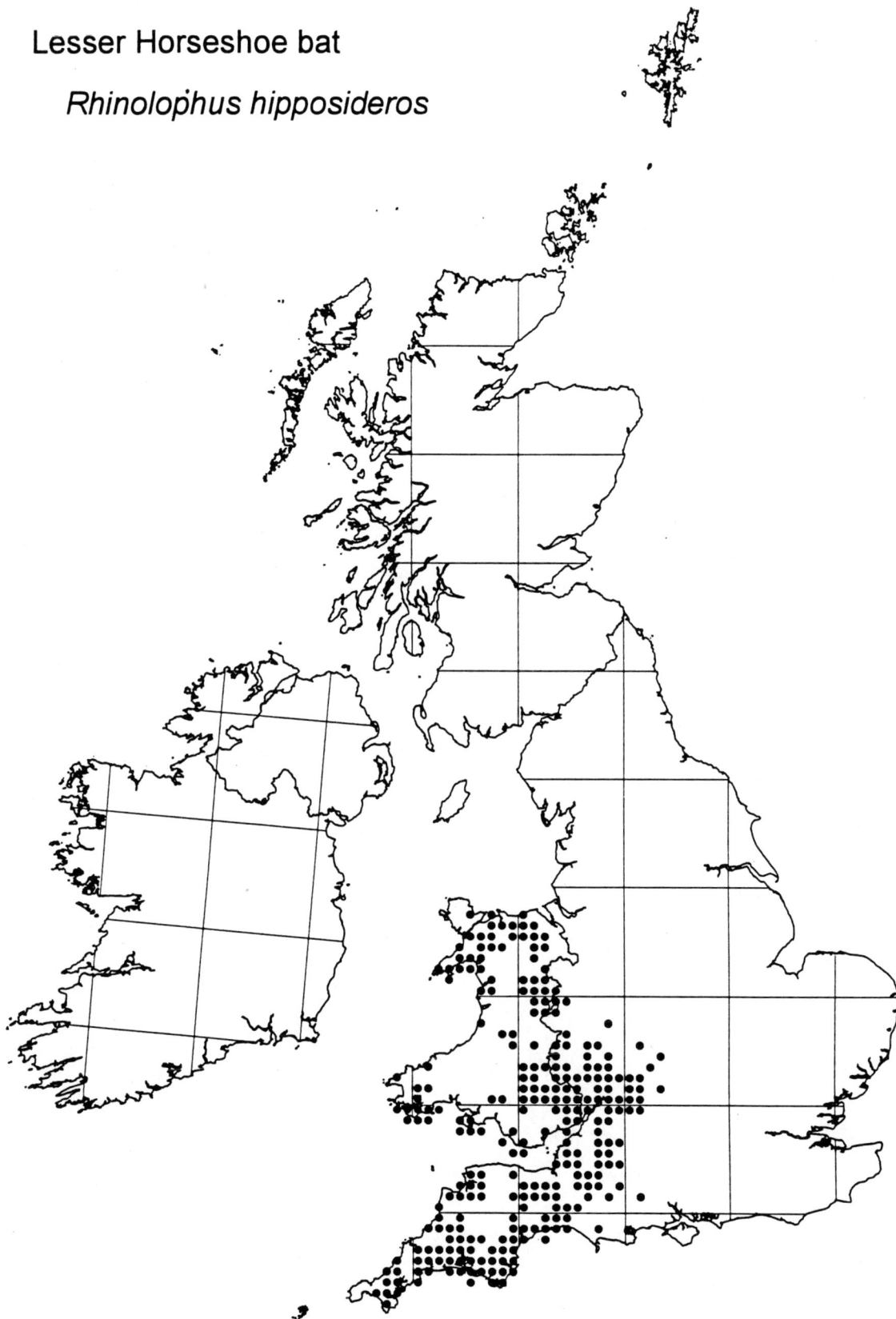

Distribution of the Lesser Horseshoe bat in Britain and Ireland, 1970-1995 (by 10 Km square).
Source: Bat Conservation Trust, English Nature

Birds

47

Marsh warbler (*Acrocephalus palustris*)
Action Plan

1. Current status

1.1 The marsh warbler is a summer migrant which formerly bred in scattered locations across southern England, but a long-term decline became apparent from the 1950s when there were probably well over 100 breeding pairs. Up until 1980 there were still around 50-80 breeding pairs. Until recently, the main breeding area was in Worcestershire in the Severn and Avon valleys, but this population declined rapidly in the 1980s and no breeding pairs were recorded there in 1989. A few pairs subsequently reappeared (including three pairs in 1993), but none was present in 1994; it is likely that the species will become extinct at this locality. A population became established on the Kent coast in the 1970s and these birds have increased slowly in numbers and range since then, to over 25 pairs in at least four sites by 1993. In addition, several other sites are now occupied in adjoining counties (including seven singing males at one site in 1994) and records of unpaired singing birds are now widespread. Elsewhere in Europe, the marsh warbler breeds mainly in the cool temperate middle latitudes, usually in lowland areas. The population is concentrated in central and eastern Europe and has spread northwards in northern Europe in recent decades.

1.2 The marsh warbler is specially protected under Schedule 1 of the Wildlife and Countryside Act 1981 and EC Birds Directive, and is listed on Appendix II of the Bern Convention.

2. Current factors causing loss or decline

2.1 The reasons for the decline in the lower Avon population are not well known but some marsh warbler sites have been lost as a result of vegetation change and riverine channel modification.

2.2 Climatic factors have been suggested as a partial cause of the long-term UK decline, since the species occurs at the northern edge of its range here, and breeds only in the warmer southern counties of England. However, many aspects of its ecology are poorly understood and numerous apparently suitable nesting areas have never been occupied.

2.3 Geographical isolation has been proposed as a possible reason for the near-extinction of the western population. However, the species has had a fragmented and scattered distribution in this country for many decades.

2.4 The marsh warbler is prone to disturbance by birdwatchers and others. The nest is relatively easy to find and a number of incidents of egg collecting have been recorded in the Worcestershire breeding area.

3. Current action

3.1 Since the mid 1980s the Worcestershire Wildlife Trust has monitored the size, distribution and breeding habitats of the western population, prevented disturbance or persecution and liaised with landowners.

3.2 The Trust has undertaken habitat management on both peripheral and core sites to maintain their suitability, even those which have been deserted.

3.3 The Severn Trent Water Authority undertook flood alleviation work in 1985 close to the core breeding area. As part of this work, management was carried out to produce areas of herbaceous vegetation which it was hoped would be colonised by marsh warblers.

3.4 Most of the former breeding sites of the marsh warbler in Worcestershire (which include the sites occupied in 1993) have been notified as SSSIs.

3.5 Since the reappearance of birds in recent years, the Worcestershire Wildlife Trust has been responsible for drawing up species management guidelines for river managers to be promoted by EA staff. It is hoped that these will also be applied to Kent, and areas where populations become established.

3.6 In Kent, little has so far been done for the marsh warbler except that local volunteers have monitored the population and provided information on features of breeding habitat. RSPB staff have also carried out small-scale habitat management.

4. Action plan objectives and targets

4.1 Maintain the marsh warbler as a British breeding species.

4.2 In the long term, encourage a natural expansion of the marsh warbler population through maintenance of suitable habitat in former, current and future breeding areas.

5. Proposed action with lead agencies

The objectives and targets for marsh warbler will be achieved by ensuring the appropriate protection and management of existing breeding sites, and those recently abandoned, in order to maintain and, where appropriate, improve their suitability for marsh warblers. Adequate population monitoring and research into the habitat requirements of the species is also necessary.

5.1 Policy and legislation

5.1.1 Incorporate appropriate riparian habitat management prescriptions into Local Environment Agency Plans (LEAPs) to benefit the marsh warbler. (ACTION: EA, EN)

5.2 Site safeguard and management

5.2.1 Safeguard existing or recently abandoned breeding sites by carrying out appropriate habitat management, particularly scrub removal and maintenance of high water tables. (ACTION: EA, EN)

5.2.2 Protect regularly occupied breeding sites from any potentially damaging developments. (ACTION: EN)

5.2.3 Where appropriate, consider notifying regular breeding sites as SSSIs. (ACTION: EN)

5.3 Species management and protection

5.3.1 Ensure that adequate wardening of occupied marsh warbler sites takes place to prevent undue disturbance and persecution by egg collectors. (ACTION: EN)

5.4 Advisory

5.4.1 Promote appropriate management of marsh warbler sites. (ACTION: EA, EN)

5.5 Future research and monitoring

5.5.1 Ensure continued monitoring of marsh warblers in Britain through the Rare Breeding Birds Panel. (ACTION: JNCC)

5.5.2 Collate information on the habitats of marsh warblers in Britain. (ACTION: EN)

5.5.3 Acquire information on marsh warbler ecology from researchers in Europe and east Africa, in order to learn more about the factors determining habitat requirements during the breeding season, and survival on migration and during winter. (ACTION: JNCC)

5.6 Communications and publicity

5.6.1 None proposed.

5.7 Links with other action plans

5.7.1 It is likely that the safeguard and management of undisturbed semi-natural riparian habitat will also benefit the European Otter.

Marsh Warbler

Acrocephalus palustris

Breeding distribution of Marsh Warbler in Britain and Ireland, 1988-1991 (by 10 Km square).
Source: Gibbons, D.W., Reid, J.B. and Chapman, R.A. (1993). The new atlas of breeding birds
in Britain and Ireland 1988-1991. Calton, U.K.: T. and A.D. Poyser.

● Record of breeding

· Record with no evidence of breeding

Nightjar (*Caprimulgus europaeus*)
Action Plan

1. Current status

1.1 The nightjar is a summer migrant that has been declining in numbers and range for much of this century, reaching a low point of 2100 males in 1981, with a decline in range of 52% between 1968-72 and 1992. There has been a partial recovery in the size of the population which had reached 3400 males in 1992. The species now breeds mainly in southern England, but there are scattered populations as far north as central Scotland. It is probably now extinct as a breeding species in Northern Ireland where its former habitats included cut-over raised bogs. Lowland heathland and young forestry plantations are now the most important habitats. An increase in forestry clear-fells as a result of major storms and forest management have assisted recent increases, with over 50% of the total population found in this habitat in the 1992 survey. In Europe the species has been declining in numbers and range since at least 1950, especially in north-west and northern Europe.

1.2 The nightjar is protected under the Wildlife and Countryside Act 1981 and Schedule 1 of the Wildlife (Northern Ireland) Order 1985, and is listed on Annex 1 of the EC Birds Directive and Appendix II of the Bern Convention.

2. Current factors causing loss or decline

2.1 The area of heathland in the UK has undergone a dramatic reduction during the course of this century due to agricultural land claim, afforestation and built development. For example, it is estimated that 40% of England's lowland heathland has been lost since the 1950s. Threats continue from housing and infra-structure developments.

2.2 Where heathland lacks appropriate management, it will become unsuitable as nesting habitat due to invasion by bushes and trees.

2.3 Nightjars require extensive areas of suitable feeding habitat, especially uncultivated land. The loss of such habitats within a few kilometres of the nesting area may result in a decline in the number of birds.

2.4 It is possible that a decline in the availability of large insects caused by changes in agriculture (such as the indirect effects of pesticides) and/or climatic change, may have affected nightjar populations.

2.5 In commercial forests, nightjars nest in the young stages of plantations, while there is still bare ground between the trees. If no other suitable habitat becomes available in other new or young stands, local population declines could occur as the recently planted blocks mature.

3. Current action

3.1 Detailed research into the ecology of nightjars nesting in Thetford Forest has been carried out by the RSPB with FC help; FE's forestry practice there is now aimed at maintaining a constant area of young plantation as good habitat for breeding nightjars.

3.2 Specific management on some nature reserves has benefited this species, as has the heathland management carried out by various county heathland projects managed by EN, RSPB and local authorities.

3.3 The nightjar has benefited from heathland management encouraged by the Breckland ESA and Countryside Stewardship Scheme.

4. Action plan objectives and targets

4.1 Maintain a population of at least 3400 churring males.

4.2 Halt the decline in range of the nightjar (there were 268 occupied ten km squares in 1992).

4.3 Increase the numbers and range of nightjar to 4000 churring males in at least 280 ten km squares by the year 2003 (an 18% population increase and 5% range increase in 10 years).

4.4 In the long term (next 20 years), restore nightjar to parts of its former range in, for example, south-west England, west Midlands, north-west England, south-west Scotland and Northern Ireland.

5. Proposed action with lead agencies

The objectives and targets for nightjar will be achieved through protecting, maintaining, restoring and re-establishing lowland heathland and associated foraging habitats; adopting sympathetic forestry management practices; and promoting extensive agriculture systems in the wider countryside. Population numbers and range will need to be monitored.

5.1 Policy and legislation

5.1.1 Include specific targets and management for the nightjar in Forest Design Plans across the species' current and former range. (ACTION: DANI, FE)

5.1.2 Take full account of the requirements of the nightjar when considering felling and restocking proposals in its current and former range. (ACTION: FA, FE)

5.1.3 Incorporate specific targets and management for nightjars in MoD site management plans in appropriate sites across the species' former range. (ACTION: MoD)

5.1.4 Seek to extend the Wildlife Enhancement Scheme to other key areas of lowland heathland in England. (ACTION: EN)

5.1.5 Support extensive low intensity agricultural systems within the historic range of the species through the appropriate agri-environment schemes. (ACTION: CCW, DANI, MAFF, SOAEFD, WOAD)

5.2 Site safeguard and management

5.2.1 Consider notifying important nesting and foraging sites as SSSI/ASSIs. (ACTION: CCW, EHS, EN, SNH)

5.2.2 Designate as SPAs areas of 'special interest' that support nationally important populations of nightjars (subject to current guidelines) and encourage their appropriate management. (ACTION: CCW, DETR, EHS, EN, SNH)

5.2.3 Seek to achieve 'favourable conservation status' of the nightjar by measures complementary to SPAs. This will include projects to maintain, enhance and restore heathland adjacent to SPAs (eg through agri-environment schemes). (ACTION: CCW, EHS, EN, SNH, DANI, MAFF, SOAEFD, WOAD)

5.2.4 Protect nationally important localities for nightjars from damaging developments through the planning process. (ACTION: CCW, EHS, EN, SNH)

5.2.5 Incorporate suitable policies for the conservation of lowland heathland and other important nightjar nesting and foraging areas into Development Plans, Regional Government Strategies, Indicative Forestry Strategies and Heathland Strategies. (ACTION: LAs)

5.2.6 Seek to secure long-term funding for county heathland management projects. (ACTION: EN, LAs)

5.3 Species management and protection

5.3.1 None proposed.

5.4 Advisory

5.4.1 Produce specific advisory material for the management of heathland and forestry plantations for nightjars. (ACTION: EN, FE)

5.5 Future research and monitoring

5.5.1 Monitor changes to the numbers and range of nightjars through a national survey every 10 years (next survey due in 2002) as part of the statutory agencies/RSPB programme of scarce bird monitoring. (ACTION: JNCC)

5.5.2 Investigate the availability of the nightjar's food supply. (ACTION: CCW, EN, SNH)

5.5.3 Evaluate the condition of heathland in the former range of nightjar and the potential for remedial management. (ACTION: EN, SNH)

5.6 Communications and publicity

5.6.1 Use the nightjar as a species to promote the conservation of heathland. (ACTION: EN)

5.7 Links with other action plans

5.7.1 It is likely that implementation of this action plan will also benefit the woodlark.

5.7.2 The plan should be considered in conjunction with those for lowland heathland and lowland acid grassland.

Nightjar ·

Caprimulgus europaeus

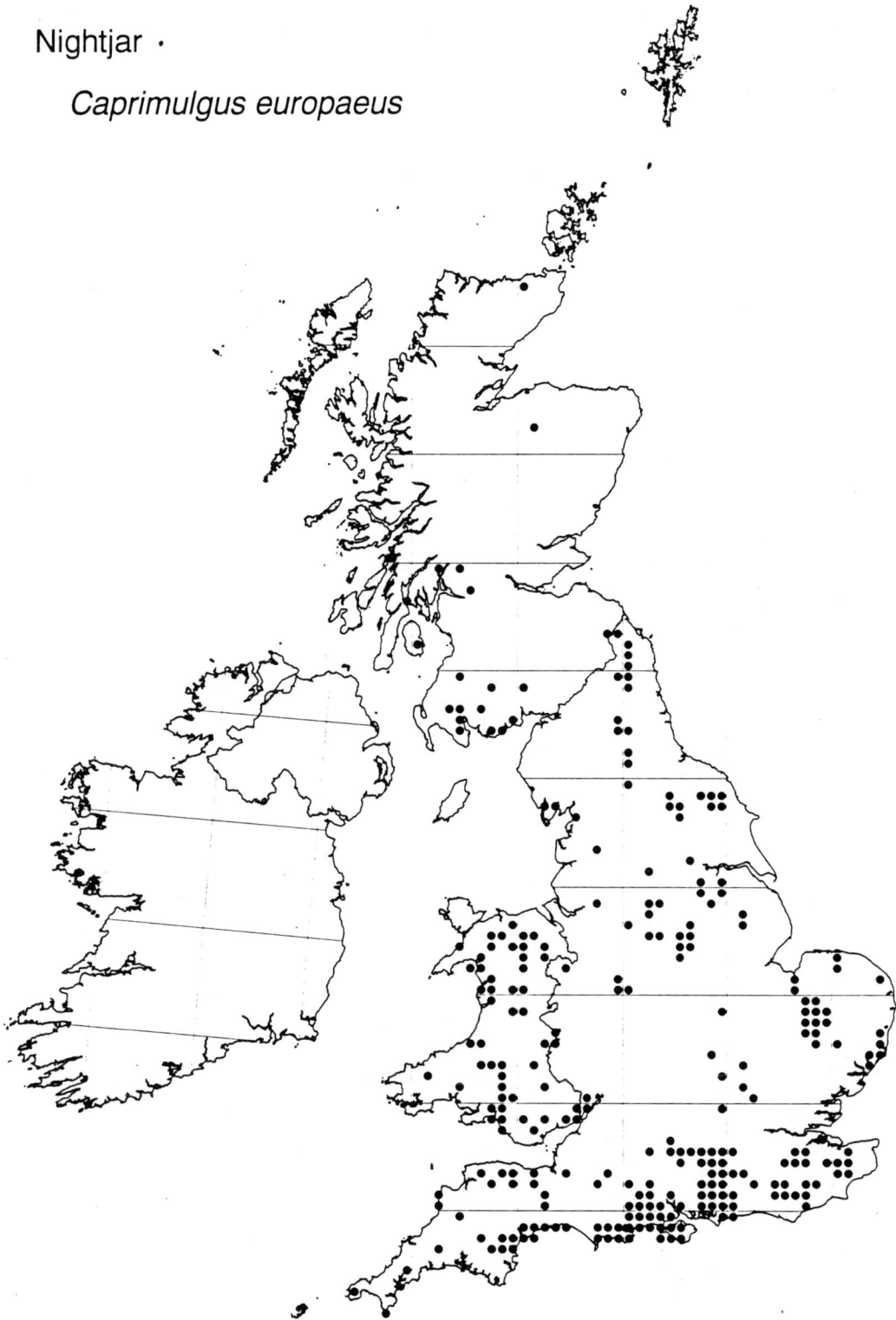

Breeding distribution of Nightjar in Britain and Ireland (by 10 Km square).
Source: RSPB, 1992 Nightjar Survey.

●·   Record of breeding

Linnet (*Carduelis cannabina*)
Action Plan

1. Current status

1.1 The linnet is a common and widespread species across the UK countryside where it uses weedy fields, hedgerows, gorse thickets, heathland and scrub (particularly near the coast). However, based on the Common Bird Census, numbers declined by 56% on farmland between 1968 and 1991. Their UK range declined only slightly over this period but was most marked in Northern Ireland. The UK population was estimated at 540,000 territories in the New Breeding Atlas (1988-91). It is widespread and common in much of Europe, though declining in some areas, particularly The Netherlands and Finland. A variable proportion of the UK breeding population winters in Spain and western France; the birds remaining in the UK are joined by breeding birds from northern Europe.

1.2 The linnet is protected under the Wildlife and Countryside Act 1981, the Wildlife (Northern Ireland) Order 1985 and EC Birds Directive, and is listed on Appendix II of the Bern Convention.

2. Current factors causing loss or decline

2.1 The recent decline of the linnet has occurred at the same time as decreases in the numbers and/or range of other farmland birds which share its diet of grass and wildflower seeds, and some cereal grains. Linnets are more dependent than other seed-eaters on wildflower seeds during the breeding season, when the chicks are also fed on seeds rather than insects. It is likely that the decline in linnets may be due to changes in agricultural practice, both in the UK and in their wintering range in south-west Europe. These include the increased use of herbicides and fertilisers, the switch from spring-sown to autumn-sown crops and the consequent loss of winter stubble fields, and the general reduction in farmland habitat diversity due to the loss of mixed farming and increased specialisation.

2.2 Changes in management of pastoral areas may also have caused declines through the increased use of fertilisers, re-seeding of species-rich fields, more intensive grazing, early cutting for silage and the loss of the small proportion of arable fields that were typically present on such farms.

2.3 The removal of hedges, gorse thickets and other unmanaged scrub, combined with the increased frequency and severity of hedge trimming and heavy grazing in some areas, will have led to losses of suitable nesting habitat.

3. Current action

3.1 Until recently, the linnet was not regarded as a high priority species for conservation action but it is likely to have benefited, incidentally, at a small number of individual sites from initiatives for other species associated with heathland and scrub habitats, particularly in coastal situations. A good example is the acquisition and management of heathland, including the establishment and management of gorse for Dartford warblers.

3.2 Large stretches of rocky coast have been brought under appropriate conservation management, which involves intensive land use on cliff-tops, particularly by the National Trust under 'Enterprise Neptune'.

3.3 The provision of rotational set-aside will have benefited the species, although this has been significantly reduced in area in recent years. New prescriptions encouraging the growing of spring cereals and retention of winter stubbles in the South Downs ESA, and the pilot Arable Stewardship Scheme, should also benefit the linnet.

3.4 Linnets may also have benefited from the provision of game cover crops and the young stages of conifer plantations.

4. Action plan objectives and targets

4.1 In the short term, halt or reverse the decline in numbers of the linnet by the year 2003 so that the Breeding Bird Survey index is at least at 1996 levels.

4.2 In the long term, see a sustained recovery in numbers so that the BBS index is at least 50% higher than 1996 levels and the range has recovered to 1968-1972 levels by 2008.

5. Proposed action with lead agencies

The priorities for linnet are to obtain a better understanding of its year-round habitat and other ecological requirements, and promote widespread sympathetic land management accordingly. It is also important that the UK population is monitored to enable trends to be identified.

5.1 Policy and legislation

5.1.1 Take account of the need to recover linnet and other farmland bird populations when developing agricultural policy and CAP reform; consider how to extend the Arable Stewardship Scheme if the pilot is successful, and how to substitute for the benefits of set-aside, if this is further reduced or abolished. Retention of coastal and other scrub habitats should be encouraged. (ACTION: DANI, MAFF, SOAEFD, WOAD)

5.1.2 Where appropriate, incorporate new management prescriptions when reviewing agri-environment schemes, especially ESAs, Countryside Stewardship,

Tir Cymen and Countryside Premium Scheme, in order to reverse some of the recent changes in farm management outlined in Section 2. (ACTION: CCW, DANI, MAFF, SOAEFD, WOAD)

5.1.3 Seek uptake of a more cautious and targeted use of herbicides and fertilisers on farmland to reduce the impacts on potential food sources for the linnet. This could include encouraging integrated crop management, organic farming and the more widespread adoption of initiatives such as the recently begun Scottish 'TIBRE' project. (ACTION: DANI, MAFF, SOAEFD, WOAD)

5.2   Site safeguard and management

5.2.1 None proposed.

5.3   Species management and protection

5.3.1 None proposed.

5.4   Advisory

5.4.1 Promote further advice to land managers on management for linnets as one of a suite of farmland birds and update that advice in the light of new policies and research findings. (ACTION: DANI, FA, MAFF, SOAEFD, WOAD)

5.4.2 Promote effective management of set-aside for breeding and wintering birds, including linnet. (ACTION: DANI, MAFF, SOAEFD, WOAD)

5.4.3 Promote the effective management of hedgerows and farmland scrub for the benefit of linnet and other farmland birds. (ACTION: DANI, MAFF, SOAEFD, WOAD)

5.5   Future research and monitoring

5.5.1 Ensure appropriate monitoring of numbers through continuation of the BTO/JNCC/RSPB Breeding Bird Survey and consider the setting up of an equivalent survey to monitor winter populations. (ACTION: CCW, EHS, EN, JNCC, SNH)

5.5.2 Study the diet of the linnet in different breeding habitats and relate this to nesting success. Information is required on the diet of adults at different stages of the year, particularly during the summer, and on the food supplied by the adults to chicks and fledglings. (ACTION: CCW, EHS, EN, FA, JNCC, SNH)

5.5.3 Investigate winter survival of linnet in relation to habitat and food availability and hence improve knowledge of the winter habitat requirements of the species. (ACTION: CCW, EHS, EN, FA, JNCC, SNH)

5.6   Communications and publicity

5.6.1 As appropriate, use the linnet as an example when highlighting the issue of declining farmland birds. (ACTION: CCW, EH, EN, SNH)

5.6.2 Promote a change in perception of wild plants on farmland as essential food sources for seed-eating farmland birds rather than as 'weeds'. (ACTION: DANI, MAFF, SOAEFD, WOAD)

5.7   Links with other action plans

5.7.1 It is likely that implementation of this action plan will also benefit the following UK BAP farmland birds: bullfinch, corn bunting, grey partridge, reed bunting, skylark, song thrush, tree sparrow, turtle dove.

5.7.2 The plan should be considered in conjunction with those for cereal field margins and ancient hedgerows.

Linnet

Carduelis·cannabina

Breeding distribution of Linnet in Britain and Ireland, 1988-1991 (by 10 Km square).
Source: Gibbons, D.W., Reid, J.B. and Chapman, R.A. (1993). The new atlas of breeding birds in Britain and Ireland 1988-1991. Calton, U.K.: T. and A.D. Poyser.

●   Record of breeding

·   Record with no evidence of breeding

Cirl bunting (*Emberiza cirlus*)
Action Plan

1. Current status

1.1 The cirl bunting is closely associated with traditional, mixed farming and was found in many parts of southern Britain in the last century. In 1938 it was still widely distributed across southern England with isolated populations as far north as north Wales. However, by 1970 the population had declined and notable gaps had appeared in its range. The population crashed in the next decade and a national survey in 1989 found only 118 pairs of which all but four were in south Devon. Since then the Devon population has begun to increase with an estimated 370 occupied territories in 1996. The species is largely sedentary and a small number of males still survive at an isolated site in Cornwall, although extinction here seems likely. Elsewhere in Europe it occurs around the Mediterranean and in temperate regions, and declines have been reported in a number of areas.

1.2 The cirl bunting is specially protected under Schedule I of the Wildlife and Countryside Act 1981 and EC Birds Directive, and is listed on Appendix II of the Bern Convention.

2. Current factors causing loss or decline

Research by RSPB since the late 1980s strongly suggests that a number of factors relating to changes in agricultural practice are largely responsible for the decline of this species. They include:

2.1 Loss of winter food. A marked reduction in cereal stubbles and other wildflower-rich fields, and the loss of stockyards and threshing yards, have greatly reduced winter food availability. The indirect effects of pesticides may have been a contributory factor at the start of the cirl bunting decline and could hinder future range expansion.

2.2 Loss of food for chicks. Chicks are predominantly fed on large insects, especially grasshoppers and crickets, which have declined due to intensive grassland management (fertilising, re-seeding, close-grazing etc) associated with dairying and livestock rearing in the south-west. This results in poor productivity due to the starvation of chicks, and it is likely that poorly-fed broods are more easily found by corvids and other predators.

2.3 Habitat loss. Built developments, removal of hedges and, in the long term, abandonment of arable land have all resulted in the loss of cirl bunting breeding and wintering sites.

2.4 Disturbance. Cirl buntings are especially prone to disturbance from birdwatchers, walkers and other visitors during the breeding season and the post-fledging period.

2.5 Weather. Cirl buntings are especially vulnerable to hard winter weather, particularly when snow cover makes food in stubble fields unavailable. This is of particular concern because the species is found in only one small area of the country. Cool, wet conditions in the breeding season result in poor breeding success although, since the cirl bunting has a protracted breeding season, it is possible for good numbers of young to be reared even when the early season weather is poor.

3. Current action

3.1 As a result of RSPB research, enough is now known about the most important requirements of cirl buntings to enable direct conservation action to be taken, mainly through a project officer funded by an RSPB/EN Species Recovery Project, with support from a range of other partners including MAFF and local authorities.

3.2 Farmers in the key areas have been persuaded to retain stubble fields through the winter and these have been well used by cirl buntings. The benefits of set-aside to the species have been widely promoted to relevant individuals and organisations. A considerable number of Countryside Stewardship agreements have been signed and implemented. Practical advice to landowners, local authorities, advisers and others on how to conserve cirl buntings has been acted upon.

3.3 A recent survey has identified potential localities in southern England (mid Somerset, Isle of Wight) which could support cirl buntings in the future but which require suitable management of farmland. Translocation to such areas may be necessary as the species shows very poor dispersal abilities.

4. Action plan objectives and targets

4.1 In the short term, maintain the upward trend in numbers and increase in distribution (within the current range) of the cirl bunting population in the UK.

4.2 Increase the UK population to 550 territories by the year 2003.

4.3 In the long term, ensure a wider geographical spread of the cirl bunting by re-establishing populations outside the current (1997) range.

5. Proposed action with lead agencies

The objectives and targets for cirl bunting will be achieved through: protecting breeding and wintering sites in south-west England from inappropriate agricultural management, development and other adverse land-use change;

promoting measures to enhance the farmland environment for the species (particularly winter stubbles, unimproved grassland and mixed farming); if appropriate, using techniques such as supplementary feeding during hard weather and reintroduction into former breeding localities; and raising the profile of cirl bunting as a bird of conservation concern without causing undue additional disturbance. Continuing the programme of cirl bunting monitoring and research is also essential.

5.1 Policy and legislation

5.1.1 Take account of the need to recover cirl bunting and other farmland bird populations when developing agricultural policy and CAP reform; consider how to extend the Arable Stewardship Scheme if the pilot is successful, and how to substitute for the benefits of set-aside, if this is further reduced or abolished. (ACTION: MAFF)

5.1.2 Where appropriate, incorporate new management prescriptions when reviewing agri-environment schemes, especially ESAs and Countryside Stewardship, in order to reverse some of the recent changes in farm management outlined in Section 2. (ACTION: MAFF)

5.1.3 Seek uptake of a more cautious and targeted use of pesticides and fertilisers on farmland to reduce the impacts on potential food sources for the cirl bunting. This could include encouraging integrated crop management and organic farming. (ACTION: MAFF)

5.2 Site safeguard and management

5.2.1 Secure a minimum of 25 new Countryside Stewardship Scheme agreements per year, for the years 1998-2000, that will deliver cirl bunting management in south Devon. This should include the provision of at least 40 ha of winter stubble per year (120 ha over three years). (ACTION: MAFF)

5.2.2 Promote positive management on existing SSSIs that support cirl buntings. (ACTION: EN)

5.2.3 Incorporate policies to assist cirl bunting conservation in appropriate development plans. (ACTION: LAs)

5.2.4 Protect key cirl bunting breeding and wintering sites from significant adverse changes due to development. (ACTION: EN)

5.3 Species management and protection

5.3.1 Continue to fund action for cirl buntings through English Nature's Species Recovery Programme. (ACTION: EN)

5.3.2 Consider reintroductions as an aid to cirl bunting conservation. (ACTION: EN)

5.3.3 Provide supplementary food for cirl buntings when hard winter weather prevents access to natural food in fields. (ACTION: EN)

5.4 Advisory

5.4.1 Promote further advice to land managers on management for cirl buntings as one of a suite of farmland birds and update that advice in the light of new policies and research findings. (ACTION: EN, MAFF)

5.5 Future research and monitoring

5.5.1 Continue the programme of cirl bunting research and monitoring including annual sampling of nesting success and periodic full surveys of the breeding population approximately every 10 years (next survey due in 1998). (ACTION: EN)

5.6 Communications and publicity

5.6.1 Promote the need for cirl bunting conservation, particularly to land managers, birdwatchers and holiday-makers. (ACTION: EN)

5.7 Links with other action plans

5.7.1 It is likely that implementation of this plan will also benefit the following UK BAP farmland birds: bullfinch, corn bunting, grey partridge, linnet, reed bunting, skylark, song thrush, turtle dove.

5.7.2 The plan should be considered in conjunction with those for cereal field margins and ancient hedgerows.

Cirl Bunting

Emberiza cirlus

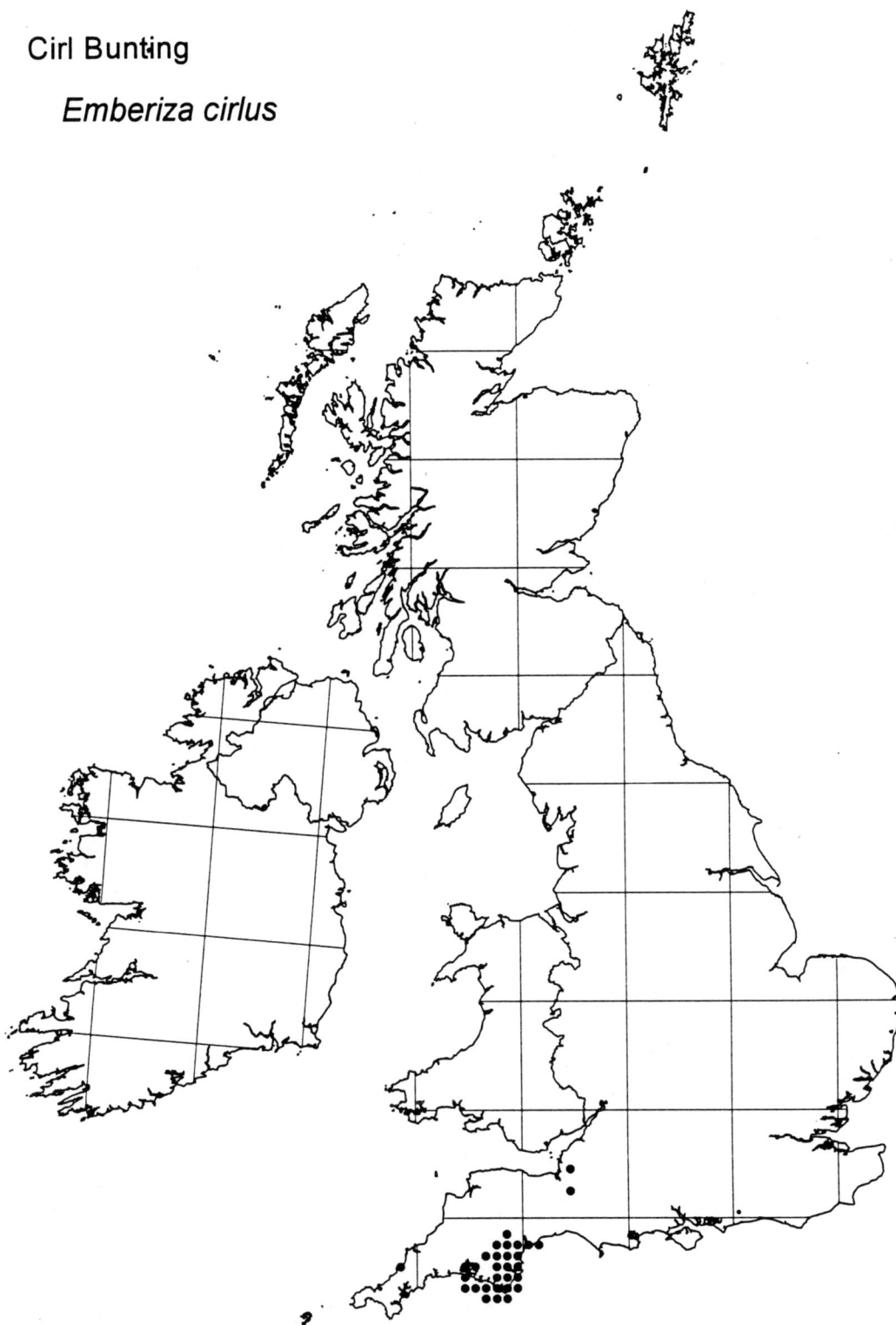

Breeding distribution of Cirl Bunting in Britain and Ireland, 1993-1995 (by 10 Km square).
Source: RSPB data (reserves, research and conservation officers).

●   Record of breeding

·   Record with no evidence of breeding

Reed bunting (*Emberiza schoeniclus*)
Action Plan

1. Current status

1.1 The reed bunting inhabits reedbeds and other wetland habitats, as well as drier farmland sites such as overgrown ditches and hedgerows. The species is found throughout Britain and Ireland, although it is scarcer in the uplands and the far north and west. There are also some gaps in distribution elsewhere but with no clear pattern. A decline in numbers has occurred in recent years. In Britain, BTO census results show a relatively high population level from the late 1960s to the mid 1970s, followed by a decrease of more than 50% to a new, more stable lower level during the early 1980s. The Waterways Bird Survey, in particular, showed a steep decline from 1974 to 1983, but little change in numbers since then. The species also decreased in range by around 12% between the two breeding atlas periods (1968-72 and 1988-91), with the UK population estimated at around 240,000 pairs during the latter period. It is not a species of conservation concern elsewhere in Europe where it is common and widespread.

1.2 The reed bunting is protected under the Wildlife and Countryside Act 1981, the Wildlife (Northern Ireland) Order 1985 and EC Birds Directive, and is listed on Appendix II of the Bern Convention.

2. Current factors causing loss or decline

These are not well known though are thought to include the following factors:

2.1 The decline of the reed bunting has occurred at the same time as decreases in the numbers and/or range of a suite of other farmland birds, many of which share its diet of cereal, grass and wildflower seeds, and also feed their young on insects. It is therefore likely that its decline on farmland may be largely due to: changes in agricultural practice, particularly the increased use of pesticides and fertilisers; the switch from spring-sown to autumn-sown crops and the consequent loss of winter stubble fields; the more intensive use of grassland; and the general reduction in habitat diversity on farmland due to the loss of mixed farming and increased specialisation.

2.2 Deterioration of wet habitats may have had a serious effect on populations. BTO census data suggest that numbers in wetland habitats have declined. Loss of small ponds, unsympathetic river engineering and the encroachment of scrub and carr are all likely to have had adverse effects on both the breeding and wintering populations. The main period of recent land drainage was 1968-85, when both arterial watercourses and field drains were modified on a large scale, leading to a loss in both the quantity and quality of the reed bunting's characteristic wetland habitats.

3. Current action

3.1 The reed bunting has not previously been regarded as a priority species for conservation action, but it is likely to have benefited incidentally from initiatives for other wetland species since it readily moves into newly-created wetlands. Conservation organisations have devoted considerable resources to the acquisition and management of reedbeds, wet grassland, saltmarsh and other wetlands.

3.2 The species has also benefited from rotational set-aside, although this has been significantly reduced in area in recent years. New prescriptions encouraging the growth of spring-sown cereals and retention of winter stubbles in the South Downs ESA, and the pilot Arable Stewardship Scheme should also benefit the reed bunting.

4. Action plan objectives and targets

4.1 In the short term, halt or reverse the decline in numbers of the reed bunting by the year 2003 so that the Breeding Bird Survey index is at least at 1996 levels.

4.2 In the long term, see a sustained recovery in numbers so that the BBS index is at least 50% higher than 1996 levels, in both wetland and farmland habitats, by 2008.

5. Proposed action with lead agencies

The priorities for reed bunting are to obtain a better understanding of the factors affecting its numbers and distribution in farmland and wetland habitats, and to identify and promote suitable management prescriptions. The UK population should be monitored to enable trends to be identified.

5.1 Policy and legislation

5.1.1 Take account of the need to recover the reed bunting and other farmland bird populations when developing agricultural policy and CAP reform; consider how to extend the Arable Stewardship Scheme if the pilot is successful, and how to substitute for the benefits of set-aside, if this is further reduced or abolished. (ACTION: DANI, MAFF, SOAEFD, WOAD)

5.1.2 Where appropriate incorporate new management prescriptions when reviewing agri-environment schemes, especially ESAs, Countryside Stewardship, Tir Cymen and Countryside Premium Scheme, in order to reverse some of the recent changes in farm management outlined in Section 2. (ACTION: CCW, DANI, MAFF, SOAEFD, WOAD)

5.1.3 Seek uptake of a more cautious and targeted use of pesticides and fertilisers on farmland to reduce the impacts on potential food sources for the reed bunting. This could include encouraging integrated crop management and organic farming and the more widespread adoption of initiatives such as the recently begun Scottish 'TIBRE' project. (ACTION: DANI, MAFF, SOAEFD, WOAD)

5.1.4 Promote sympathetic management of watercourses for reed bunting. (ACTION: EA, EHS, SEPA)

5.2   Site safeguard and management

5.2.1 None proposed.

5.3   Species management and protection

5.3.1 None proposed.

5.4   Advisory

5.4.1 Promote further advice to land managers on management for reed buntings as one of a suite of farmland birds, and update that advice in the light of new policies and research findings. (ACTION: DANI, MAFF, SOAEFD, WOAD)

5.4.2 Promote effective management of set-aside for breeding and wintering birds, including the reed bunting. (ACTION: DANI, MAFF, SOAEFD, WOAD)

5.4.3 Promote advice on the sympathetic management of freshwater wetlands and farmland watercourses to landowners and managers. (ACTION: DANI, EA, MAFF, SEPA, SOAEFD, WOAD)

5.5   Future research and monitoring

5.5.1 Ensure appropriate monitoring of the breeding population through continuation of the BTO/JNCC/RSPB Breeding Bird Survey and consider setting up an equivalent survey to monitor winter populations. (ACTION: CCW, EHS, EN, JNCC, SNH)

5.5.2 Analyse information on breeding habitats on farmland which was gathered during the BTO corn bunting survey. (ACTION: CCW, EHS, EN, JNCC, SNH)

5.5.3 Consider the need for a detailed study into the ecology of the reed bunting. (ACTION: CCW, EHS, EN, JNCC, SNH)

5.6   Communications and publicity

5.6.1 As appropriate, use the reed bunting as an example when highlighting the issue of declining farmland birds. (ACTION: CCW, DANI, EHS, EN, JNCC, MAFF, SNH, SOAEFD, WOAD)

5.6.2 Promote a change in perception of wild plants on farmland as essential food sources for seed-eating farmland birds, rather than as 'weeds'. (ACTION: CCW, DANI, EHS, EN, JNCC, MAFF, SNH, SOAEFD, WOAD)

5.7   Links with other action plans

5.7.1 It is likely that implementation of this action plan will benefit the following UK BAP farmland species: bullfinch, corn bunting, grey partridge, linnet, skylark, song thrush, tree sparrow, turtle dove.

5.7.2 The plan should be considered in conjunction with those for cereal field margins, reedbeds, grazing marsh and coastal salt marsh.

Reed Bunting

Emberiza schoeniclus

Breeding distribution of Reed Bunting in Britain and Ireland, 1988-1991 (by 10 Km square). Source: Gibbons, D.W., Reid, J.B. and Chapman, R.A. (1993). The new atlas of breeding birds in Britain and Ireland 1988-1991. Calton, U.K.: T. and A.D. Poyser.

●   Record of breeding

·   Record with no evidence of breeding

Wryneck (*Jynx torquilla*)
Action Plan

1. Current status

1.1 The wryneck was formerly common in central and south-east England, breeding north to Durham and Cumbria, and west to Devon and Wales. The population declined to 150-400 pairs in south-east England by 1954-1958, 20-30 pairs in 1966 and one pair in 1973. Since then there has been only sporadic breeding in England. Habitat was typically orchards or over-mature woodland close to unimproved grassland rich in ants, their main prey. In Scotland, birds (probably of Scandinavian origin) were first recorded in Highland pine and birch woods in 1951. Breeding was first confirmed in 1969 with a peak of seven pairs in 1977. Colonisation has since faltered, with no more than one pair confirmed in any year since 1985. It bred successfully in 1993, but there was no recorded breeding in 1994. The wryneck is a regular migrant to sites in eastern Britain. The European population is estimated at 350,000-1,000,000 pairs.

1.2 The wryneck is specially protected under Schedule 1 of the Wildlife and Countryside Act 1981 and is listed on Appendix II of the Bern Convention. It is protected as a migratory species under the EC Birds Directive.

2. Current factors causing loss or decline

2.1 Loss of feeding habitat. This has been due to ploughing of downland and unimproved grassland, and degradation of pasture due to myxomatosis and the decline of rabbits. The latter changed ant populations, reduced ant densities, or made them unavailable.

2.2 Loss of nesting habitat, especially the felling of orchards and over-mature trees, which were replaced by orchards of young trees or converted to arable.

2.3 Increasing use of pesticides. In common with a number of other species, the wryneck population decline coincided with the increasing use of agricultural chemicals in lowland habitats. It seems likely that this reduced the amount of insect food available.

3. Current action

3.1 Any breeding pairs discovered are monitored and protected.

3.2 The encouragement of Caledonian pine forest expansion and other mature, native woodland in Scotland is likely to provide core breeding and feeding areas.

4. Action plan objectives and targets

4.1 Retain the wryneck as a regular breeding species in the UK.

4.2 Ensure that sufficient suitable habitat in the Scottish breeding area is maintained to support a population of wrynecks.

5. Proposed action with lead agencies

Meeting the objectives for this species will depend primarily on availability of suitable breeding and feeding habitat, as well as protection of individual nest locations.

5.1 Policy and legislation

5.1.1 Ensure the protection of remaining fragments of mature pine and broadleaved forest in Strathspey and the restoration or expansion of these habitats into appropriate areas. (ACTION: SNH, FA, FE)

5.2 Site safeguard and management

5.2.1 Ensure that appropriate protection is given to any regularly used nesting localities. (ACTION: SNH, FE)

5.2.2 Manage or encourage management of Caledonian Pine Forest reserves to promote mature and overmature components, with a high proportion of standing dead trees. (ACTION: SNH, FA)

5.2.3 In the light of the conclusions of 5.5.2, consider whether a programme of experimental habitat management of appropriate sites is necessary. (ACTION: SNH, EN)

5.3 Species management and protection

5.3.1 Ensure that breeding pairs of wrynecks found in Scotland or England in future years are monitored, and protected from disturbance or persecution. (ACTION: SNH, EN)

5.4 Advisory

5.4.1 None proposed.

5.5 Future research and monitoring

5.5.1 Ensure all recent nest sites are checked annually and monitor all breeding attempts. Liaise with the Rare Birds Breeding Panel to obtain additional information. (ACTION: SNH, EN)

5.5.2 Investigate wryneck ecology through a desk study of food and habitat requirements of European populations, particularly Scandinavian. (ACTION: SNH, EN)

5.6   Communications and publicity

5.6.1 Ensure that breeding sites of wrynecks are kept confidential, in liaison with bird information services. (ACTION: SNH, EN)

5.7   Links with other action plans

5.7.1 It is likely that wryneck will benefit from actions arising from the native pinewood and possibly lowland wood pastures and parklands habitat action plans.

Wryneck

Jynx torquilla

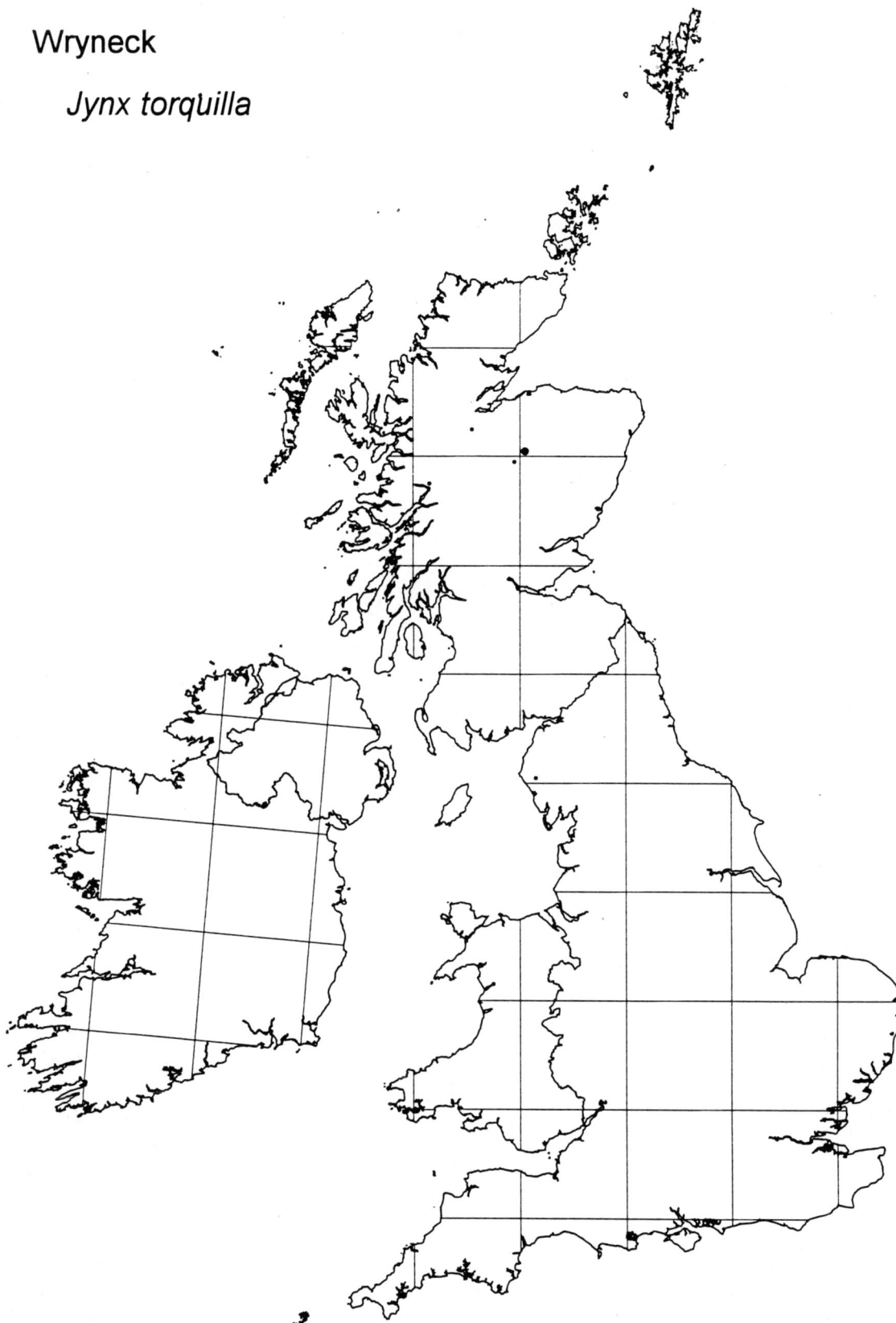

Breeding distribution of Wryneck in Britain and Ireland, 1988-1991 (by 10 Km square).
Source: Gibbons, D.W., Reid, J.B. and Chapman, R.A. (1993). The new atlas of breeding birds in Britain and Ireland 1988-1991. Calton, U.K.: T. and A.D. Poyser.

●　　　Record of breeding

·　　　Record with no evidence of breeding

71

Red-backed shrike (*Lanius collurio*)
Action Plan

1. Current status

1.1 The red-backed shrike is a summer migrant that was formerly widespread in farmland, scrub and heathland over much of England and Wales. Following a dramatic decline, it is no longer a regular breeder in the UK. As late as the first breeding atlas (1968-72) there was confirmed breeding in 65 ten km squares. However, by 1980 the population was almost confined to heathland in East Anglia and, in 1989, there was no confirmed breeding for the first time. Since then, nesting in England has been sporadic. The occurrence of six to eight pairs in three successive summers (1977-79) in Scotland gave rise to hopes of colonisation from Scandinavia but there has been only occasional breeding since then. In Europe it is widely distributed but is declining throughout much of its range, especially in north-west Europe (eg a 50% decline in Sweden over the last 20 years). The species winters in east and south Africa and migrates via south-east Europe.

1.2 The red-backed shrike is specially protected under Schedule 1 of the Wildlife and Countryside Act 1981 and is listed on Annex 1 of the EC Birds Directive and Appendix II of the Bern Convention.

2. Current factors causing loss or decline

These are not well known, but are thought to include the following:

2.1 Habitat loss. Red-backed shrikes formerly bred in a range of habitats including commons, waste ground, overgrown hedgerows, young plantations and other scrubby habitats, as well as on heathland. In its latter years, the population was concentrated on lowland heathland. It has been shown that, at a local level, habitat loss in the form of scrub clearance resulted in double the rate of population decline compared with that in other areas. However, since the decline in numbers has set in, areas where the habitat has remained have been deserted for reasons as yet unknown. Research in Europe has suggested that a mosaic of suitable feeding habitats is important.

2.2 Food supply. The species feeds primarily on large flying insects whose abundance has probably been reduced by agricultural intensification, including habitat loss and change, and the increased use of pesticides and fertilisers. Declines in invertebrate food may have been exacerbated by habitat loss but may also have occurred where former breeding habitat remains apparently unaltered. Changes to habitat and food supply in the wintering and migration areas may have affected the population in a similar way.

2.3 Demographic effects, in particular reduced mating opportunities. There is evidence that potential breeding birds have struggled to find a mate as breeding densities were reduced, and ringed adults have been observed to move considerable distances from their previous nesting areas, which is unusual for passerines.

2.4 Egg collection. Red-backed shrike clutches appear to hold a special attraction to egg collectors. Between 1960 and 1970, the population within areas subjected to egg collecting was believed to have decreased twice as rapidly compared with areas not subjected to either this threat or habitat destruction.

2.5 Disturbance. The species attracts attention from birdwatchers in considerable numbers if it nests in a publicly accessible place. Although the species is tolerant of people on the continent and at nest sites in the UK, it is prone to desert their food caches or 'larders' if they are inspected.

3. Current action

3.1 RSPB, FC and others have been involved in wardening breeding sites to prevent disturbance by birdwatchers and liaise with landowners.

3.2 A literature review of possible factors affecting the population has been completed and a CASE studentship into the ecology of the species (part-funded by RSPB and Sheffield University) is currently being carried out in Austria.

4. Action plan objectives and targets

4.1 Ensure the success of any pairs of red-backed shrikes which attempt to breed in the UK and therefore maximise the chances of recolonisation.

5. Proposed action with lead agencies

Learning more about the habitat needs and therefore management requirements of this species is crucial to assist re-colonisation. Other priorities for the species are to provide wardening to protect breeding pairs (but only where a clear need is identified) and, where necessary, to keep the whereabouts of any breeding pairs confidential (except to landowners and to statutory agency/NGO staff).

5.1 Policy and legislation

5.1.1 None proposed.

5.2 Site safeguard and management

5.2.1 Where the species is found to occur, ensure that its conservation needs are actively considered in development policies and proposals. (ACTION: EN, LAs, SNH)

5.3   Species management and protection

5.3.1   Maintain nest site confidentiality (but see 5.6.1 below) and investigate all reliable reports of egg collecting. (ACTION: CCW, EN, SNH, Police Authorities)

5.3.2   Consider wardening of sensitive, accessible sites to prevent undue disturbance from birdwatchers or members of the public. (ACTION: CCW, EN, SNH)

5.4   Advisory

5.4.1   Provide advice to landowners/site managers on the prevention of disturbance and habitat management to maintain and, if possible, enhance habitat suitability of breeding sites. (ACTION: CCW, EN, SNH)

5.5   Future research and monitoring

5.5.1   Monitor breeding attempts through the Rare Breeding Birds Panel. (ACTION: JNCC)

5.5.2   Encourage research into the ecology and management needs of this species throughout the year in order to improve the chances of re-colonisation and the success of any breeding attempts. (ACTION: CCW, EN, JNCC, SNH)

5.6   Communications and publicity

5.6.1   In cooperation with landowners/occupiers, consider providing a public viewing facility where nesting occurs in a popular public site and where some form of wardening effort is required. (ACTION: CCW, EN, SNH)

5.7   Links with other action plans

5.7.1   None proposed.

Red-backed Shrike

Lanius collurio

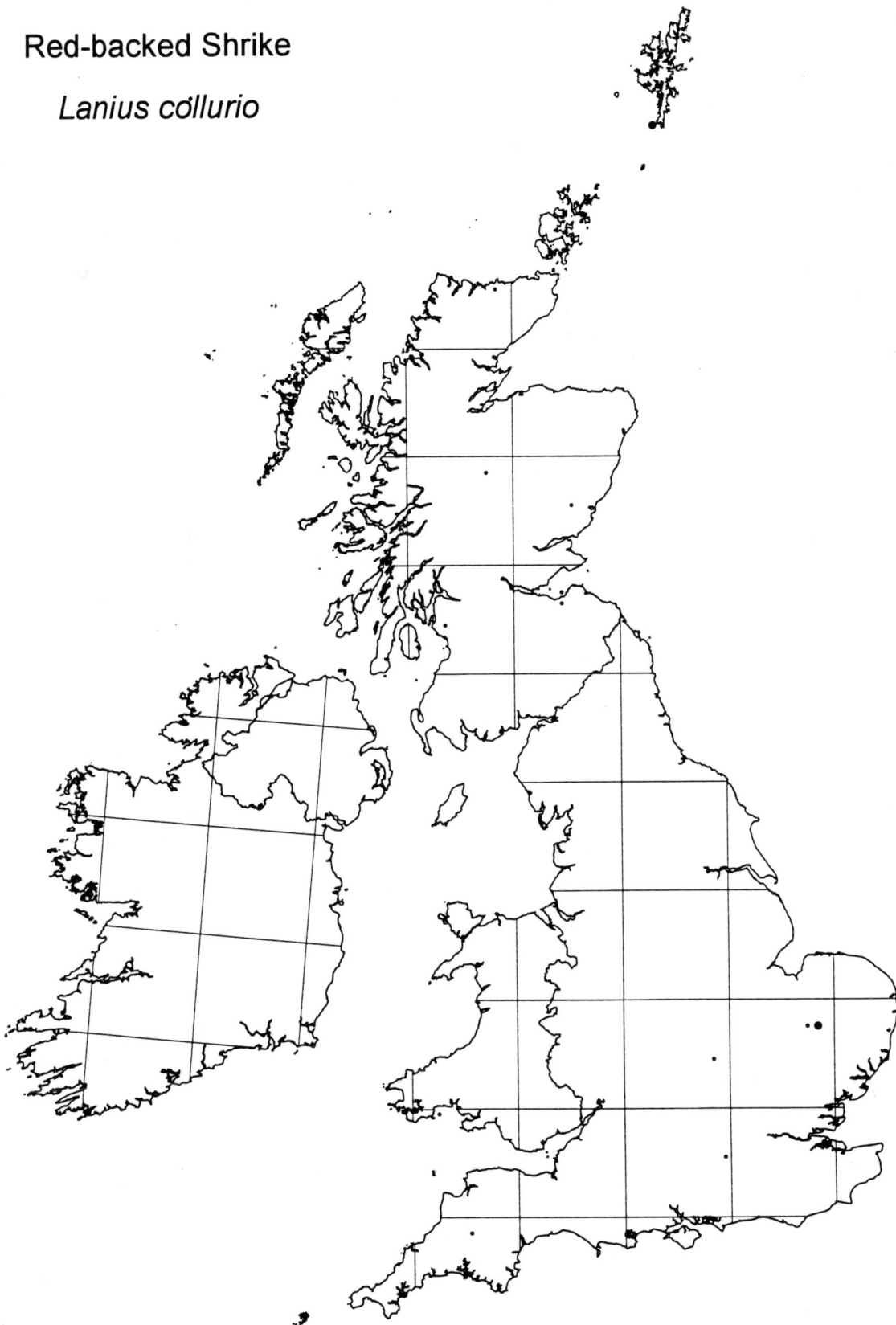

Breeding distribution of Red-backed Shrike in Britain and Ireland, 1988-1991 (by 10 Km square). Source: Gibbons, D.W., Reid, J.B. and Chapman, R.A. (1993). The new atlas of breeding birds in Britain and Ireland 1988-1991. Calton, U.K.: T. and A.D. Poyser.

●   Record of breeding

·   Record with no evidence of breeding

Woodlark (*Lullula arborea*)
Action Plan

1. Current status

1.1 The woodlark was formerly found across Britain, south from Yorkshire, and in Northern Ireland, but is now largely restricted to five core areas: Devon, east Dorset/south Hampshire (including the New Forest), the Surrey/Hampshire border, Breckland and the Suffolk coast. The number of ten km squares occupied in the breeding season decreased by 62% (from 198 to 73 ten km squares) between 1968-72 and 1988-91. However, since 1986 (when the population was estimated to be around 250 pairs) the population has increased with up to 620 pairs breeding in 1993, and the 1997 survey has recorded around 1500 pairs. The nesting habitats are varied and include farmland, recently felled forestry plantations (mainly in East Anglia) and heathland in southern England and the Suffolk coast. Early results from the 1997 survey suggest that around 50% of breeding pairs across the country are now nesting on set-aside and other weedy fields. The recent increase in the population has largely resulted from the provision of new plantation habitats within the current core areas. Little is known of the woodlark's winter requirements and distribution, although there appears to be some movement southwards within England and to the continent. In Europe the woodlark is declining in both numbers and range.

1.2 The woodlark is protected under Schedule 1 of the Wildlife and Countryside Act 1981 and listed on Annex 1 of the EC Birds Directive and Appendix II of the Bern Convention.

2. Current factors causing loss or decline

2.1 An estimated 40% of England's lowland heathland has been lost since the 1950s. This has led to a loss of feeding and nesting habitats for woodlarks. Whilst losses to afforestation and agriculture have declined, threats from roads and housing developments continue.

2.2 Woodlarks require a mosaic of bare ground or short vegetation for feeding, and tussocks of vegetation with disturbed ground for nest sites. Lack of appropriate management can lead to sites becoming unsuitable for the species. Rabbits play a key role in creating bare ground and short grass at many sites, and their decline following myxomatosis in the 1950s may have played a significant part in the decline of the woodlark.

2.3 In Devon woodlarks breed on farmland, using mosaics of set-aside, arable and horticultural crops, unimproved rough pasture and other marginal habitats. Most of the territories are on moderate to steep slopes. More intensive management, for example reseeding and fertiliser application which would decrease bare ground feeding areas, or conversion to other uses, have been cited as causes of the decline in Devon.

2.4 Severe winter weather and, in particular, snow cover has had an adverse impact on winter survival. The hard winters of 1962/63 and 1981/82 had considerable impact on woodlark populations on the southern heathlands.

3. Current action

3.1 Woodlarks occur on a number of heathland nature reserves which are managed partly for their benefit.

3.2 Research has been carried out by RSPB and FC on the habitat use of woodlarks in restocked conifer plantations in Breckland. This has allowed the impact of changes in the age-structure of forests to be predicted, enabling Design Plans in Thetford Forest to be modified and so maintain good numbers of woodlarks.

3.3 The work of county heathland projects (managed by EN, RSPB and local authorities), including the introduction of fire breaks, increasing areas of short heather following tree removal and other management, has assisted this species on a number of heathland sites in Dorset, the Suffolk Sandlings, Surrey, north-east Hampshire and west Sussex.

3.4 The woodlark has also benefited from heathland management encouraged by the Breckland ESA and Countryside Stewardship Scheme.

3.5 The woodlark has also benefited incidentally from the provision of set-aside (see 1.1).

3.6 An RSPB leaflet on woodlarks in Devon has been produced for farmers in the county.

4. Action plan objectives and targets

4.1 Maintain a population of around 1500 breeding pairs of woodlark within the existing range of around 90 ten km squares.

4.2 Increase the range of the woodlark from 90 to 120 ten km squares, including the recolonisation of Wales and south-west England, by 2008, coupled with further increases in the population.

5. Proposed action with lead agencies

The objectives and targets above are to be achieved by protecting, maintaining, restoring and re-establishing lowland heathland; encouraging the maintenance/restoration of extensively managed, mixed agricultural systems; and ensuring the adoption of sympathetic management of afforested land. Population size and range needs to be monitored.

5.1 Policy and legislation

5.1.1 Ensure that clear targets for the woodlark are incorporated into appropriate site management plans, particularly land managed by the MoD and local authorities. (ACTION: EN, LAs, MoD)

5.1.2 Prepare and implement an Endangered Species Action Plan for woodlarks on FE land, to include specific targets for woodlarks in Forest Design Plans in forests within their current and former range. (ACTION: FE)

5.1.3 Take full account of the requirements of the woodlark when considering felling and restocking proposals. (ACTION: FA, FE)

5.1.4 Encourage the development of extensively-managed, mixed agricultural systems to provide suitable rough grassland and spring-sown cereals with winter stubbles, through appropriate agri-environment schemes. (ACTION: MAFF, WOAD)

5.1.5 Encourage the uptake of schemes supporting the reversion of arable land to heathland through ESAs and Countryside Stewardship. (ACTION: MAFF)

5.1.6 Seek to extend the Wildlife Enhancement Scheme (WES) to other key areas of lowland heathland in England. (ACTION: EN)

5.2 Site safeguard and management

5.2.1 Consider notifying heathland sites important for woodlarks as SSSI/ASSIs. (ACTION: EN)

5.2.2 Designate as SPAs areas of 'special interest' that support nationally important populations of woodlarks (subject to current guidelines) and encourage their appropriate management. (ACTION: DETR, EN)

5.2.3 Seek to achieve 'favourable conservation status' of the woodlark by measures complementary to SPAs. This will include projects to maintain, enhance and restore heathland adjacent to SPAs (eg through agri-environment schemes). (ACTION: DETR, EN, MAFF)

5.2.4 Protect nationally important localities for woodlarks from damaging developments and land use change using the planning process. (ACTION: EN)

5.2.5 Incorporate suitable policies for the conservation of lowland heathland into Development Plans, Regional Government Strategies, Indicative Forestry Strategies and Heathland Strategies. (ACTION: LAs)

5.2.6 Seek to secure long-term funding for county heathland management projects. (ACTION: DETR, EN, LAs)

5.2.7 Introduce or continue management for woodlarks on heathland nature reserves. (ACTION: EN, LAs)

5.3 Species management and protection

5.3.1 None proposed.

5.4 Advisory

5.4.1 Produce specific advisory material for the management of heathland and forestry plantations for woodlarks. (ACTION: EN, FA, FE)

5.4.2 Revise the leaflet produced for farmers in Devon in the light of new information from the 1997 breeding survey. (ACTION: EN, MAFF)

5.4.3 Promote effective management of set-aside for breeding and wintering birds, including woodlark. (ACTION: MAFF, WOAD)

5.5 Future research and monitoring

5.5.1 Monitor the UK breeding population of woodlarks every 10 years through the statutory agencies'/RSPB programme of scarce bird monitoring (next survey due in 2007). (ACTION: JNCC)

5.5.2 Consider the need for habitat usage survey and monitoring in the south-west. (ACTION: EN)

5.6 Communications and publicity

5.6.1 Use the woodlark as a species to support the conservation of heathland and extensively managed mixed farmland. (ACTION: EN)

5.7 Links with other action plans

5.7.1 It is likely that implementation of this action plan will also benefit the nightjar.

5.7.2 The plan should be considered in conjunction with those for lowland heathland and lowland acid grassland.

Woodlark

Lullula arborea

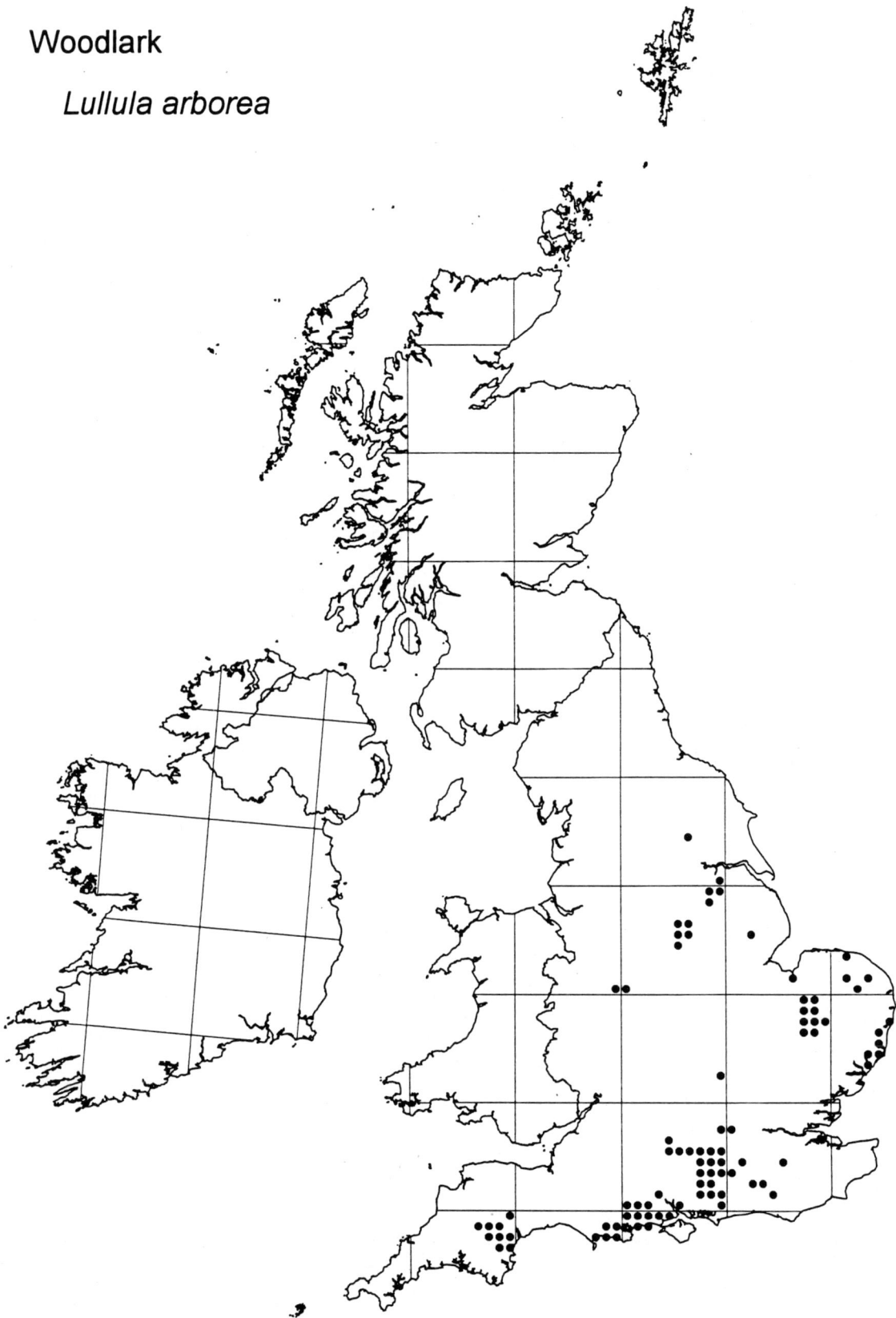

Breeding distribution of Woodlark in Britain and Ireland, 1995-1996 (by 10 Km square).
Source: RSPB data, 1997 Woodlark Survey.

●   Record of arbeding

Common scoter (*Melanitta nigra*) breeding & wintering Action Plan

1.   Current status

1.1   The UK breeding population of common scoter has declined by more than 50% in the last 25 years. In Northern Ireland, 150 pairs in 1967 declined to zero in the early 1990s. All existing breeding pairs are in Scotland. Detailed survey in 1995 found 89 females in Scotland (and 111 in the Republic of Ireland). In eight years common scoters in the Flow Country have declined by 49%, from 55 pairs in 1988 to only 28 in 1996. Breeding habitat includes mesotrophic lochs, blanket bog and heather moorland.

1.2   Common scoters have important moulting and wintering localities in the UK, with 25,000-30,000 distributed in inshore waters. Most of these birds originate in Fennoscandia and western Siberia. The wintering areas of British breeding common scoters are unknown.

1.3   The common scoter is specially protected under Schedule 1 of the Wildlife and Countryside Act 1981 and the Wildlife (Northern Ireland) Order 1985. It is protected as a migratory species under the EC Birds Directive and is listed on Appendix III of the Bern Convention.

2.   Current factors causing loss or decline

2.1   Wintering concentrations of common scoters are extremely vulnerable to large-scale oil spills.

2.2   Eutrophication may detrimentally affect food availability. Water clarity and level, and weed growth are also potentially important factors.

2.3   Fish stocking may have led to increased competition for invertebrate food in some breeding lakes.

2.4   Predation by mink may have been responsible for a steady change in sex-ratio in favour of males in Lower Lough Erne. Foxes are also a problem in some areas.

2.5   Afforestation, and its secondary effects such as sedimentation and increased access, are a possible threat to the Scottish population.

2.6   Modern commercial harvesting of sand-dwelling shellfish may threaten common scoters' food resources.

3.   Current action

3.1   Some 81% of Flow Country common scoters nest in protected areas, and on Islay all but one site is designated. Reserves have been established at Lower Lough Erne and Forsinard. Part of the common scoter population occurs within the Shetland and Argyll Islands ESAs.

3.2   Two conservation schemes operate in the Flow Country (LIFE-nature scheme and the SNH Peatland Management Scheme). Both should assist the conservation of common scoter.

3.3   Statutory and voluntary bodies have been seeking improvement of procedures for coastal oil transportation.

4.   Action plan objectives and targets

4.1   In Scotland, increase the breeding population to at least 100 pairs by 2008, and maintain at least the existing range.

4.2   Regain common scoter as a breeding species in Northern Ireland.

4.3   Safeguard the current range and distribution of moulting and wintering common scoters.

5.   Proposed action with lead agencies

There is an urgent need to support research and monitoring into ecological factors that affect the distribution and population trends of breeding common scoter. Other essential actions include protecting important breeding and wintering sites, and encouraging appropriate habitat management.

5.1   Policy and legislation

5.1.1   Seek the implementation of effective legislation to enable site protection of important common scoter marine wintering sites. (ACTION: DETR, EHS, SOAEFD)

5.1.2   Consider the adoption of improved pollution prevention and control measures, including MEHRAs, and shipping management measures. (ACTION: CCW, DETR, DTI, EA, EHS, EN, Harbour authorities, JNCC, LAs, MCA, SEPA, SNH)

5.1.3   Take forward enforcement of MARPOL limits on deliberate discharges, port waste management plans and oil spill contingency planning. (ACTION: CCW, DETR, DTI, EA, EHS, EN, Harbour authorities, JNCC, LAs, MCA, SEPA, SNH)

5.1.4   Ensure that licensing of offshore oil and gas blocks does not detrimentally affect important wintering or moulting sites of common scoters. (ACTION: CCW, DTI, EHS, EN, JNCC, SNH)

5.1.5   Seek the introduction of improved shellfish harvesting and monitoring practices which recognise important and/or designated common scoter areas. (ACTION: DANI, MAFF, SOAEFD, WOAD)

5.1.6 Consider the potential impacts of afforestation proposals on mesotrophic lochs, flows and heather moorland in common scoter areas. (ACTION: DANI(FS), FC, SEPA)

5.2 Site safeguard and management

5.2.1 Encourage positive management of peatlands and moorland around common scoter nesting sites. (ACTION: DANI, EHS, SAC, SNH, SOAEFD)

5.2.2 Designate important breeding, moulting and wintering sites as SSSI/ASSI and SPA for common scoters, and encourage their appropriate management. (ACTION: CCW, DETR, EHS, EN, SNH, SOAEFD)

5.2.3 Liaise with the Republic of Ireland over the impact of the Ballyshannon hydro-electric power station on common scoters and the potential for recolonisation. (ACTION: EHS)

5.2.4 Ensure that detrimental effects of development proposals on regular breeding sites and key wintering/moulting sites for common scoters are minimised. (ACTION: CCW, EHS, EN, LAs, SNH, SOAEFD)

5.2.5 Identify forestry sites adjacent to breeding common scoter sites where undesirable impacts could be remedied. (ACTION: FC, SNH)

5.2.6 Seek to enhance water quality in Lower Lough Erne to improve chances of common scoter recolonisation. (ACTION: DANI, EHS)

5.3 Species management and protection

5.3.1 Monitor the impact of predators on breeding populations of common scoters, and consider control if necessary. (ACTION: SNH)

5.4 Advisory

5.4.1 Provide advice to wetland owners and managers about the requirements of common scoters. (ACTION: EHS, SNH)

5.5 Future research and monitoring

5.5.1 Revise methods of survey and monitoring of wintering common scoters. (ACTION: CCW, EHS, EN, JNCC, SNH)

5.5.2 Pass information gathered during survey and monitoring of this species to JNCC and the Rare Breeding Birds Panel. (ACTION: CCW, EHS, EN, SNH)

5.5.3 Investigate the ecology, food sources and origin of wintering and moulting common scoters. (ACTION: CCW, EHS, EN, SNH)

5.5.4 Investigate the ecology of breeding common scoters, including food availability, water quality, competitors, predators, and habitat, and clarify impacts of afforestation. (ACTION: FC, SEPA, SNH)

5.5.5 Promote research into the wintering grounds of UK breeding birds and the origins of birds wintering in UK waters. (ACTION: CCW, EHS, EN, JNCC, SNH)

5.6 Communications and publicity

5.6.1 Raise the profile of common scoter as a species that has recently become extinct as a breeder in Northern Ireland and is under threat from land-use changes in the Flow Country. (ACTION: CCW, EHS, EN, JNCC, SNH)

5.7 Links with other action plans

5.7.1 Common scoter may benefit from actions arising out of the eutrophic and mesotrophic standing waters habitat action plans.

Common Scoter

Melanitta nigra

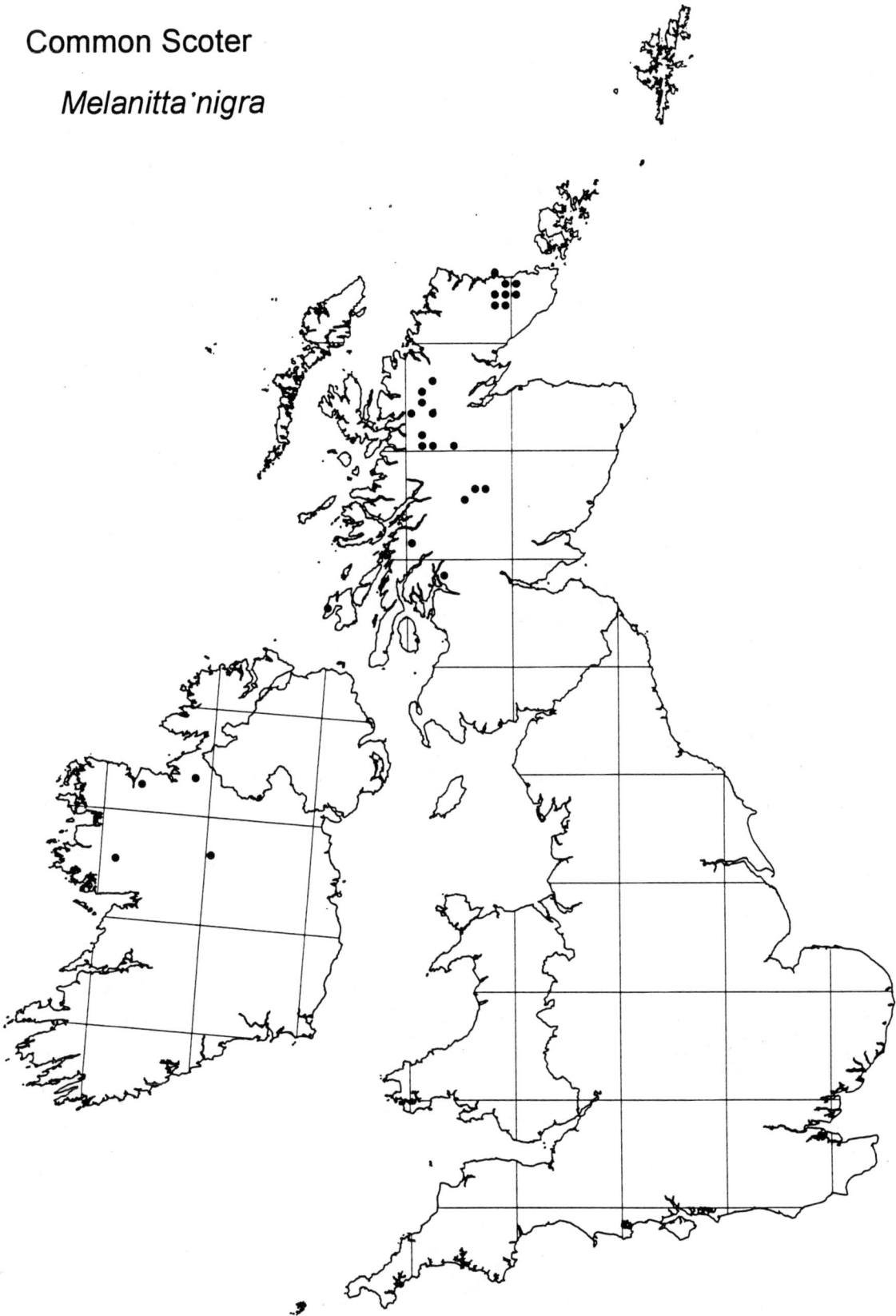

Breeding distribution of Common Scoter in Britain and Ireland, 1995-1996 (by 10 Km square). Source: Wildfowl and Wetlands Trust, Slimbridge. Report to the Sea Empress Environmental Evaluation Committee (1996).

●   Record of breeding

83

Common Scoter

Melanitta nigra

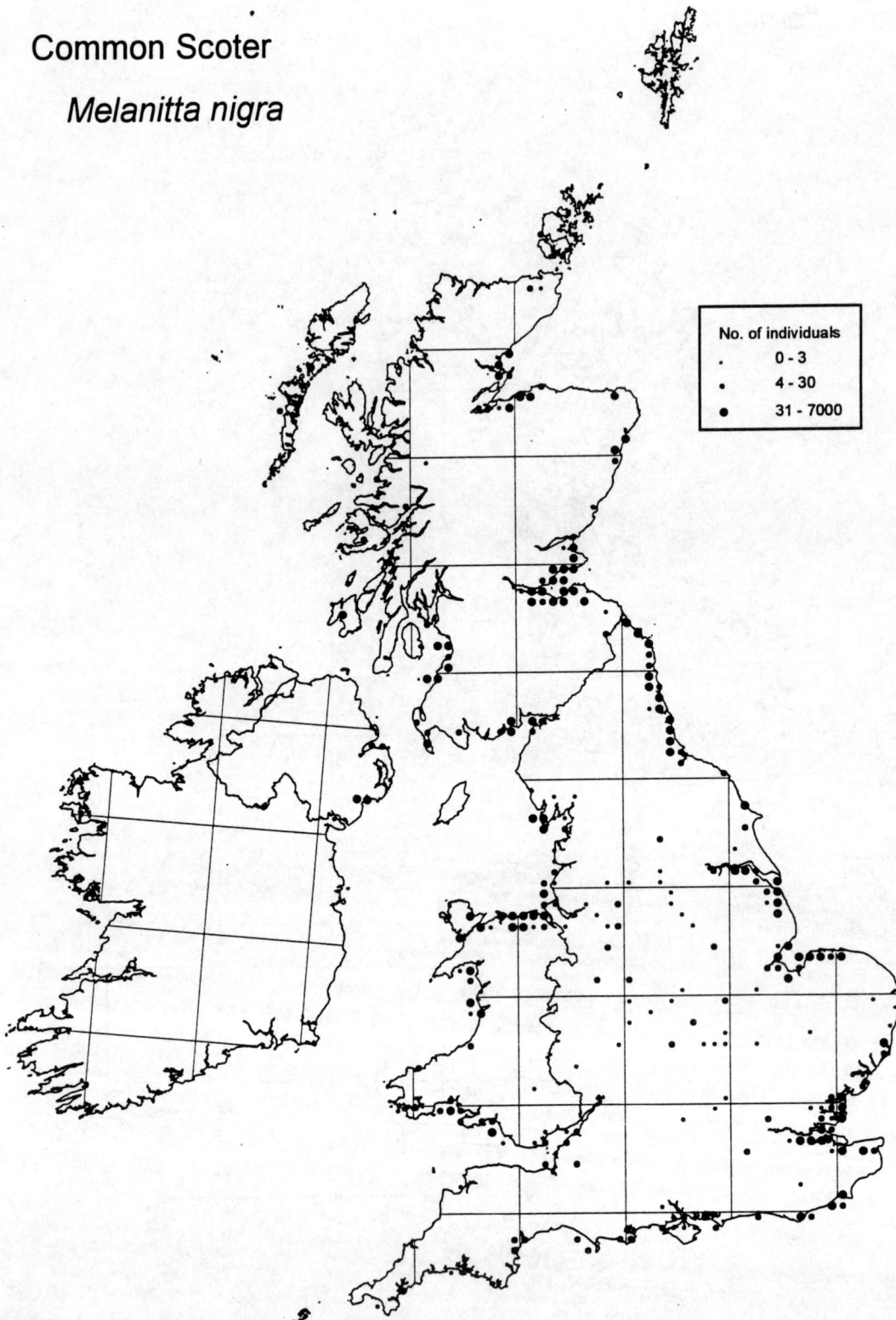

No. of individuals
.   0 - 3
•   4 - 30
●   31 - 7000

Wintering distribution of Common Scoter in Britain and Ireland, 1991-1997 (by 10 Km square).
Source: Wetland Bird Survey (WeBS).

Note: This data is compiled from the data supplied by volunteers for the Wetland Bird Survey.
As such, this is not a dedicated Common Scoter survey and does not represent a complete coverag

84

Corn bunting (*Miliaria calandra*)
Action Plan

1. Current status

1.1 The corn bunting is a characteristic resident species of lowland arable farmland and is one of the few British species largely dependent on cropped land. Its distribution is curious with the bulk of the population found across southern and eastern England but with small outlying groups as far away as Cornwall, the Outer Hebrides and north-east Scotland. Its numbers and distribution have been declining in some areas since the last century and steadily, in most places, since the early 1970s, a trend which appears to be continuing. The results of the Common Bird Census suggest that there was a 76% decline in the breeding population between 1968 and 1991. In addition, a decline of 32% in its British range between the two breeding atlas periods (1968-72 and 1988-91) has led to further fragmentation of the remaining high density areas and the loss of the species from many areas such as Devon, Shetland, and parts of the West Midlands and south-east England. The Farmland Bunting Survey, organised by the BTO in 1993, recorded only around 20,000 territories remaining in Britain, with no confirmed breeding in Wales. None was found breeding in Northern Ireland during the 1988-91 atlas survey. The species is declining over much of north-west Europe but remains common and widespread in southern Europe.

1.2 The corn bunting is protected under the Wildlife and Countryside Act 1981, Schedule 1 of the Wildlife (Northern Ireland) Order 1985 and the EC Birds Directive.

2. Current factors causing loss or decline

2.1 Although the precise factors remain unclear, the loss of extensive mixed farming would appear to be the key to the decline of the corn bunting.

2.2 Loss of winter food is thought to be a probable cause of the population decline. The BTO's winter corn bunting survey, in 1992/93, showed that weedy stubble fields were by far the most important feeding habitat during the winter. The area of winter stubbles has been greatly reduced in recent decades due to the switch from spring-sown to autumn-sown cereals, the decline in mixed farming and the disappearance of undersowing. In addition, increased herbicide and fertiliser use has reduced the abundance of wildflower seeds.

2.3 Reduced breeding productivity. The intensification of farming practices, such as the increased use of pesticides and fertilisers, has reduced the availability of insects which are essential as chick food. Changes in grazing/mowing regimes may reduce nest site availability and breeding success on grassland, and the decline in mixed farming has led to the disappearance of insect-rich (and reduced input) undersown spring cereals.

3. Current action

3.1 Until recently the corn bunting was not regarded as a species of conservation concern and, hence, little direct action has been taken to help it.

3.2 Census work by the BTO has highlighted the plight of the species and a current GCT/EN/RSPB research project is investigating the causes of the decline, particularly with respect to agricultural intensification.

3.3 Rotational set-aside will have benefited the species, although this has been significantly reduced in area in recent years. New prescriptions encouraging the growth of undersown spring-sown cereals and retention of winter stubbles in the South Downs ESA, and the pilot Arable Stewardship Scheme, should also benefit the corn bunting.

4. Action plan objectives and targets

4.1 In the short term, halt or reverse the decline in numbers of the corn bunting by the year 2003 so that the Breeding Bird Survey index is at least at 1996 levels.

4.2 In the long term, see a sustained recovery in numbers, so that the BBS index is at least 50% higher than 1996 levels with a measurable increase in range by 2008.

5. Proposed action with lead agencies

The objectives and targets will be delivered through: identifying the causes of the decline of the corn bunting; encouraging beneficial changes in agricultural land management through government mechanisms; and ensuring monitoring is in place to assess the benefits of agricultural schemes to corn buntings.

5.1 Policy and legislation

5.1.1 Take account of the need to recover the corn bunting and other farmland bird populations when developing agricultural policy and CAP reform; consider how to extend the Arable Stewardship Scheme if the pilot is successful, and how to substitute for the benefits of set-aside, if this is further reduced or abolished. (ACTION: DANI, MAFF, SOAEFD, WOAD)

5.1.2 Where appropriate, incorporate new management prescriptions when reviewing agri-environment schemes, especially ESAs, Countryside Stewardship, Tir Cymen and Countryside Premium Scheme, in order to reverse some of the recent changes in farm management outlined in Section 2. (ACTION: CCW, DANI, MAFF, SOAEFD, WOAD)

5.1.3 Seek uptake of a more cautious and targeted use of pesticides and fertilisers on farmland to reduce the impacts on potential food sources for the corn bunting. This could include encouraging integrated crop management, organic farming and the more widespread adoption of initiatives such as the recently begun Scottish 'TIBRE' project. (ACTION: DANI, MAFF, SOAEFD, WOAD)

5.2 Site safeguard and management

5.2.1 None proposed.

5.3 Species management and protection

5.3.1 None proposed.

5.4 Advisory

5.4.1 Promote further advice to land managers on management for corn bunting as one of a suite of farmland birds and update that advice in the light of new policies and research findings. (ACTION: DANI, MAFF, SOAEFD, WOAD)

5.4.2 Promote effective management of set-aside for breeding and wintering birds, including corn bunting. (ACTION: DANI, MAFF, SOAEFD, WOAD)

5.5 Future research and monitoring

5.5.1 Carry out further studies to gain an adequate understanding of the ecological requirements of the corn bunting, including the role of different factors in the decline of the species in different parts of the UK. (ACTION: CCW, DANI, EHS, EN, JNCC, MAFF, SNH, SOAEFD, WOAD)

5.5.2 Ensure appropriate monitoring of the breeding population through continuation of the BTO/JNCC/RSPB Breeding Bird Survey and consider setting up an equivalent survey to monitor winter populations. (ACTION: CCW, EHS, EN, JNCC, SNH)

5.5.3 Consider including corn bunting in any future work which assesses the effects of set-aside, ESAs, the pilot Arable Stewardship Scheme and other mechanisms which may encourage farmland birds. (ACTION: DANI, MAFF, SOAEFD, WOAD)

5.6 Communications and publicity

5.6.1 As appropriate, use the corn bunting as an example when highlighting the issue of declining farmland birds. (ACTION: CCW, DANI, EHS, EN, JNCC, MAFF, SNH, SOAEFD, WOAD)

5.6.2 Promote the importance of traditional crofting with cattle and mixed cultivation for the conservation of corn buntings in western Scotland, and of traditional ley farming elsewhere in the UK. (ACTION: CCW, DANI, EHS, EN, JNCC, MAFF, SNH, SOAEFD, WOAD)

5.6.3 Promote a change in perception of wild plants on farmland as essential food sources for seed-eating farmland birds, rather than as 'weeds'. (ACTION: CCW, DANI, EHS, EN, JNCC, MAFF, SNH, SOAEFD, WOAD)

5.7 Links with other action plans

5.7.1 It is likely that implementation of this action plan will also benefit the following UK BAP farmland birds: bullfinch, grey partridge, linnet, reed bunting, skylark, song thrush, tree sparrow, turtle dove.

5.7.2 The plan should be considered in conjunction with that for cereal field margins.

Corn Bunting

Miliaria calandra

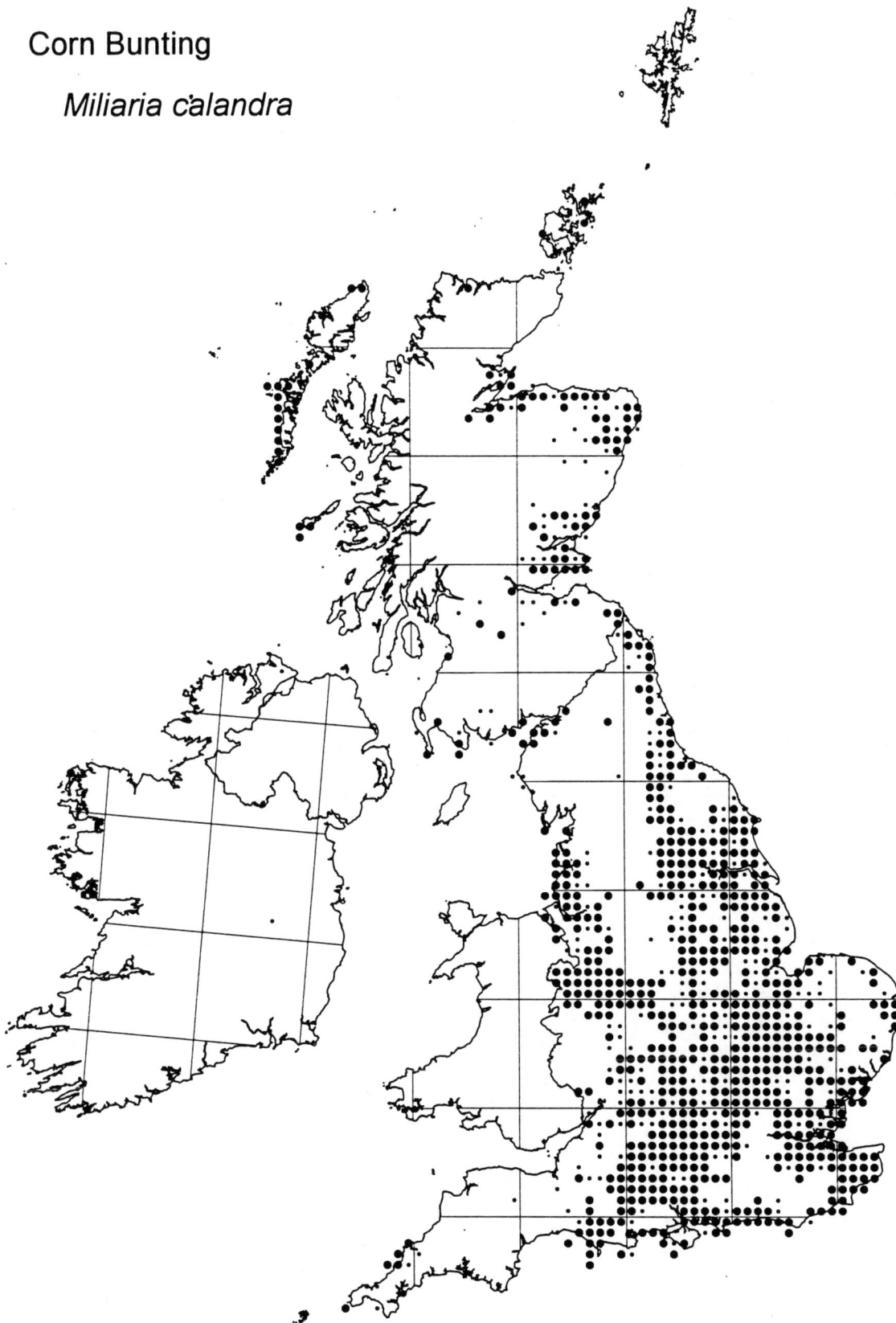

Breeding distribution of Corn Bunting in Britain and Ireland, 1988-1991 (by 10 Km square).
Source: Gibbons, D.W., Reid, J.B. and Chapman, R.A. (1993). The new atlas of breeding birds
in Britain, and Ireland 1988-1991. Calton, U.K.: T. and A.D. Poyser.

●   Record of breeding

·   Record with no evidence of breeding

Spotted flycatcher (*Muscicapa striata*)
Action Plan

1. Current status

1.1 The spotted flycatcher is an insectivorous summer migrant which breeds in open wooded habitats throughout the UK. Preferred habitats are mature broadleaved woodland (though it will also use mature conifers), hedgerows with mature trees, parkland and large gardens. The species is scarcer in the far north and west and is almost absent from the Western and Northern Isles. There are additional gaps in distribution elsewhere but with no clear pattern. The species has been in decline since the early 1960s. Common Bird Census data show a 62% decline in woodland and a 70% decline in farmland between 1968 and 1991, though the range had reduced by only 6.6% between the two breeding atlases (1968-72 and 1988-91). The UK population estimate derived from the New Breeding Bird Atlas is 130,000 territories which represents only one quarter of the estimate in the first atlas. The species is a common and widespread summer visitor across mainland Europe, except northern Scandinavia and densely forested, arid or mountainous areas. Numbers are fluctuating in some countries, such as Sweden and The Netherlands, and there is evidence of recent declines in others including Finland, Germany and Spain.

1.2 The spotted flycatcher is protected under the Wildlife and Countryside Act 1981, Wildlife (Northern Ireland) Order 1985 and EC Birds Directive.

2. Current factors causing loss or decline

These are not well known, but may include one or more of the following:

2.1 Weather effects. These appear to be important and could have population impacts if long-term climate change occurs. The key factor appears to be summer weather conditions as more birds breed early if temperatures are warmer, and one study found that clutch sizes are larger when there is more sunshine.

2.2 Drought in the Sahel region. This has been implicated in the declines of a number of trans-Saharan migrants. The spotted flycatcher passes through the Sahel region en route to wintering grounds in southern Africa. Changes in conditions in the Sahel or the wintering areas could be a factor in the species' decline but no clear link has been established.

2.3 Changes in agriculture. Firm data on the importance of this for spotted flycatcher are lacking, but there is growing evidence that a range of birds found on lowland farmland are affected by low invertebrate availability during the summer.

2.4 Loss of nest sites. Many spotted flycatchers nest in large trees and there has been a large-scale loss of these in woodland, parks and hedgerows (especially following Dutch elm disease), which are favoured habitats. However, there are no quantitative data on the effect of these losses.

3. Current action

3.1 Until recently the spotted flycatcher was not regarded as a species of conservation concern, so little action for it has been taken. However, some aspects of broadleaved woodland management, particularly the creation and maintenance of clearings and wide rides, will have benefited the species.

3.2 Provision of nest-boxes (usually for other species) will also have helped spotted flycatchers, particularly in areas with a dearth of natural nest sites.

4. Action plan objectives and targets

4.1 In the short term, halt or reverse the decline in numbers of the spotted flycatcher by the year 2003 so that the Breeding Bird Survey index is at least at 1996 levels.

4.2 In the long term, see a sustained recovery in numbers, so that the BBS index is at least 50% higher than 1996 levels, by 2008.

5. Proposed action with lead agencies

The priority for spotted flycatcher is to obtain a better understanding of its requirements and then promote sympathetic habitat management accordingly. The UK population will need to be monitored to enable trends to be identified.

5.1 Policy and legislation

5.1.1 No action proposed until the outcome of research actions is available. However, it is expected that the species will benefit from the policy actions proposed for other declining farmland birds.

5.2 Site safeguard and management

5.2.1 None proposed.

5.3 Species management and protection

5.3.1 Consider the requirements of nesting spotted flycatchers when providing nest-boxes in nature reserves, country parks and other protected areas. (ACTION: CCW, EHS, EN, FA, LAs, SNH)

5.4   Advisory

5.4.1   Consider the needs of spotted flycatchers in general advice on woodland management. These should include encouraging the provision of broadleaved stands with an open canopy and open spaces, including rides and tree fall gaps. (ACTION: CCW, EHS, EN, FA, SNH)

5.5   Future research and monitoring

5.5.1   Analyse BTO Nest Record Cards from the 1960s to look for changes in productivity which might explain the recent population decline. (ACTION: CCW, EHS, EN, JNCC, SNH)

5.5.2   Undertake a study into the summer ecology and habitat use of spotted flycatchers, including an investigation of the relationship between diet/insect availability, the growth/survival of chicks and fledging success. (ACTION: CCW, EHS, EN, FC, JNCC, SNH, WOAD)

5.5.3   Ensure appropriate monitoring of spotted flycatcher numbers through continuation of the BTO/JNCC/RSPB Breeding Bird Survey. (ACTION: CCW, EHS, EN, JNCC, SNH, WOAD)

5.6   Communications and publicity

5.6.1   No action proposed until the results of research actions are available.

5.7   Links with other action plans

5.7.1   This action plan should be considered in conjunction with those for cereal field margins, ancient hedgerows, and other wooded priority habitats.

Spotted Flycatcher

Muscicapa striata

Breeding distribution of Spotted Flycatcher in Britain and Ireland, 1988-1991 (by 10 Km square). Source: Gibbons, D.W., Reid, J.B. and Chapman, R.A. (1993). The new atlas of breeding birds in Britain and Ireland 1988-1991. Calton, U.K.: T. and A.D. Poyser.

●   Record of breeding

·   Record with no evidence of breeding

Tree sparrow (*Passer montanus*)
Action Plan

1. Current status

1.1 The tree sparrow is patchily distributed on farmland across Britain and Ireland, being scarcer in the uplands, and the far north and west. The main populations are now found across the Midlands, southern and eastern England, with the species almost absent from the south-west, Wales and the north-west. The tree sparrow appears to undergo irregular fluctuations in numbers. In Britain, there was a high population from the 1880s to the 1930s, but numbers then decreased to a low point around 1950, around which time it became extinct in Ireland. Numbers then increased again from 1960 to 1978, possibly due to an influx of birds from mainland Europe. However, based on the Common Bird Census, there was a decline of 85% in numbers in Britain between the two breeding atlas periods (1968-72 and 1988-91), the largest decline of any common species during this period. The tree sparrow also decreased in range by 20% over the same period, with particular losses in Wales and Scotland. The species is still common and widespread across mainland Europe with population trends differing between countries. Populations are mainly sedentary but large-scale autumnal movements occasionally occur, particularly from the more northerly parts of the range.

1.2 The tree sparrow is protected under the Wildlife and Countryside Act 1981, Wildlife (Northern Ireland) Order 1985 and EC Birds Directive.

2. Current factors causing loss or decline

2.1 Little is known about the factors affecting numbers of tree sparrows, but their recent decline has occurred at the same time as decreases in the numbers and/or ranges of other farmland birds which share its diet of grass, wildflower and cereal seeds, and also feed their young on insects. It is therefore likely that its decline is due to changing agricultural practices, particularly the increased use of herbicides; the shift from spring-sown to autumn-sown crops and the consequent loss of winter stubble fields; the more intensive management of grassland; and the general reduction of habitat diversity on farmland due to the loss of mixed farming and increased specialisation.

2.2 As a colonial or semi-colonial hole-nesting species, the availability of nest sites may be a limiting factor, and the fact that nest boxes are readily occupied supports this. The loss of elm trees from lowland Britain during the late 1970s and 1980s would doubtless have removed large numbers of potential nest sites from favoured areas.

3. Current action

3.1 Little direct conservation work for the tree sparrow has been carried out, although nest-box schemes in a number of areas have been implemented.

3.2 Rotational set-aside will have benefited the species, although this has been significantly reduced in area in recent years. New prescriptions encouraging the growth of spring-sown cereals and retention of winter stubbles in the South Downs ESA, and the pilot Arable Stewardship Scheme, should also benefit the tree sparrow.

4. Action plan objectives and targets

4.1 In the short term, halt or reverse the decline in numbers of the tree sparrow by the year 2003 so that the Breeding Bird Survey index is at least at 1996 levels.

4.2 In the long term, see a sustained recovery, so that the BBS index is at least 50% higher than 1996 levels, and a measurable increase in range is achieved, by 2008.

5. Proposed action with lead agencies

The objectives and targets for tree sparrow will be delivered through improving our knowledge of the factors causing the decline in numbers and promoting sympathetic land management to facilitate population recovery. It will be a priority to monitor the UK population to enable trends to be identified.

5.1 Policy and legislation

5.1.1 Take account of the need to recover tree sparrow and other farmland bird populations when developing agricultural policy and CAP reform; consider how to extend the Arable Stewardship Scheme if the pilot is successful, and how to substitute for the benefits of set-aside, if this is further reduced or abolished. Retention of appropriately managed hedgerow trees and farm woodland should be encouraged. (ACTION: DANI, FA, MAFF, SOAEFD, WOAD)

5.1.2 Where appropriate, incorporate new management prescriptions when reviewing agri-environment schemes, especially ESAs, Countryside Stewardship, Tir Cymen and Countryside Premium Scheme, in order to reverse some of the recent changes in farm management outlined in Section 2. (ACTION: CCW, DANI, MAFF, SOAEFD, WOAD)

5.1.3 Seek uptake of a more cautious and targeted use of pesticides and fertilisers on farmland to reduce the impacts on potential food sources for the tree sparrow. This could include encouraging integrated crop management, organic farming and the more widespread adoption of initiatives such as the recently begun Scottish 'TIBRE' project. (ACTION: DANI, MAFF, SOAEFD, WOAD)

5.2 Site safeguard and management

5.2.1 Consider implementing site safeguard measures for a small number of large tree sparrow colonies (ie those in excess of 20 pairs). (ACTION: CCW, EHS, EN, SNH)

5.2.2 Undertake management measures for tree sparrows within protected areas (especially nature reserves) and, where possible, promote them on adjoining farmland. Measures will include nest-box schemes, retention of dead trees and provision of winter feeding habitat. (ACTION: CCW, EHS, EN, SNH)

5.3 Species management and protection

5.3.1 See 5.2.2.

5.4 Advisory

5.4.1 Promote further advice to land managers on management for tree sparrows as one of a suite of farmland birds and update that advice in the light of new policies and research findings. (ACTION: DANI, MAFF, SOAEFD, WOAD)

5.4.2 Promote effective management of set-aside for breeding and wintering birds, including the tree sparrow. (ACTION: DANI, MAFF, SOAEFD, WOAD).

5.5 Future research and monitoring

5.5.1 Carry out an historical review of the species, including analysis of existing BTO Nest Record Cards, in order to investigate the possible reasons for decline. (ACTION: CCW, EHS, EN, JNCC, SNH)

5.5.2 Undertake an autecological study of the tree sparrow in order to determine its requirements and investigate the factors causing the population decline. (ACTION: CCW, EHS, EN, SNH)

5.5.3 Ensure appropriate monitoring of numbers through continuation of the BTO/JNCC/RSPB Breeding Bird Survey and consider the setting up of an equivalent survey to monitor winter populations. (ACTION: CCW, EHS, EN, JNCC, SNH)

5.6 Communications and publicity

5.6.1 As appropriate, use the tree sparrow as an example when highlighting the issue of declining farmland birds. (ACTION: CCW, EHS, EN, SNH)

5.6.2 Promote a change in perception of wild plants on farmland as essential food sources for seed-eating farmland birds, rather than as 'weeds'. (ACTION: DANI, MAFF, SOAEFD, WOAD)

5.7 Links with other action plans

5.7.1 It is likely that implementation of this action plan will also benefit the following UK BAP farmland birds: bullfinch, corn bunting, grey partridge, linnet, reed bunting, skylark, song thrush, turtle dove.

5.7.2 The plan should be considered in conjunction with that for cereal field margins, ancient hedgerows and other wooded priority habitats.

Tree Sparrow

Passer montanus

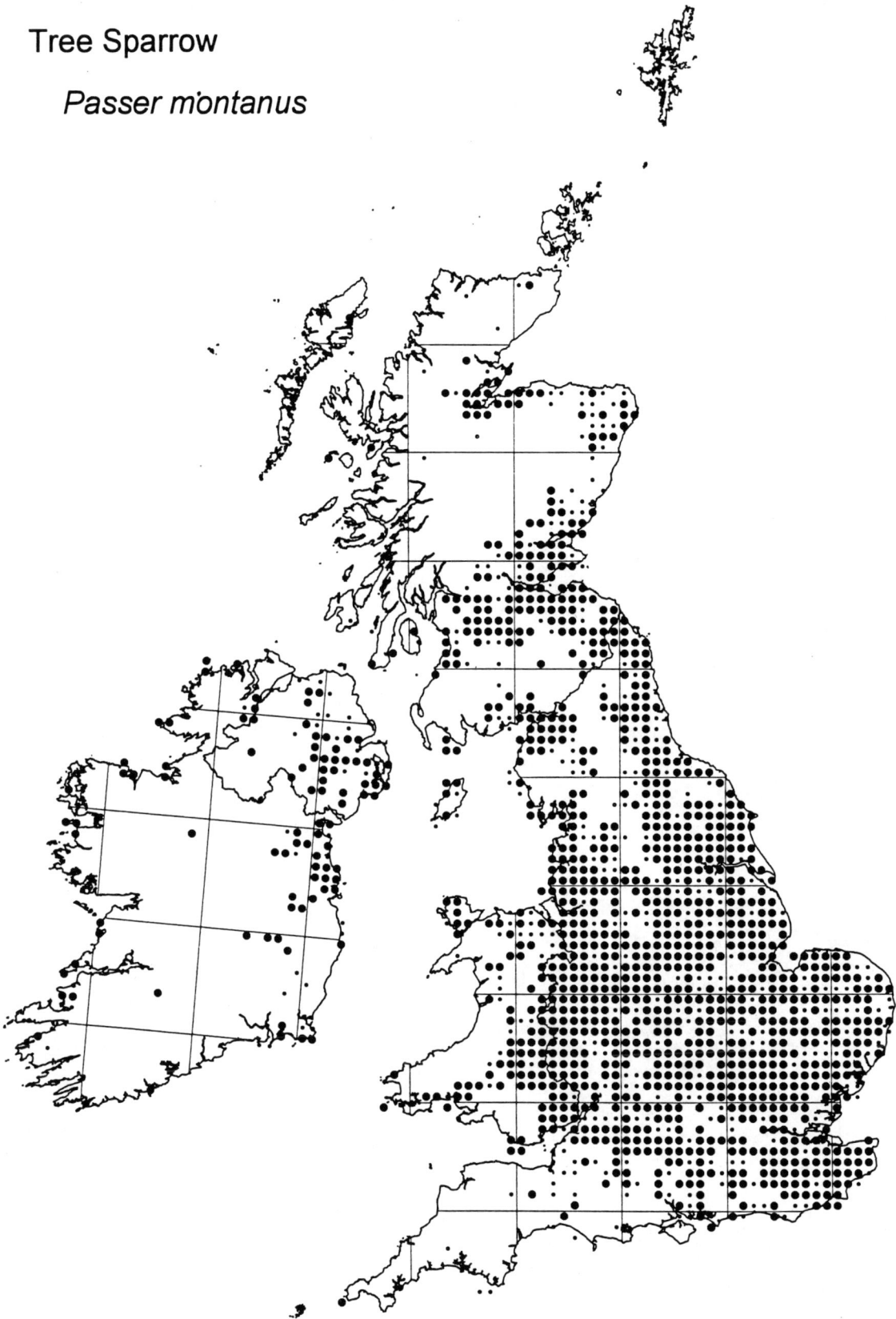

Breeding distribution of Tree Sparrow in Britain and Ireland, 1988-1991 (by 10 Km square).
Source: Gibbons, D.W., Reid, J.B. and Chapman, R.A. (1993). The new atlas of breeding birds
in Britain and Ireland 1988-1991. Calton, U.K.: T. and A.D. Poyser.

- ●   Record of breeding
- ·   Record with no evidence of breeding

Red-necked phalarope (*Phalaropus lobatus*)
Action Plan

1. Current status

1.1 The red-necked phalarope is a rare species with fewer than 50 breeding males recorded at a small number of sites (mires with areas of open water and emergent vegetation), all within Scotland. It has been lost this century from the Inner Hebrides, the Uists, Orkney, the southern half of Shetland and mainland Scotland. On Fetlar and Unst, the population dropped below 15 breeding males in the late 1980s, but has recently revived, with 37 breeding males in 1997. Three to five breeding males are recorded at another regularly used site on Lewis.

1.2 The red-necked phalarope is specially protected under Schedule 1 of the Wildlife and Countryside Act 1981 and Annex 1 of the EC Birds Directive, and is listed on Appendix II of the Bern Convention.

2. Current factors causing loss or decline

2.1 Succession of vegetation within breeding mires resulting in loss of open water. Cessation of grazing may also have contributed to this.

2.2 Changes in water levels and drainage of pool systems, particularly in the Hebrides and Mainland Shetland.

2.3 Eutrophication of pool systems through agricultural improvement is implicated in the Republic of Ireland. Similar changes may have affected some Scottish sites.

2.4 Predation may have contributed to the decline in Shetland.

2.5 The reasons for decline in Outer Hebrides are unclear; there still appears to be a number of suitable breeding sites on the Uists.

3. Current action

3.1 Most of the Fetlar breeding sites are protected within SSSIs and SPA.

3.2 About 85% of the British red-necked phalarope population breeds on sites managed by the RSPB; these are being actively managed to maintain suitable pool systems and emergent vegetation.

3.3 Management agreements over further mires in Shetland, potentially suitable for red-necked phalaropes, are presently being negotiated by RSPB.

3.4 Research into phalarope habitat requirements has been conducted by RSPB in the early 1980s and between 1993 and 1996. The results of the latter studies are now being implemented.

4. Action plan objectives and targets

4.1 In the short term, maintain the red-necked phalarope as a breeding species in the UK, with at least 35-40 breeding males at 10 sites.

4.2 By 2003, increase the north Shetland breeding population to 55-60 breeding males at 16 sites on Fetlar and Unst.

4.3 By 2005, increase the breeding population in the Hebrides to 10 breeding males on at least three sites.

4.4 Enable range expansion to a number of previously occupied sites within mainland Shetland, north Orkney and Tiree.

5. Proposed actions with lead agencies

The objectives and targets will be achieved through appropriate management of breeding habitat at existing sites and re-creating suitable habitat at other locations. Attention will also need to be paid to gaining further understanding of species habitat and management requirements.

5.1 Policy and legislation

5.1.1 Ensure that changes in agricultural systems within breeding areas do not cause deterioration in nesting habitat, water levels or water quality. (ACTION: NoSWA, SAC, SEPA, SNH, SOAEFD)

5.1.2 Ensure that prescriptions for Shetland, Western Isles and Argyll Islands ESAs produce good wetland habitat for breeding red-necked phalaropes in the traditional range. (ACTION: NoSWA, SAC, SNH, SOAEFD)

5.2 Site safeguard and management

5.2.1 Ensure that any regular breeding sites are appropriately protected by statutory mechanisms or voluntary agreements. (ACTION: SNH, SOAEFD)

5.2.2 Review the management of sites for red-necked phalaropes, and ensure appropriate grazing and management of vegetation succession. (ACTION: SAC, SNH, SOAEFD)

5.2.3 Continue to negotiate management agreements over existing and potentially suitable breeding sites for phalaropes in the traditional range. (ACTION: SNH)

5.2.4 Ensure that existing water management and drainage at breeding sites are appropriate, and that changes do not adversely affect any existing or potential breeding sites. (ACTION: SAC, SEPA, SNH, SOAEFD)

5.3   Species management and protection

5.3.1 Establish exclosures around phalarope nesting pools to prevent trampling during the nesting season. (ACTION: SNH, SOAEFD)

5.3.2 Ensure disturbance to red-necked phalaropes from birdwatchers is minimised. (ACTION: SNH)

5.4   Advisory

5.4.1 Ensure landowners and managers are aware of the presence, legal status and conservation requirements of this species, and promote appropriate habitat management. (ACTION: SAC, SNH, SOAEFD)

5.5   Future research and monitoring

5.5.1 Undertake annual monitoring of phalarope numbers and productivity, and provide information to the Rare Breeding Birds Panel. (ACTION: SNH)

5.5.2 In conjunction with NGOs, review results of their large-scale experimental management; disseminate and implement findings accordingly. (ACTION: SNH).

5.5.3 Undertake regular vegetation monitoring at existing and potential breeding sites to ensure that suitable breeding habitat is maintained. (ACTION: SNH)

5.6   Communications and publicity

5.6.1 Retain viewing facilities over a successful breeding site on Mires of Funzie, Fetlar. (ACTION: SNH)

5.6.2 Provide information to highlight the decline and importance of the species. (ACTION: SNH)

5.7   Links with other action plans

5.7.1 None proposed.

Red-necked Phalarope

Phalaropus lobatus

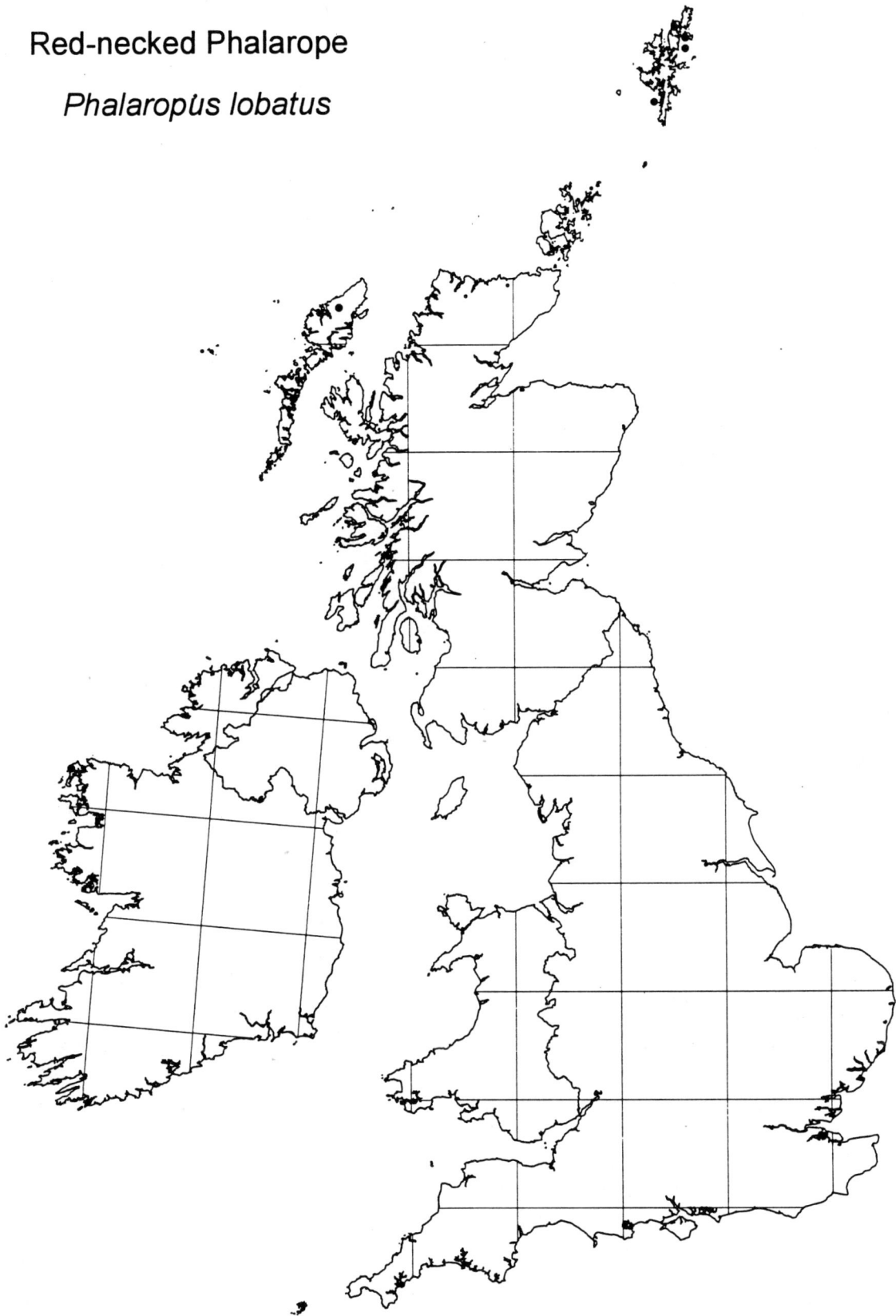

Breeding distribution of Red-necked Phalarope in Britain and Ireland, 1988-1991 (by 10 Km square). Source: Gibbons, D.W., Reid, J.B. and Chapman, R.A. (1993). The new atlas of breeding birds in Britain and Ireland 1988-1991. Calton, U.K.: T. and A.D. Poyser.

●   Record of breeding

·   Record with no evidence of breeding

Bullfinch (*Pyrrhula pyrrhula*)
Action Plan

1. Current status

1.1 The bullfinch is a fairly common and widespread resident species found in woodland, in orchards and on farmland, where it is closely associated with dense shrubs, scrub and untrimmed hedges. It occurs throughout most of the UK, although it is scarce in the far north and west, and almost absent from the Western and Northern Isles. There are some gaps in distribution elsewhere which are typically in areas with a dearth of woodland, such as the Fens and parts of north-west Scotland. Whilst there has been only a small decrease in range between the two atlas periods (1968-72 and 1988-91), numbers in Britain have decreased from an estimated population of 300-350,000 pairs in 1984 to 190,000 by 1988-91. The Common Bird Census indicates that there has been a 75% decline on farmland and a 47% decline in woodland between 1968 and 1991. The species is common and widespread across much of mainland Europe and may be expanding in the north and west of the range.

1.2 The bullfinch is protected under the Wildlife and Countryside Act 1981. Under licence, it may be killed (usually by shooting) or taken in cage traps for the purpose of preventing serious damage to the buds of fruit trees. A general licence was issued for commercial fruit growers in Kent for the 1996/97 winter; elsewhere, growers may apply for individual licences. Bullfinch is also protected under the Wildlife (Northern Ireland) Order 1985 and EC Birds Directive.

2. Current factors causing loss or decline

Recent analyses of long-term data sets by BTO and RSPB have not pinpointed definite causes of the bullfinch decline. An analysis of CBC data has not found a correlation between the decline and the increase in the populations of sparrowhawk and magpie. Nor has ongoing work on ringing recoveries and nest record card data found strong evidence for a link between the decline and variations in breeding performance or survival. The bullfinch decline is likely instead to involve one or more of the following:

2.1 Removal of farmland trees and hedgerows, and reduction in quality of remaining hedges due to frequent trimming. The main impact on bullfinches has been loss of nesting habitat, particularly hedges and thickets, and loss of food sources (buds, seeds and fruits).

2.2 The loss of winter food sources through the use of herbicides and loss of winter stubble fields (in common with other declining seed-eating farmland birds). However, the bullfinch does not forage far from hedgerows and woods, and so is much more confined to field margins than other farmland species.

2.3 Trapping. Despite its recent large decline, bullfinches are still being trapped. The numbers taken each year vary according to the availability of other food sources, particularly ash seeds, and on the severity of winter weather (eg in Kent over 1000 were taken in 1990/91, and 300 in 1996/97 - MAFF data). Under new licensing arrangements, which came into force in October 1996, trapping under general licence is only permitted in Kent. This level of mortality is unlikely to have an effect at the UK population level, but local impacts are possible.

3. Current action

3.1 Until very recently the bullfinch was not regarded as a species in need of assistance and targeted conservation action. However, establishment and management of broadleaved and mixed woodland will have benefited it, especially if plantings included native seed- and berry-bearing species.

3.2 The new Hedgerows Regulations will protect the hedges most likely to be favoured by the bullfinch. Sympathetic hedgerow management (eg hedge laying, coppicing, gapping up, replanting and less regular trimming) is encouraged by agri-environment schemes such as Countryside Stewardship and ESAs. Some elements of these schemes, most notably the pilot Arable Stewardship Scheme, also encourage land management that may benefit the bullfinch, for example, the sympathetic management of field margins.

3.3 The species is also likely to benefit from the Orchard Scheme recently begun by CCW, which seeks to restore management to neglected orchards and encourage new planting.

4. Action plan objectives and targets

4.1 In the short term, halt or reverse the decline in numbers of the bullfinch by the year 2003 so that the Breeding Bird Survey index is at least at 1996 levels.

4.2 In the long term, see a sustained recovery in numbers, so that the BBS index is at least 50% higher than 1996 levels by 2008.

5. Proposed action with lead agencies

The main priorities for bullfinch are: the promotion of sympathetic habitat management on farmland and in lowland broadleaved and mixed woodland;

the study of the requirements of the species; working towards a reduction in the level of trapping of bullfinches in orchards through the development and promotion of alternative methods of crop protection; and ensuring licensing policy is appropriate to the status of the species. It will also be important to monitor the UK population to enable trends to be identified.

5.1 Policy and legislation

5.1.1 Take account of the need to recover bullfinch and other farmland bird populations when developing agricultural policy and CAP reform; consider how to extend the Arable Stewardship Scheme if the pilot is successful, and how to substitute for the benefits of set-aside, if this is further reduced or abolished. Retention of hedgerows, thickets and other scrub/wooded habitats on farmland should be encouraged. (ACTION: DANI, FA, MAFF, SOAEFD, WOAD)

5.1.2 Where appropriate, incorporate new management prescriptions when reviewing agri-environment schemes, especially ESAs, Countryside Stewardship, Tir Cymen and Countryside Premium Scheme, in order to reverse some of the recent changes in farm management outlined in Section 2. (ACTION: CCW, DANI, MAFF, SOAEFD, WOAD)

5.1.3 Seek uptake of a more cautious and targeted use of pesticides and fertilisers on farmland to reduce the impacts on potential food sources for the bullfinch. This could include encouraging integrated crop management, organic farming, and the more widespread adoption of initiatives such as the recently begun Scottish 'TIBRE' project. (ACTION: DANI, MAFF, SOAEFD, WOAD)

5.1.4 Review licensing procedures regularly to ensure that they remain appropriate to the status of the bullfinch. (ACTION: MAFF, SOAEFD, WOAD)

5.2 Site safeguard and management

5.2.1 None proposed.

5.3 Species management and protection

5.3.1 None proposed (but see 5.1.4 above).

5.4 Advisory

5.4.1 Promote methods other than trapping to fruit growers as a means of reducing the problem of bullfinches in orchards. (ACTION: MAFF)

5.4.2 Consider producing advisory material for orchard owners on the provision of alternative sources of natural food for bullfinches. (ACTION: CCW, DANI, MAFF, SOAEFD)

5.4.3 Promote the sympathetic management of hedgerows and farmland scrub for the benefit of bullfinch and other farmland birds. (ACTION: DANI, MAFF, SOAEFD, WOAD)

5.5 Future research and monitoring

5.5.1 Ensure appropriate monitoring of numbers through continuation of the BTO/JNCC/RSPB Breeding Bird Survey and consider the setting up of an equivalent survey to monitor winter populations. (ACTION: CCW, EHS, EN, JNCC, SNH)

5.5.2 Undertake an autecological study of the bullfinch to identify appropriate habitat management. (ACTION: CCW, EHS, EN, FC, JNCC, SNH)

5.5.3 Ensure completion of analyses of long-term data sets on ringing recoveries and nest record cards to help determine the causes of the bullfinch decline. (ACTION: JNCC)

5.6 Communications and publicity

5.6.1 Promote the bullfinch as a species in need of conservation assistance. (ACTION: CCW, EHS, EN, JNCC, SNH)

5.7 Links with other action plans

5.7.1 It is likely that implementation of this action plan will also benefit the following UK BAP farmland birds: corn bunting, grey partridge, linnet, reed bunting, skylark, song thrush, spotted flycatcher, tree sparrow, turtle dove.

5.7.2 The plan should be considered in conjunction with those for cereal field margins, ancient hedgerows, and other wooded priority habitats.

Bullfinch
Pyrrhula pyrrhula

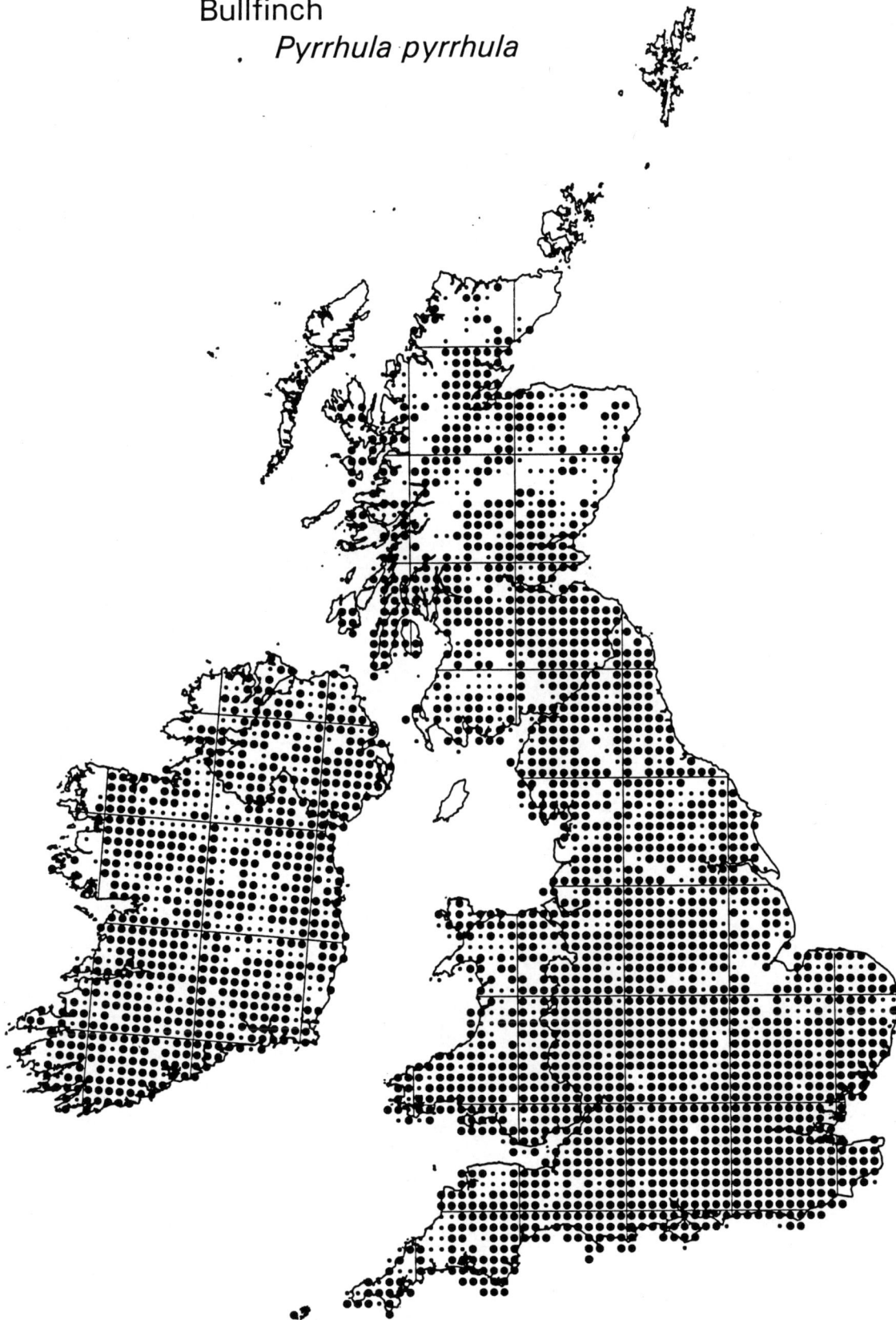

Breeding distribution of Bullfinch in Britain and Ireland, 1988-1991 (by 10 Km square).
Source: Gibbons, D.W., Reid, J.B. and Chapman, R.A. (1993). The new atlas of breeding birds in Britain and Ireland 1988-1991. Calton, U.K.: T. and A.D. Poyser.

●   Record of breeding

·   Record with no evidence of breeding

Roseate tern (*Sterna dougallii*)
Action Plan

1. Current status

1.1 The roseate tern has a highly fragmented breeding range in the north-east Atlantic. Its European stronghold is the Azores (Portugal) which supports 1170 pairs, representing around 60% of the north-east Atlantic population. Elsewhere the species breeds only very locally in Britain, Ireland and France. In 1996 there were 677 pairs at the two sites in the Republic of Ireland (including 557 at Rockabill, the main colony in the British Isles since 1986), around 100 pairs in Brittany, France and 64 pairs at five main sites in the UK. It is therefore one of the UK's rarest breeding seabirds. Although the UK population has declined greatly (from 1000 pairs in 1969 to 210 pairs in 1989), many of the birds have moved to the growing colony at Rockabill. Productivity at this colony is good and has been a major factor in the recent increase in the north-west European population as a whole. The key wintering area for birds breeding in the UK is west Africa, particularly Ghana.

1.2 The roseate tern is specially protected under Schedule 1 of the Wildlife and Countryside Act 1981 and Schedule 1 of Wildlife (Northern Ireland) Order 1985, and is listed on Annex I of the EC Birds Directive and Appendix II of the Bern Convention.

2. Current factors causing loss or decline

2.1 Most, if not all, of the decrease in UK breeding numbers is due to a change in distribution, since the colony at Rockabill, in the Irish Republic, has shown a corresponding increase in numbers. The reasons for this re-distribution are not well known. The overall trend for the species in north-west Europe is upward.

2.2 Outside the breeding season, the trapping of terns for sport or food in west Africa has been suggested as a major cause of mortality. Also, long-term changes in sea-surface temperature may be partly responsible for the consistent and continued decline of fish stocks, eg *Sardinella*, in coastal west Africa and the Gulf of Guinea. As the winter progresses, *Sardinella* become less available to terns in this region and the whereabouts of roseate terns and the composition of their diet in the December to May period remain unknown.

2.3 Some competition may occur between early nesting roseate and late nesting common terns, at sites with few crevices or long vegetation. At some sites, there is a possibility of competition between terns and gulls for nesting areas.

2.4 Predation, particularly by foxes and rats, may restrict nesting to offshore islands. Even on remote sites, predation by the larger species of gulls may threaten breeding attempts.

2.5 Flooding of nesting areas has been a problem at some sites.

3. Current action

3.1 The most important roseate tern colonies in the UK are now within nature reserves and a number have been designated as SPAs.

3.2 Management for the benefit of roseate terns has been implemented at all regularly-used sites and destruction of gull eggs has taken place at several roseate tern islands.

3.3 A colour-ringing scheme is established throughout Britain and Ireland, and a roseate tern coordinator has recently begun work in the Republic of Ireland.

3.4 RSPB and BirdLife International have funded an education programme by the Government of Ghana to try to reduce the incidence of winter trapping there.

4. Action plan objectives and targets

4.1 Increase the UK roseate tern population to 200 pairs by 2008.

4.2 Maintain favourable conditions at current and historical breeding sites in the UK to ensure there are a minimum of five colonies with at least ten pairs in each by 2008.

5. Proposed action with lead agencies

The objectives and targets should be achieved by ensuring the management and protection of existing and former roseate tern breeding sites throughout the UK; and by encouraging international cooperation and action to ensure that the north-east Atlantic roseate tern population is conserved.

5.1 Policy and legislation

5.1.1 None proposed.

5.2 Site safeguard and management

5.2.1 Ensure that the protection of breeding colonies is actively considered in development policies and proposals. (ACTION: CCW, EHS, EN, SNH)

5.2.2 Maintain and, where appropriate, enhance species management measures at all regularly used breeding sites and a suite of formerly used sites. (ACTION: CCW, EHS, EN, SNH)

5.3 Species management and protection

5.3.1 Assess levels of predation at breeding sites and, where necessary, carry out programmes of predator control. (ACTION: CCW, EHS, EN, SNH)

5.4 Advisory

5.4.1 None proposed.

5.5 Future research and monitoring

5.5.1 Continue to monitor the UK population through the Seabird Monitoring Programme. (ACTION: JNCC)

5.5.2 Ensure continued international cooperation on research, monitoring and management of the north-east Atlantic roseate tern population. (ACTION: EHS, JNCC)

5.6 Communications and publicity

5.6.1 Use the roseate tern as an example of a bird under pressure from factors operating outside the UK in order to reduce persecution in the wintering grounds in west Africa. (ACTION: JNCC)

5.7 Links with other action plans

5.7.1 None proposed.

Roseate Tern

Sterna dougallii

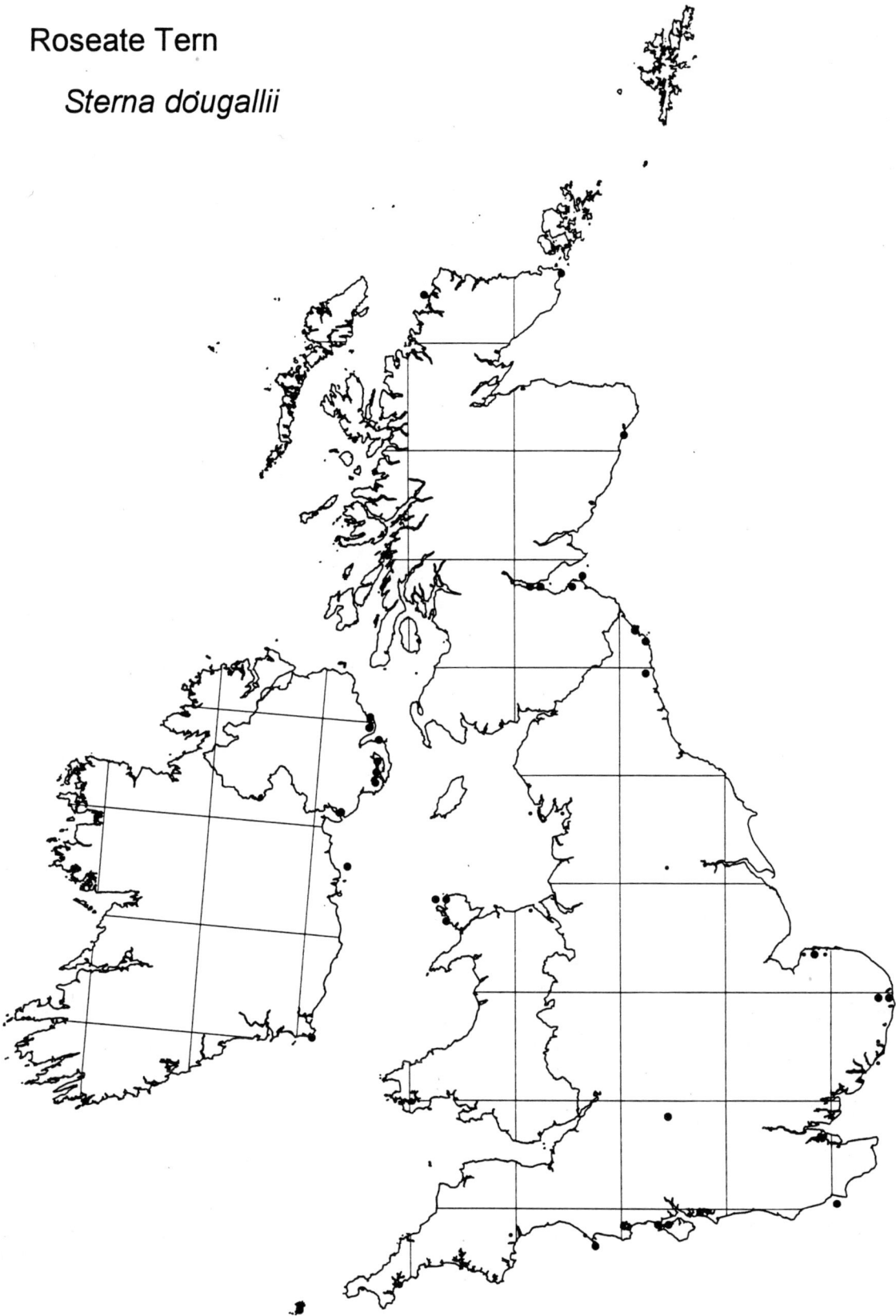

Breeding distribution of Roseate Tern in Britain and Ireland, 1993-1996 (by 10 Km square).
Source: RSPB data, National Tern Monitoring Surveys (1993-1996).

●   Record of breeding

·   Record with no evidence of breeding

Turtle dove (*Streptopelia turtur*)
Action Plan

1. Current status

1.1 The turtle dove is a summer migrant that breeds at the northern edge of its range in the UK. It is confined largely to the south and east of England and is associated with fertile arable farmland in warm, dry situations. The population was at a high at the time of the first breeding atlas (1968-72). However, the Common Bird Census index has indicated a fall of around 60% in the population since this time, and the new breeding atlas (1988-91) shows a marked decrease in range of around 25%. The latest population estimate, taken from the new atlas, is approximately 75,000 territories. The turtle dove is declining in many parts of Europe although it is still common and widespread in the lowlands of central and southern Europe. It generally occurs below 350 m in a variety of fairly dry, sunny, sheltered habitats.

1.2 The turtle dove is protected under the Wildlife and Countryside Act 1981 and Schedule 1 of the Wildlife (Northern Ireland) Order 1985. It is a traditional quarry species in Mediterranean countries and, as such, is listed on Annex II of the EC Birds Directive.

2. Current factors causing loss or decline

2.1 The decline of the turtle dove has occurred at the same time as decreases in the numbers and/or range of other farmland birds which share its diet of grass and weed seeds. It is therefore likely that its decline may be due, at least in part, to changes in agricultural practice such as the increased use of herbicides and fertilisers, which have reduced the quantity and variety of wildflowers on arable land.

2.2 Turtle doves nest in large hedges and mature scrub, and also retreat to the safety of this dense vegetation when disturbed. The loss of features such as overgrown hedgerows and hawthorn thickets on farmland is likely to have had an adverse effect on the population.

2.3 As a long-distance migrant, the turtle dove faces threats, particularly from hunting, outside the UK. It is heavily shot in France and the Iberian peninsula. Tens of thousands of birds are also shot in their wintering areas, mainly Senegal, and many more are killed on migration through Morocco.

2.4 In the UK, turtle doves are associated with light soils in the drier parts of the country and the decrease in range of the species has been most marked in the north and west. It is therefore possible that some climatic factor may be operating.

2.5 Little is known of the effects of habitat or climatic changes in the wintering grounds of the species. Turtle doves spend part of the year, particularly February and March, in acacia scrub in the Sahel region, and recent drought conditions and habitat destruction there have coincided with a steep decline in numbers.

3. Current action

3.1 Until recently the turtle dove was not regarded as a species of conservation concern, so little action for it has been carried out. Rotational set-aside will have benefited the species, although this has been significantly reduced in area in recent years. New prescriptions encouraging the growth of spring-sown cereals and retention of winter stubbles in the South Downs ESA, and the pilot Arable Stewardship Scheme, should also benefit the turtle dove.

3.2 EN/GCT have undertaken a pilot study into the summer ecology and habitat use of the turtle dove which has made recommendations for a full study that will determine the importance of agricultural factors in the decline of the population.

3.3 The EC and French government are under pressure to ensure that the legislation on hunting is enforced. The turtle dove is one of a number of species identified for a Species Management Plan by the EC. The plan is being funded by the EC and coordinated by the Office National de la Chasse. GCT is undertaking an analysis of European ringing recoveries of the turtle dove in an attempt to investigate trends in hunting pressure and survival.

4. Action plan objectives and targets

4.1 In the short term, halt or reverse the decline in numbers of the turtle dove by the year 2003 so that the Breeding Bird Survey index is at least at 1996 levels.

4.2 In the long term, see a sustained recovery in numbers so that the BBS index is at least 50% higher than 1996 levels by 2008.

5. Proposed action with lead agencies

It will be important to gain a better understanding of the requirements of the turtle dove in the UK. Other priorities are the promotion of sympathetic land management techniques in the light of the better knowledge, and the improvement of the survival rates of British turtle doves outside the UK by promoting habitat conservation and a reduction in shooting pressure. The UK population should be monitored to enable trends to be identified.

5.1 Policy and legislation

5.1.1 Take account of the need to recover turtle dove and other farmland bird populations when developing agricultural policy and CAP reform; consider how to extend the Arable Stewardship Scheme if the pilot is successful, and how to substitute for the benefits of set-aside, if this is further reduced or abolished. Retention of appropriately managed hedgerow trees and farm woodland should be encouraged. (ACTION: DANI, FA, MAFF, SOAEFD, WOAD)

5.1.2 Where appropriate, incorporate new management prescriptions when reviewing agri-environment schemes, especially ESAs, Countryside Stewardship, Tir Cymen and Countryside Premium Scheme, in order to reverse some of the recent changes in farm management outlined in Section 2. (ACTION: CCW, DANI, MAFF, SOAEFD, WOAD)

5.1.3 Seek uptake of a more cautious and targeted use of pesticides and fertilisers on farmland to reduce the impacts on potential food sources for the turtle dove. This could include encouraging integrated crop management, organic farming and the more widespread adoption of initiatives such as the recently begun Scottish 'TIBRE' project. (ACTION: DANI, MAFF, SOAEFD, WOAD)

5.1.4 Support the European Commission in its efforts to enforce Article 7 of the Birds Directive on the hunting of the turtle dove. (ACTION: DETR, FCO)

5.2 Site safeguard and management

5.2.1 Ensure appropriate management of areas of scrub on protected sites (including nature reserves) within the existing and former range of the turtle dove. (ACTION: CCW, EN)

5.3 Species management and protection

5.3.1 None proposed.

5.4 Advisory

5.4.1 Promote further advice to land managers on management for turtle dove as one of a suite of farmland birds and update that advice in the light of new policies and research findings. (ACTION: MAFF, WOAD)

5.4.2 Promote effective management of set-aside for breeding birds, including turtle dove. (ACTION: MAFF, WOAD)

5.4.3 Promote the sympathetic management of hedgerows and farmland scrub for the benefit of turtle dove and other farmland birds. (ACTION: DANI, MAFF, SOAEFD, WOAD)

5.5 Future research and monitoring

5.5.1 Compare Nest Record Cards from the 1960s with those from recent years in order to look for possible explanations for the population decline. (ACTION: CCW, EN)

5.5.2 Undertake a study into the summer ecology and habitat use of turtle doves, including an assessment of diet and a comparison with a study carried out in the 1960s. (ACTION: CCW, EN)

5.5.3 Ensure appropriate monitoring of turtle dove breeding numbers through continuation of the BTO/JNCC/RSPB Breeding Bird Survey. (ACTION: CCW, EN, JNCC)

5.6 Communications and publicity

5.6.1 Use the turtle dove as an example of a bird under pressure from factors operating outside the UK in order to promote increased protection and beneficial habitat management throughout its range. (ACTION: JNCC)

5.7 Links with other action plans

5.7.1 It is likely that implementation of this plan will also benefit the following UK BAP farmland birds: bullfinch, corn bunting, grey partridge, linnet, reed bunting, skylark, song thrush, tree sparrow.

5.7.2 This action plan should be considered in conjunction with those for cereal field margins and ancient hedgerows.

Turtle Dove

Streptopélia turtur

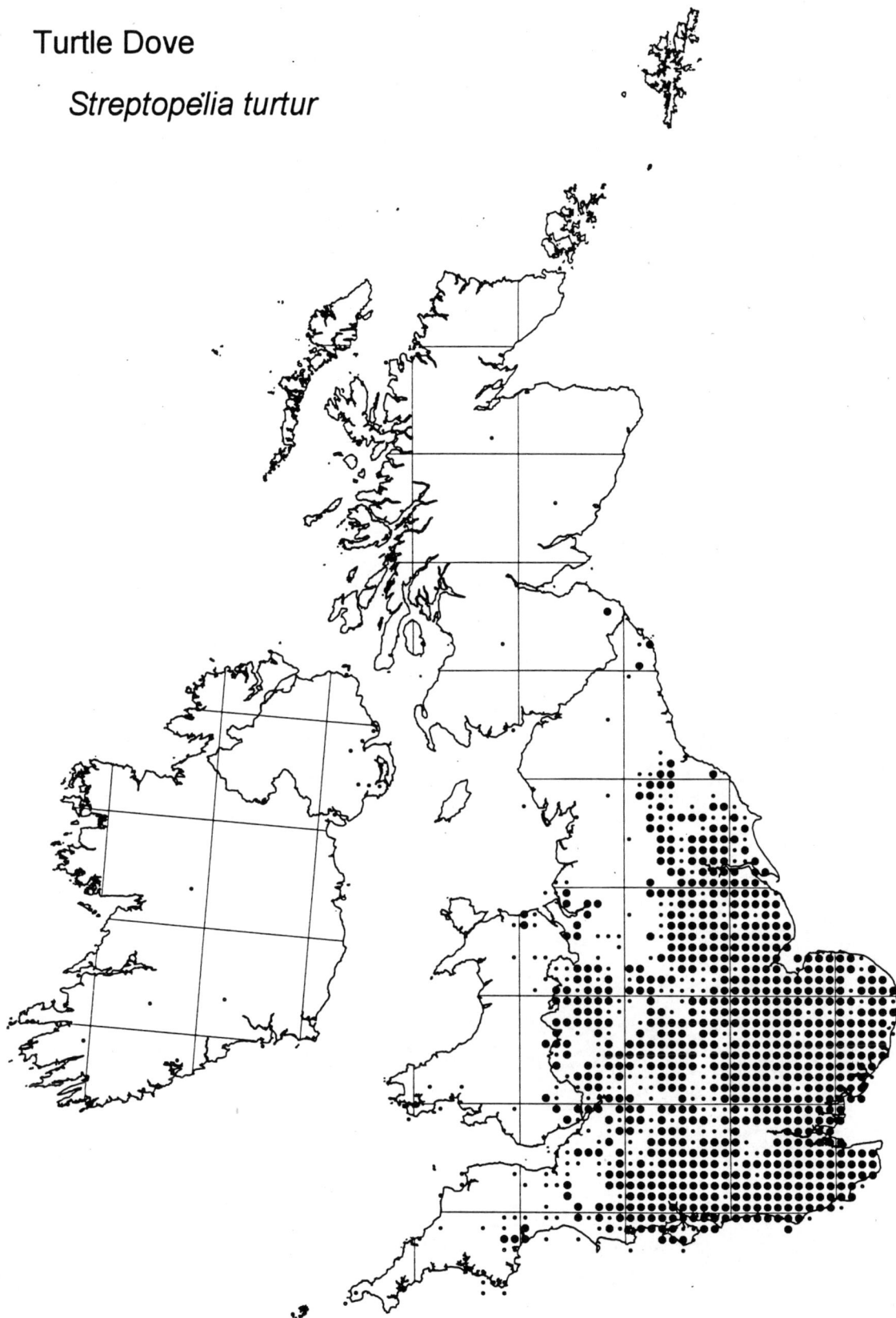

Breeding distribution of Turtle Dove in Britain and Ireland, 1988-1991 (by 10 Km square).
Source: Gibbons, D.W., Reid, J.B. and Chapman, R.A. (1993). The new atlas of breeding birds in Britain and Ireland 1988-1991. Calton, U.K.: T. and A.D. Poyser.

●   Record of breeding

·   Record with no evidence of breeding

Amphibian

Pool frog (*Rana lessonae*)
Action Plan

1. Current status

1.1 The pool frog is a member of the 'green frog complex'. It often occurs together with other green frogs, notably the edible frog (*Rana kl. esculenta*), which is a hybrid of the pool frog and marsh frog (*R. ridibunda*). Pool frogs usually exist as metapopulations dependent on multiple ponds quite close together and interconnected by suitable terrestrial habitat. Pool frog tadpoles can overwinter but survival is often low. The species relies heavily on the best summers for recruitment of new juveniles.

1.2 The status of the pool frog in Britain is uncertain, but a series of factors indicate that it may be native and not simply a recent introduction. The possibly native populations of this species may now be extinct in the wild in Britain. At potentially the last remaining native UK site for the species, in Norfolk, there have been no confirmed sightings since 1993 and only a single male animal from that population exists in captivity. Pool frog is found across much of central Europe, as far north as south-west Sweden and Norway and as far east as Asia.

1.3 The pool frog is listed on Annex IV of the EC Habitats and Species Directive.

2. Current factors causing loss or decline

The reasons for the decline of this species are largely unknown, but several factors are suspected and these may now be providing constraints on its recovery. These factors include:

2.1 Reduction in the number and quality of suitable ponds in close proximity to each other. This can be caused by encroachment of scrub, presence of fish, atmospheric pollution (eg nitrogen pollution) leading to reduced breeding success, drought and/or lowered water tables.

2.2 Reduction in quality of terrestrial habitat due to succession to woodland.

2.3 Increased numbers of water fowl, notably geese (which will overgraze grasses, foul water and eat frogs and tadpoles).

2.4 Small populations are vulnerable to grass snake predation and collecting.

3. Current action

3.1 This species is the subject of a Species Recovery Programme project coordinated by English Nature, which involves work on a number of areas including:

3.1.1 Habitat management. Small areas around the ponds that yielded the last sightings are being opened up with a view to creating suitable habitat for re-establishment of the species.

3.1.2 Survey of the last known site in Norfolk and other possible sites (in Cambridgeshire and Northamptonshire).

3.1.3 Captive breeding. The one surviving 'native' male has bred with pool frogs of different origins. Attempts to find other native origin animals have been initiated and a captive breeding programme using Swedish origin animals has begun.

3.1.4 Investigation of native status using a variety of approaches including bioacoustics, genetics, palaeoarchaeology and literature review.

4. Action plan objectives and targets

The following objectives and targets apply if definitive evidence can be found to support the thesis that pool frogs are native to Britain. If research indicates that it is not a native species, then no further conservation action would be necessary.

4.1 Recover the population at the Norfolk site (if not already extinct).

4.2 Restore viable populations to three suitable sites in the likely former range of the species through (re)introduction by 2003. This should only be undertaken if the native status of the pool frog is confirmed.

5. Proposed action with lead agencies

It is important that reliable conclusions about the native status of pool frog in Britain are reached as quickly as possible. Meanwhile, practical work should focus on the development of an *ex-situ* breeding programme and habitat management in preparation for reintroductions which should be undertaken if the species is confirmed to be native. Surveys at the Norfolk site and other former sites should continue.

5.1 Policy and legislation

5.1.1 If the native status of this species is confirmed, and if extant populations are found or reintroductions undertaken, then add the species to Schedule 5 of the Wildlife and Countryside Act 1981. (ACTION: DETR, JNCC)

5.1.2 Review legislative mechanisms for restricting release to, and movement in, the wild of pool frogs of non-native origin (eg through Wildlife and Countryside

115

Act 1981 Section 9 or 14, and Schedule 9 review). (ACTION: EN, JNCC)

5.1.3 Determine the most suitable approach to reintroduction of the species in the light of studies on its native status. (ACTION: EN, JNCC)

5.2   Site safeguard and management

5.2.1 Ensure appropriate management at a core area of the Norfolk site to allow the persistence of any remaining animals and prepare for possible reintroduction. (ACTION: EN)

5.3   Species management and protection

5.3.1 Continue to develop a captive breeding programme to maintain native origin animals (or at least to preserve some genetic material) and provide animals that could be used for release into the wild. This action should follow the proposals outlined in the Species Recovery Programme and, if necessary, captive breeding work should be extended to other suitable institutions. (ACTION: EN)

5.3.2 Following management to re-create suitable habitat, reintroduce the pool frog at three suitable former sites (subject to outcome of research on native status). (ACTION: EN)

5.4   Advisory

5.4.1 Produce guidance on suitable management for pool frog habitats and distribute to landowners and managers at extant and restored sites, and sites where the species has been recorded in the recent past. (ACTION: EN)

5.4.2 Provide guidance on the management of non-native populations of pool frogs. This action should be informed by the work outlined under 5.5.4. (ACTION: EN)

5.4.3 Ensure that relevant agri-environment scheme Project Officers and members of regional agri-environment consultation groups are advised of actual or potential sites for this species, its importance and management needed for its conservation. (ACTION: EN)

5.5   Future research and monitoring

5.5.1 Continue with research to determine whether the pool frog is native to Britain. A number of lines of investigation should be pursued including genetic studies, literature research, archaeological study and archiving of reference bone material, study of calls, behaviour and morphology. (ACTION: EN)

5.5.2 Ensure the completion of the current initiative to survey all known former sites and to determine whether an extant population remains in Norfolk. (ACTION: EN)

5.5.3 Undertake a thorough survey of green frog populations with a view to identifying colonies of pool frogs that have so far gone undetected. (ACTION: EN)

5.5.4 Review studies of habitat requirements and management needs, looking particularly at effects of numbers and sizes of ponds, shading, fish and pollution. (ACTION: EN)

5.5.5 Undertake monitoring of water quality and water levels at the Norfolk site. This should be carried out with a view to maintaining suitable habitat. If necessary, action should be taken to curtail pollution and excessive water abstraction. (ACTION: EA, EN)

5.5.6 If non-native populations of the pool frog are discovered, assess the threat that they may pose to the genetic identity of any reintroduced pool frog colonies. (ACTION: EN, JNCC)

5.6   Communications and publicity

5.6.1 Continue to develop links with relevant European experts with a view to exchanging information on conservation management and *ex-situ* breeding techniques. (ACTION: EN)

5.6.2 Depending on the outcome of the studies on native status and subsequent conservation actions/decisions, publicise the presence and conservation importance of a 'new' British species. (ACTION: EN)

5.7   Links with other action plans

5.7.1 There may be benefit in considering this action plan with that for fens.

(No map provided, as there is only one possible native site.)

Vascular plants

Alchemilla minima (an alchemilla)
Action Plan

1. Current status

1.1 *Alchemilla minima* is a small, apomictic, perennial plant which grows in moist grassland, generally above 300 m in altitude. It is well adapted to heavy grazing, being able to set seed in very closely grazed turf. The taxonomy of this alchemilla is in dispute. It was first recognised as a distinct species in 1947. However, there is an alternative view that it is best treated as a dwarf variant of the more widespread *A. filicaulis*. The extreme dwarf characters are apparently lost after a long period of cultivation.

1.2 This alchemilla is believed to be endemic to two fells in the Yorkshire Dales (Ingleborough and Whernside), although there are doubtful records from farther afield, particularly from the northern Pennines. It is a difficult plant to identify in the field which suggests that it may be under-recorded. New localities are still being found within its limited range.

1.3 This species is classified as *Vulnerable*. It receives general protection under the Wildlife and Countryside Act 1981.

2. Current factors causing loss or decline

2.1 Any newly discovered populations outside of SSSIs and NNRs will continue to be at risk from inappropriate grazing management and agricultural improvement.

3. Current action

3.1 All known populations of this species in the Yorkshire Dales lie within SSSIs.

4. Action plan objectives and targets

4.1 Maintain viable populations at all known sites.

4.2 Establish an *ex-situ* programme to protect genetic diversity, create a reserve population and provide experimental material.

5. Proposed action with lead agencies

Alchemilla minima is a rare species and probably always has been. The priority action is to clarify the taxonomic status of the taxon. An assessment of its distribution and ecology is urgently needed to inform and secure beneficial management for all populations.

5.1 Policy and legislation

5.1.1 When reviewing agri-environment schemes, including Countryside Stewardship and ESAs, consider whether changes are needed to increase their potential benefits for this species. (ACTION: EN, MAFF)

5.2 Site safeguard and management

5.2.1 Seek to protect all sites from inappropriate grazing management and agricultural improvement. (ACTION: EN, MAFF, Yorkshire Dales National Park)

5.3 Species management and protection

5.3.1 Following completion of the research outlined under 5.5.2, produce guidelines on good management practice for this species and provide mechanisms to enable them to be implemented on all known sites. Until the research is completed, seek to retain current grazing regimes on all sites. (ACTION: EN, MAFF)

5.3.2 Collect seed from all extant native sites and deposit in the Millenium Seed Bank at Wakehurst Place (Kew). (ACTION: EN, RBG Kew)

5.4 Advisory

5.4.1 Advise relevant landowners and managers of the importance of this plant, specific management for its conservation, and potentially damaging activities. When management guidelines have been prepared (see 5.3.1), ensure that they are distributed and explained as necessary. (ACTION: EN)

5.4.2 As far as possible, ensure that all relevant agri-environment project officers are advised of locations of this species, its importance, management requirements and potential threats. (ACTION: EN, MAFF)

5.5 Future research and monitoring

5.5.1 Establish a consensus on the taxonomy of this species through discussion with the relevant experts and, if necessary, genetic screening. (ACTION: EN, JNCC)

5.5.2 Undertake research into the ecological and grazing management requirements of this species and factors which may be limiting its population size. This is a high priority and should be undertaken with a view to preparing guidelines on good management practice for the species. (ACTION: EN, JNCC)

5.5.3 Undertake a thorough survey of the Whernside and Ingleborough area to update records of known sites and to search for colonies which are as yet unrecorded. Also survey sites outside this area where the plant has previously been recorded (such as the northern Pennines) in order to determine its present status in these areas. An assessment of any current threats at each site should also be made. (ACTION: EN)

5.5.4 Carry out frequent monitoring of all populations. (ACTION: EN)

5.6 Communications and publicity

5.6.1 Publicise the importance of this species through articles in conservation and land management publications and encourage botanists to report any new records, eg through Atlas 2000 recording. (ACTION: EN)

5.6.2 Seek to involve relevant local organisations (such as the Yorkshire Wildlife Trust) in conservation work for this species. (ACTION: EN)

5.7 Links with other action plans

5.7.1 This action plan should be considered in conjunction with that for upland calcareous grassland.

Alchemilla minima

■	3	0
●	0	0
○	0	0
✕	0	0
+	0	0

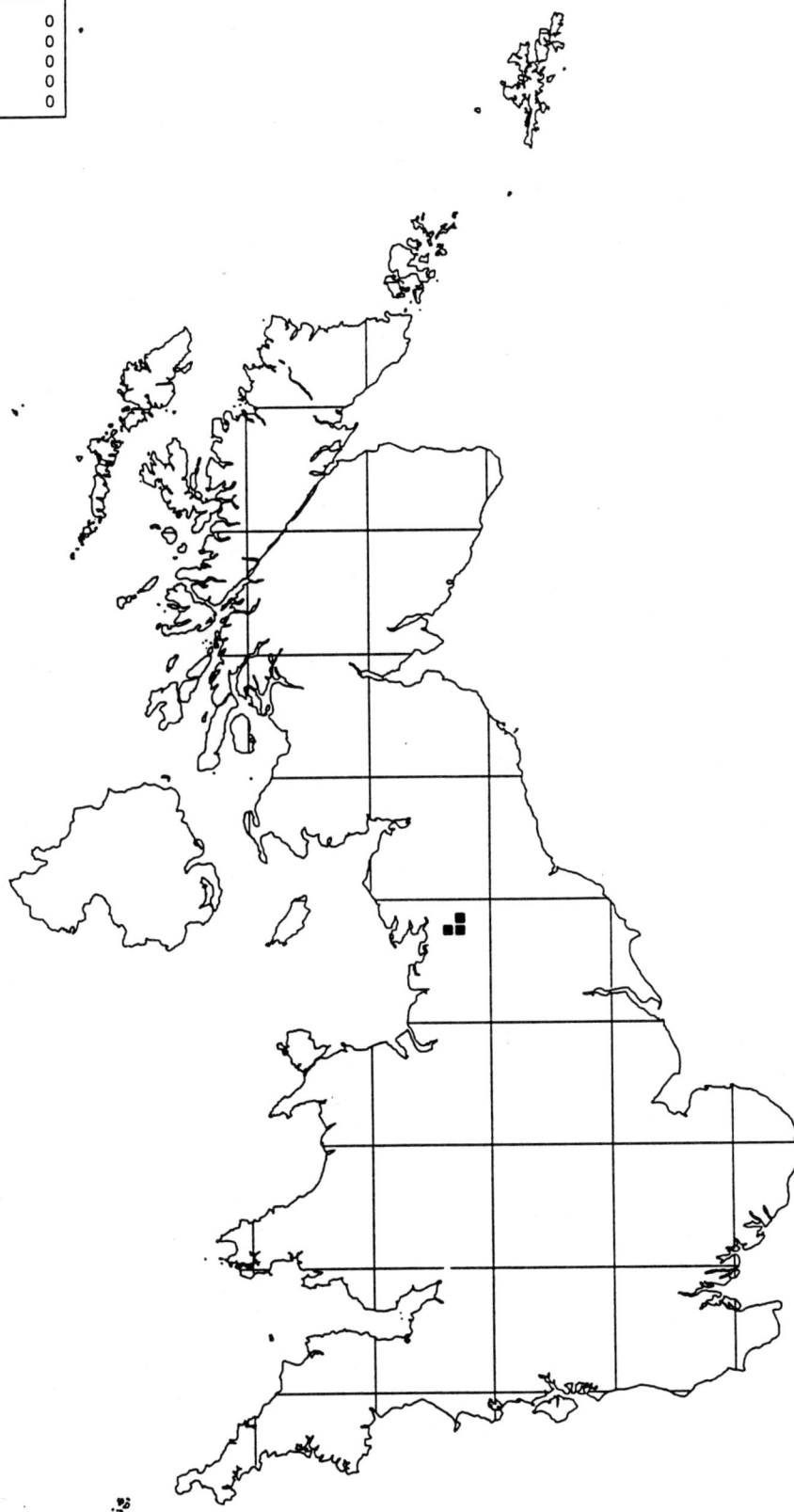

Distribution of Alchemilla minima - an alchemilla in Britain & N.Ireland, (by 10km square).

Source: British Red Data Book - Vascular plants, 1998, 3rd edition.

■ - records post 1980
● - records 1970 - 1987
○ - records pre 1970
✕ - introduced records post 1970
+ - introduced records pre 1970

Tower mustard (*Arabis glabra*)
Action Plan

1. Current status

1.1 Tower mustard is a biennial or sometimes short-lived perennial member of the cabbage family which generally favours light, nutrient-poor sandy soils often over chalk or limestone. Plants germinate in spring, spending at least one season in a vegetative state before flowering the following May-June. It can produce abundant seeds, which appear to remain viable for many years with plants often reappearing on old sites after long periods of absence. As a mobile and opportunistic species, it appears to be well matched to the traditional Breckland management cycle of extensive grazing with occasional arable cultivation.

1.2 Formerly recorded from 142 ten km squares, it has been recorded from only 31 of these since 1970. The most significant cause of its decline has been agricultural intensification on heathlands. However, it has been able to colonise areas of newly created habitat in Breckland, such as clear-felled conifer plantations, and here it may actually be increasing in numbers (there are 12 known sites in Norfolk). There are five sites in south-east England, and an unknown number scattered throughout the rest of England and eastern Wales. It is widespread elsewhere in Europe, and is also found in western Asia.

1.3 In GB this species is now classified as *Vulnerable*. It receives general protection under the Wildlife and Countryside Act 1981.

2. Current factors causing loss or decline

2.1 Habitat destruction due to agricultural intensification and building development. The former would appear to be the main reason for the continued decline of this species.

2.2 Habitat neglect, which results in a lack of open ground for regeneration and the development of coarse competing vegetation.

2.3 Overgrazing by rabbits has been suggested. Although tower mustard is a Breckland species there is evidence that it is susceptible to high levels of rabbit grazing.

3. Current action

3.1 Conservation work for this species is ongoing under Plantlife's 'Back from the Brink' project which is supported by English Nature's Species Recovery Programme. The following work has already been undertaken for sites in Surrey and Hampshire:

3.1.1 A survey of all known sites.

3.1.2 Habitat management including scrub clearance and ground disturbance.

3.1.3 Seed has been collected and kept in cultivation.

4. Action plan objectives and targets

This action plan is largely supported by work proposed under English Nature's Species Recovery Programme.

4.1 Maintain the natural range of this species in Britain.

4.2 Restore populations to five suitable historic sites by 2008.

4.3 Establish an *ex-situ* programme to protect genetic diversity, create a reserve population and provide experimental material.

5. Proposed action with lead agencies

Conservation action should recognise the opportunistic nature of tower mustard by facilitating more natural population dynamics, for example ensuring that appropriate habitat is available in the vicinity of extant sites to allow natural colonisation. Experimental management aimed at regenerating this species from the seed-bank at historic sites is also a high priority. These actions must be supported by the completion of a national survey of existing and historic sites. A better understanding of the ecological requirements of this species, and the threats to it, will underpin the above processes.

5.1 Policy and legislation

5.1.1 Ensure that the needs of this species are considered during reviews of the Breckland ESA Scheme. (ACTION: EN, MAFF)

5.2 Site safeguard and management

5.2.1 Consider notifying as SSSIs sites holding key populations of tower mustard. (ACTION: EN)

5.2.2 Where possible, ensure that heathland localities of tower mustard receive management that is beneficial to its conservation, eg through management agreements on SSSIs, Countryside Stewardship or the Breckland ESA Scheme. (ACTION: EN, MAFF)

5.2.3 Maintain suitable conditions for viable roadside and plantation ride populations. (ACTION: EN, FA, LAs)

5.2.4 Ensure maintenance of suitable areas of habitat for this species within managed forests and woodlands in its range. (ACTION: EN, FA)

5.3 Species management and protection

5.3.1 Undertake trial management at five suitable historic sites with the aim of regenerating this species from the seed-bank. Management is likely to include scrub clearance, coppicing and ground disturbance. (ACTION: EN)

5.3.2 Assess the feasibility and desirability of reintroducing tower mustard at selected sites should regeneration from the seed-bank prove unsuccessful. (ACTION: EN, JNCC)

5.3.3 Ensure the development of an *ex-situ* conservation programme. Seed should be collected from a representative number of sites in different parts of the range of this species and deposited in the Millenium Seed Bank at Wakehurst Place (Kew). Plants should also be propagated for reintroductions if necessary. (ACTION: EN, RBG Kew)

5.4 Advisory

5.4.1 Advise relevant landowners and managers of the presence and importance of this species and appropriate management for its conservation. (ACTION: EN, FA, LAs)

5.4.2 As far as possible, ensure that relevant agri-environment project officers are advised of locations for this species, its importance and management for its conservation. This is particularly important for the Breckland ESA. (ACTION: EN, MAFF)

5.4.3 Advise foresters working in the vicinity of extant sites for this species of its importance and steps which could be taken to encourage natural colonisation of their plantations. (ACTION: EN, FA)

5.5 Future research and monitoring

5.5.1 Complete a national survey of extant and historic sites, identify the main threats at each and assess the ecological requirements of the plant. (ACTION: EN, JNCC)

5.6 Communications and publicity

5.6.1 Raise awareness of the conservation value of arable and intermittently disturbed, open habitats particularly within the range of this species. This publicity should be targeted at farmers and the general public. (ACTION: EN, FA, LAs, MAFF)

5.7 Links with other action plans

5.7.1 It is likely that implementation of this action plan will benefit *Bromus interruptus* and *Scleranthus perennis* ssp *prostratus*.

5.7.2 The plan should be considered in conjunction with those for cereal field margins, lowland heathland, lowland dry acid grassland, and lowland calcareous grassland.

Arabis glabra

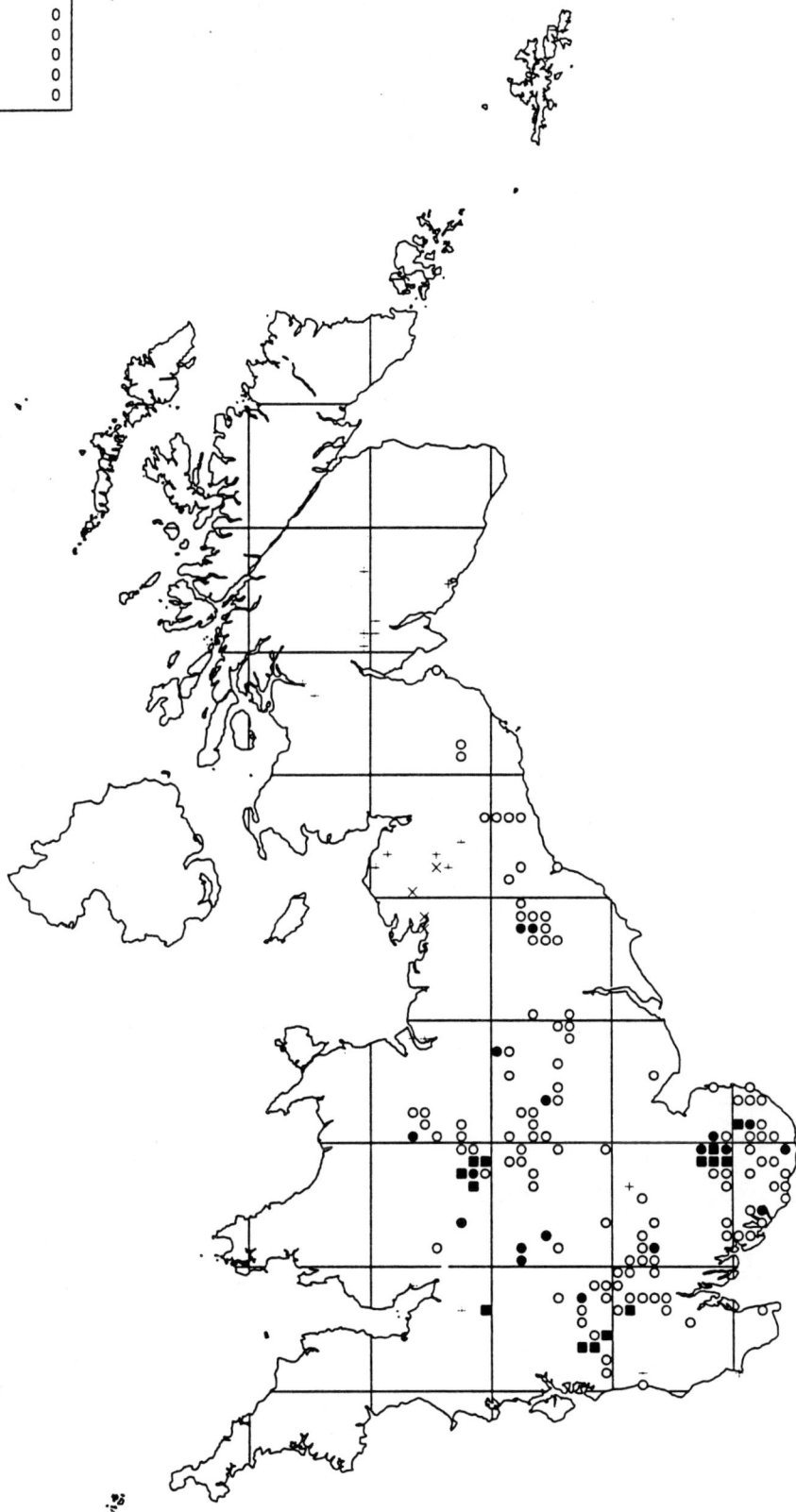

■	14	0
●	18	0
○	112	0
×	4	0
-	21	0

Distribution of Arabis glabra - tower mustard in Britain & N.Ireland, (by 10km square).
Source: British Red Data Book - Vascular plants, 1998, 3rd edition.

■ - records post 1980
● - records 1970 - 1987
○ - records pre 1970
× - introduced records post 1970
+ - introduced records pre 1970

127

Wild asparagus (*Asparagus officinalis* ssp *prostratus*) Action Plan

1. Current status

1.1 Wild asparagus is a plant of coastal dunes and clifftops and is endemic to western Europe. Genetic research has indicated that there may be justification for treating this taxon as a separate species from garden asparagus (*A. officinalis* ssp *officinalis*), an argument which strengthens the case for greater protection.

1.2 In Britain, wild asparagus, which has always been rare, is now known to survive at approximately five sites in western Cornwall, one in Dorset, three in west Glamorgan and one in southern Pembrokeshire. All of these populations are small. It has disappeared from a number of other sites in south-west England and Wales. The plant has also been recorded from dunes and cliff-tops in south-east Ireland and the Channel Isles, where it is rare and declining, the coasts of northern Spain and western France, Belgium (where there are no recent records), The Netherlands and Germany, where its present status is uncertain.

1.3 In GB wild asparagus is classified as *Vulnerable*. It receives general protection under the Wildlife and Countryside Act 1981.

2. Current factors causing loss or decline

2.1 Erosion of cliff-top habitats due to high levels of trampling by visitors. This is a particularly important factor at one Welsh site, compromising both the survival of mature plants and the recruitment of new individuals to the population.

2.2 Lack of grazing or other beneficial management. This is apparent at two of the Welsh sites which have become dominated by dense grass swards.

2.3 Gradual loss of genetic variation.

2.4 Low levels of seed production. Wild asparagus is dioecious and insect pollinated. A combination of small numbers of plants, sparse flower production, and the naturally low proportion of female plants in many populations results in frequent failure or very low levels of pollination and seed production.

2.5 Low levels of recruitment. In addition to low levels of seed production, vegetative spread is very slow.

2.6 Invasion of Hottentot fig (*Carpobrotus edulis*), threatens some of the Cornish populations.

3. Current action

3.1 A draft action plan has been produced for the Welsh populations by CCW. Several of the proposals have been implemented and a report on progress has recently been prepared.

3.2 Most extant Cornish and all extant Welsh populations are within SSSIs.

3.3 English Nature and National Trust teams have modified their management practices in line with those recommended by the CCW study.

3.4 A report is currently being prepared for CCW on the current status of wild asparagus in continental Europe.

4. Action plan objectives and targets

This plan summarises actions planned in Wales and, in addition, includes recommendations for new work in England, and the development of an overall perspective for the conservation of this taxon.

4.1 Maintain the population size at all known sites.

4.2 Enhance the population size at all known sites with the aim of doubling the wild population by 2008.

4.3 Establish two new viable populations by 2008.

4.4 Establish an *ex-situ* programme to protect genetic diversity, create a reserve population and provide experimental material.

5. Proposed action with lead agencies

This species is threatened not only because of the small number of sites at which it occurs, but also because of the low numbers of plants at each site. The recommended action therefore aims to protect and provide beneficial management for existing populations, to undertake experimental work with a view to boosting the numbers of plants at selected sites, and to establish new populations. Further survey is needed to refine conservation action for this species.

5.1 Policy and legislation

5.1.1 If wild asparagus is found to be threatened in Europe (see 5.5.4), reconsider it for protection under Schedule 8 of the Wildlife and Countryside Act 1981. (ACTION: DETR, JNCC)

5.2 Site safeguard and management

5.2.1 Provide mechanisms to ensure that a beneficial management regime is implemented on all extant sites (eg through considering sites for notification as SSSIs, and management agreements on existing SSSIs). On Welsh sites, management should follow proposals set out in the CCW report. (ACTION: CCW, EN)

5.2.2 Ensure that all sites are protected as far as possible from excessive trampling and the activities of rock-climbers. (ACTION: CCW, EN)

5.2.3 Ensure successful completion of the SAC designation for the candidate sites which include sections of the Gower Coast in Wales and the Lizard NNR in Cornwall, both of which support populations of the plant. (ACTION: CCW, DETR, EN, JNCC)

5.3   Species management and protection

5.3.1 Conserve the current level of genetic variation by developing a seed-bank for the species at Wakehurst Place (Kew) and perhaps the new Welsh botanic garden. Material collected from the Welsh and English sites should be kept separately and cultivated plants introduced only in the region from which they originated. (ACTION: CCW, EN, RBG Kew).

5.3.2 Continue the ongoing pollination work in Wales and consider a similar project in England if monitoring programmes (see 5.5.2) indicate poor pollination rates are occurring at particular sites. (ACTION: CCW, EN)

5.3.3 If suitable locations can be found, (re)introduce cultivated material at selected Welsh and English sites with the aim of establishing two new viable populations. (ACTION: CCW, EN)

5.4   Advisory

5.4.1 Provide land managers with appropriate advice on the conservation of wild asparagus. (ACTION: CCW, EN)

5.5   Future research and monitoring

5.5.1 Expand the survey of all extant and historic sites in Wales already carried out for CCW, by undertaking field surveys to establish current population numbers, status and distribution at English sites. Collate this information with field survey work recently carried out and in progress in Wales. (ACTION: CCW, EN, JNCC)

5.5.2 Monitor all extant populations in England and Wales to record data on population health, growth, flowering and fruiting. (ACTION: CCW, EN, JNCC)

5.5.3 Monitor the progress of any newly established populations. (ACTION: CCW, EN, JNCC)

5.5.4 Incorporate relevant findings from the ongoing review of the European status of wild asparagus into revisions of this plan. (ACTION: CCW, EN, JNCC)

5.5.5 Establish a consensus on the taxonomy of wild asparagus through discussion with the relevant experts. (ACTION: CCW, EN, JNCC)

5.6   Communications and publicity

5.6.1 Raise awareness of the importance of this rare taxon. Articles should be written for magazines of relevant local and national conservation groups. (ACTION: CCW, EN)

5.7   Links with other action plans

5.7.1 None proposed.

Asparagus officinalis subsp. prostratus

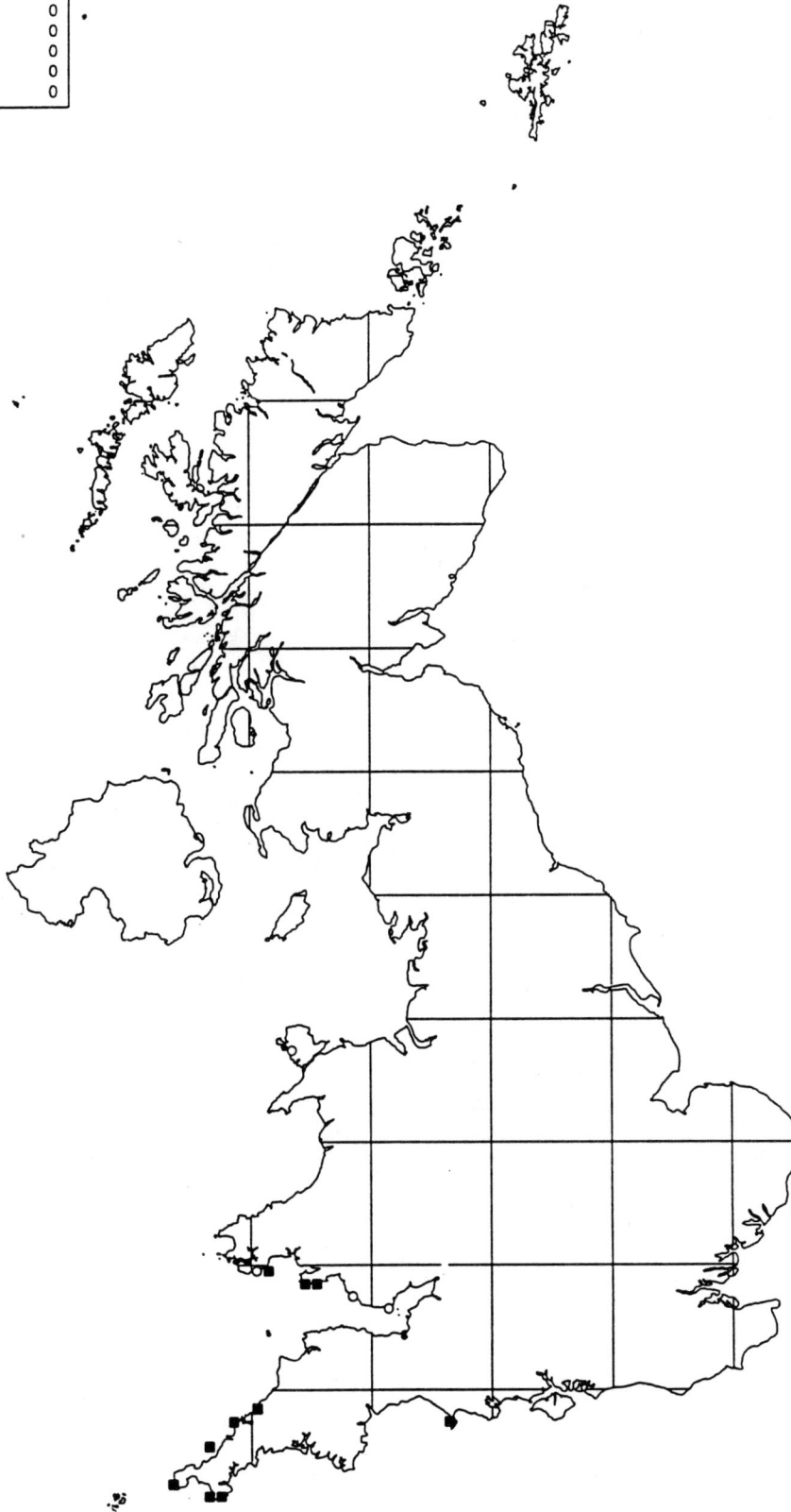

Distibution of Asparagus officinalis ssp. prostratus - wild asparagus in Britain & N.Ireland, (by 10km square). Source: British Red Data Book - Vascular plants, 1998, 3rd edition.

■ - records post 1980
● - records 1970 - 1987
O - records pre 1970
X - introduced records post 1970
+ - introduced records pre 1970

Interrupted brome (*Bromus interruptus*)
Action Plan

1. Current status

1.1 Interrupted brome is a species of arable and waste ground, especially as a weed in sainfoin, rye-grass and clover fields. This species was first discovered in 1849 and further finds soon followed, so that by 1920 the grass had been recorded from sites scattered throughout the southern third of England. The rapid spread of the plant was characteristic of an introduced species, but it is now known that this is not the case. Although interrupted brome is very different from others of its genus, it almost certainly arose in the 19th century as a new species through a major and sudden genetic change.

1.2 As a native species, interrupted brome is endemic to England and formerly occurred in south-central and south-east England from east Kent and north Somerset to south Lincolnshire. However, it is believed to be extinct in the wild, having last been seen in Cambridgeshire in 1972. Its decline was probably due to the use of improved seed-cleaning methods. It now grows only in cultivation in the UK, but it was introduced to The Netherlands and is apparently now well-established there.

1.3 This species is classified as *Extinct in the wild*.

2. Current factors causing loss or decline

2.1 Not applicable, as this species is extinct in the wild.

3. Current action

3.1 Seeds are held, and occasionally cultivated, at several botanic gardens including RBG Kew, Cambridge, Ness, and RBG Edinburgh.

3.2 A PhD study has been undertaken on the ecology of interrupted brome at the University of Liverpool.

3.3 Unsuccessful attempts were made to regenerate interrupted brome from the seed-bank at its last known site in Cambridgeshire.

4. Action plan objectives and targets

4.1 If considered feasible and desirable, restore populations of interrupted brome to three sites in its former range by 2003.

4.2 Support the conservation of this species through coordination of its *ex-situ* programme.

5. Proposed action with lead agencies

The priority for this species is to collate ecological and historical information and then to consider the feasibility and desirability of undertaking (re)introductions. Meanwhile, measures should be taken to coordinate its *ex-situ* conservation.

5.1 Policy and legislation

5.1.1 Encourage the development of relevant agri-environment schemes, such as the pilot Arable Stewardship Scheme, as a potential means of re-establishing interrupted brome in the countryside. When reviewing such schemes, consider whether changes are needed to increase their potential benefits for interrupted brome and threatened arable species. (ACTION: EN, MAFF)

5.2 Site safeguard and management

5.2.1 None proposed.

5.3 Species management and protection

5.3.1 Assess the feasibility and desirability of restoring self-sustaining wild populations of interrupted brome within its former range. Then, if appropriate, undertake experimental (re)introductions at three carefully selected sites. (ACTION: EN, JNCC, RBG Kew)

5.4 Advisory

5.4.1 Ensure that landowners and managers of any (re)introduction sites are advised on the management requirements of this species, and any activities which may be damaging to it. (ACTION: EN)

5.4.2 As far as possible, ensure that all relevant agri-environment project officers are advised of any sites where this species is restored, its management requirements and potential threats. (ACTION: EN, MAFF)

5.5 Future research and monitoring

5.5.1 Undertake a literature search and collate information to refine understanding of the history and ecology of this species. (ACTION: JNCC, RBG Kew)

5.5.2 Consult botanists in The Netherlands in order to determine the status of interrupted brome there. Exchange information on its ecological requirements and obtain advice on management which might be appropriate for its conservation in Britain. (ACTION: JNCC, RBG Kew)

5.5.3 Monitor any re-established populations for at least 10 years. (ACTION: EN, JNCC, RBG Kew)

5.6   Communications and publicity

5.6.1 Publicise the plight of this and threatened arable species. Articles should be written for relevant conservation and farming magazines and newsletters. (ACTION: EN, RBG Kew)

5.6.2 Establish arable conservation display and education centres with the aim of raising public awareness of this threatened group of the UK flora. (ACTION: EN, RBG Kew)

5.7   Links with other action plans

5.7.1 It is likely that implementation of this action plan will have benefits for other arable species, including *Arabis glabra*, *Centaurea cyanus*, *Filago lutescens*, *Filago pyramidata*, *Fumaria occidentalis*, *Fumaria purpurea*, *Galeopsis angustifolia*, *Galium tricornutum*, *Scandix pecten-veneris*, *Silene gallica*, *Torilis arvensis* and *Valerianella rimosa*.

5.7.2 The plan should be considered in conjunction with that for cereal field margins.

(No map provided, as the species is extinct in the wild.)

Scottish small-reed (*Calamagrostis scotica*)
Action Plan

1. Current status

1.1 Scottish small-reed is a tall grass currently recorded from a single locality in a rush-dominated mire pasture on the bed of a former loch in Caithness. The species is distinguished from the more widespread (but still rare) narrow small-reed by subtle differences in flower anatomy.

1.2 Scottish small-reed is endemic to Scotland. The population was estimated in 1995 at a minimum of 1000 flowering culms. The species is now extinct at its only other recorded site.

1.3 This species is classified as *Vulnerable* and is considered to be globally threatened by the World Conservation Monitoring Centre. It receives general protection under the Wildlife and Countryside Act 1981.

2. Current factors causing loss or decline

2.1 Both intensive grazing and lack of grazing have caused losses in different areas of the known site.

2.2 It is believed that the fen is flooding for an increased period each year and that this is likely to have an effect upon the population.

2.3 River bank erosion has caused loss of part of the population.

3. Current action

3.1 The site is notified as an SSSI.

3.2 The location and significance of the species has been made known to the landowners.

3.3 Seed has been collected for long-term storage at the Royal Botanic Garden's facilities in Wakehurst Place.

4. Action Plan objectives and targets

4.1 Maintain all stands of the species and ensure that all populations are regenerating successfully.

4.2 Unless the species is located elsewhere, establish the species at a second site by 2008 to reduce the risk of chance extinction.

5. Proposed action with lead agencies

The survival of this species depends on successful management of grazing and the hydrological regime (water level) at its single site. With little information on the requirements of the species, a relatively small population, and flooding of the site precluding winter grazing as an option, management experiments would be difficult and could be damaging. Instead, detailed monitoring should be used to inform the management of the SSSI. Improving the information available to botanists on the identification of the species could reveal unknown sites, especially from fieldwork taking place for Atlas 2000. The re-establishment of a second site would seem a wise precaution if additional sites for this species are not found.

5.1 Policy and legislation

5.1.1 None proposed.

5.2 Site safeguard and management

5.2.1 Seek cooperation with landowners over varying site management if essential changes to the extant population are identified by 5.5.1. (ACTION: SNH)

5.2.2 Prevent major changes to the hydrology of the site. (ACTION: SEPA)

5.3 Species management and protection

5.3.1 Assess potential locations and suitable methodologies for (re)introduction to a second site. (ACTION: SNH)

5.3.2 Establish a second population subject to the results of 5.3.1. (ACTION: SNH)

5.4 Advisory

5.4.1 Advise site owners regularly on the current status of the species, providing them with an opportunity to feed back information on any changes in management of the area. (ACTION: SNH)

5.5 Future research and monitoring

5.5.1 Monitor species performance and environmental factors until the response of the species to current management is understood. (ACTION: SNH)

5.5.2 Relate variation in grazing and water levels to plant performance recorded in 5.5.1. (ACTION: SNH)

5.5.3 Undertake a critical review of herbarium material of the small-reeds, with the aim of facilitating its identification in the field and identifying potential sites from herbarium material. (ACTION: RBG Edinburgh)

5.5.4 Encourage further survey for unknown populations of the Scottish small-reed, particularly at known locations for the narrow small-reed, using information gathered in 5.5.3. (ACTION: SNH)

5.5.5 Attempt to establish a molecular test for providing critical confirmation of any new populations of Scottish small-reed discovered (see 5.5.4). (ACTION: RBG Edinburgh)

5.6 **Communications and publicity**

5.6.1 Publicise the results of 5.5.3 and 5.5.5 to seek the involvement of local botanists in the survey of potential Scottish small-reed sites (see action 5.5.5). (ACTION: SNH)

5.7 **Links with other action plans**

5.7.1 This action plan should be considered in conjunction with that for purple moor grass and rush pasture.

Calamagrostis scotica

■	1	0
●	0	0
○	0	0
×	0	0
+	0	0

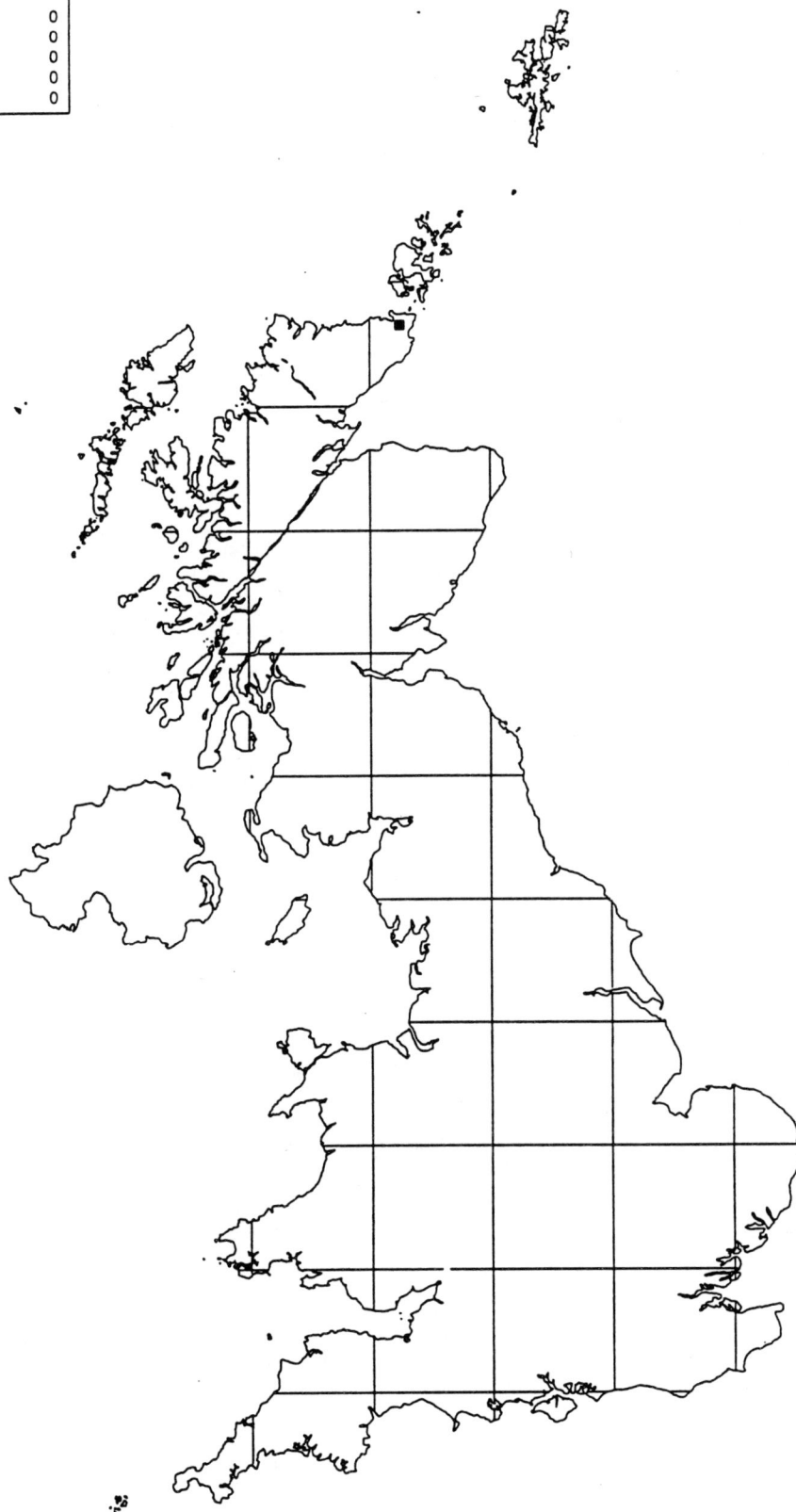

Distribution of Calamagrostis scotica - Scottish small-reed in Britain & N.Ireland, (by 10km sqaure).
Source: British Red Data Book - Vascular plants, 1998, 3rd edition.

■ - records post 1980
● - records 1970 - 1987
○ - records pre 1970
× - introduced records post 1970
+ - introduced records pre 1970

Prickly sedge (*Carex muricata* ssp *muricata*)
Action Plan

1. Current status

1.1 Prickly sedge occurs in a range of habitats including steep slopes and ledges, bushy and grassy areas. Most of its known sites have been on limestone. It seems to thrive where there is limited competition from other plant species, for example where there is occasional soil disturbance or thin drought-prone soils. The sedge grows in tufts up to 100 cm tall but is usually much shorter. It has exacting requirements, being intolerant both of excessive grazing and of competition and shading when grazing is absent.

1.2 Formerly recorded from six localities in Britain, it has recently been seen at only four: three in North Yorkshire (including two 'clumps' at Colt Park Wood NNR and 12 plants at a site in Swaledale) and one in Denbighshire (approximately 20-30 plants). It is possible that this plant has been under-recorded as it is very similar to spiked sedge (*Carex spicata*). A thorough survey of potential habitats for prickly sedge may, therefore, prove fruitful. Prickly sedge is not threatened in Europe as a whole, where it is the commoner taxon in central and eastern regions.

1.3 In GB this species is classified as *Critically Endangered* because of its exceptionally small population size. It receives general protection under the Wildlife and Countryside Act 1981.

2. Current factors causing loss or decline

2.1 Inappropriate grazing levels. Prickly sedge has suffered from both excessive grazing and under-grazing with the latter constituting the principal current threat. Two populations have been fenced to exclude grazing animals and one of these was almost lost due to subsequent scrub encroachment.

2.2 Increased soil erosion caused by the activities of walkers and rock-climbers seems to have been a factor in the extinction of prickly sedge at one site.

2.3 The Denbighshire site is on the edge of a quarry, although there are currently no approved plans for quarry expansion.

3. Current action

3.1 An introduction was attempted at a site close to Woodchester in west Gloucestershire, but was unsuccessful. Further (re)introductions are proposed.

3.2 An attempt is being made to reinforce the Swaledale population with plants grown from locally-collected seed.

3.3 Attempts have been made to protect plants from grazing in Swaledale. However, this has proved to be inappropriate, as fenced patches have declined more markedly than unfenced patches due to vigorous growth of the sward.

3.4 Seeds have been collected and deposited at Wakehurst Place (Kew).

3.5 The North Yorkshire sites for the species include one NNR and an SSSI (Swaledale). The Denbighshire site is also included within an SSSI.

4. Action plan objectives and targets

4.1 Develop and maintain viable populations at all extant sites.

4.2 Attempt the restoration of prickly sedge populations at all suitable historic sites, with experimental management in place by 2003.

4.3 Reinforce the population at Colt Park Wood NNR (if management fails to encourage the appearance of new plants) by 2003.

4.4 Establish an *ex-situ* programme to protect genetic diversity, create a reserve population and provide experimental material.

5. Proposed action with lead agencies

Management for this species at its remaining sites has not always been appropriate. Therefore, it is vital that steps are taken to ensure all sites receive beneficial management in the future. Also, because of the low numbers of plants at each site, experimental management and where appropriate reinforcements and (re)introductions should be undertaken with a view to enhancing existing populations and restoring populations at historic sites. As prickly sedge is an under-recorded species, a thorough survey is urgently required to assess its current status.

5.1 Policy and legislation

5.1.1 Consider the inclusion of this taxon on Schedule 8 of the Wildlife and Countryside Act 1981 at the earliest possible opportunity. (ACTION: DETR, JNCC)

5.2 Site safeguard and management

5.2.1 Ensure that all extant sites are considered for notification as SSSIs where this is necessary to secure their long-term protection. (ACTION: CCW, EN)

5.2.2 Ensure that all extant populations for this taxon receive management which is beneficial to its conservation. (ACTION: CCW, EN)

5.2.3 Where relevant, ensure that populations are protected from the activities of walkers and climbers. (ACTION: EN, LAs)

5.2.4 Seek full protection of the Denbighshire site from any future quarrying operations, through negotiation with all relevant parties. (ACTION: CCW, LAs)

5.3   Species management and protection

5.3.1 Undertake trial management on all suitable historic sites with the aim of regenerating plants from the seed-bank. (ACTION: EN)

5.3.2 In conjunction with the Gloucester Plant Group (BSBI) explore the potential for introducing prickly sedge at Woodchester Park. This site could offer opportunities to investigate autecological issues such as seed-bank and population dynamics. (ACTION: EN)

5.3.3 Assess the feasibility and desirability of (re)introducing prickly sedge at other suitable sites should regeneration from the seed-bank prove unsuccessful. (ACTION: CCW, EN)

5.3.4 If further survey of Colt Park Wood NNR reveals no new colonies of prickly sedge, undertake experimental reinforcements using seed collected from the plants remaining on site. Consider extending this approach to the Swaledale site. (ACTION: EN)

5.3.5 Establish an *ex-situ* seed collection for this taxon in the Millenium Seed Bank at Wakehurst Place (Kew). Plants should also be propagated for reinforcements and (re)introductions if necessary. (ACTION: CCW, EN, RBG Kew)

5.4   Advisory

5.4.1 Advise all landowners and managers on extant and restored sites of the presence of prickly sedge and appropriate management for its conservation. Consultation with landowners should also be undertaken throughout the planning of any restoration work. (ACTION: CCW, EN)

5.4.2 As far as possible, ensure that all relevant agri-environment project officers are advised of locations of this species, its importance and management needed for its conservation. (ACTION: CCW, EN, MAFF, WOAD)

5.5   Future research and monitoring

5.5.1 Survey all extant, historic and potential sites for this species in order to determine its current status.

An assessment of current threats should be made at each site. (ACTION: CCW, EN, JNCC)

5.5.2 Devise and implement a monitoring programme for all extant and restored populations. (ACTION: CCW, EN)

5.5.3 Investigate aspects of the seed biology of this species. (ACTION: CCW, EN, JNCC)

5.6   Communications and publicity

5.6.1 Raise awareness of this *Critically Endangered* taxon amongst the botanical community, as it is possible that several sites for this species remain to be discovered. Botanists should be encouraged to survey potential sites for this plant. (ACTION: CCW, EN)

5.7   Links with other action plans

5.7.1 This action plan should be considered in conjunction with that for lowland calcareous grassland.

Carex muricata subsp.muricata

■	5		0
●	0		0
○	1		0
×	0		0
-	0		0

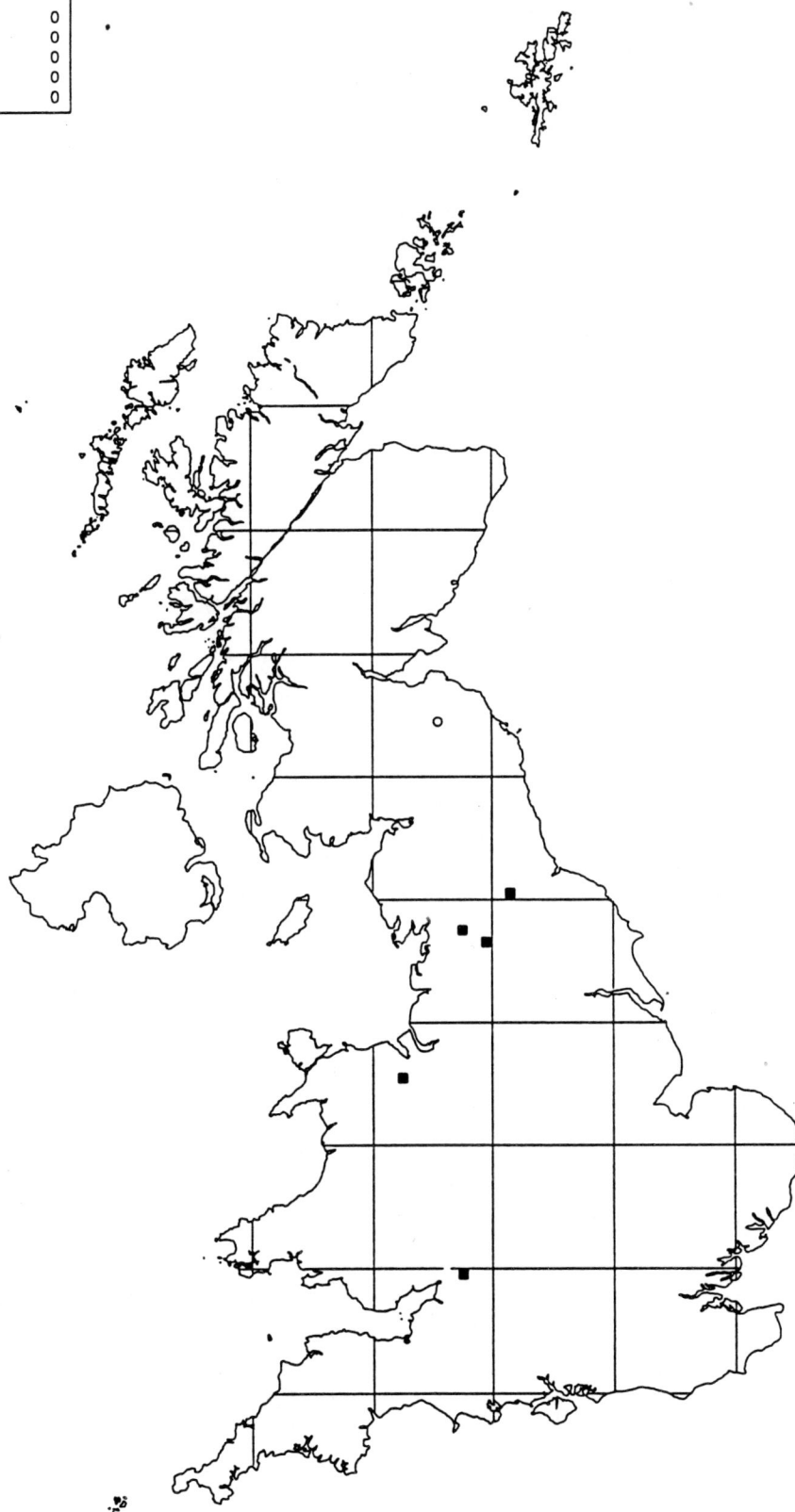

Distribution of Carex muricata subsp.muricata - prickly sedge in Britain & N.Ireland, (by 10km square). Source: British Red Data Book - Vascular plants, 1998, 3rd edition.

■ - records post 1980
● - records 1970 - 1987
○ - records pre 1970
× - introduced records post 1970
+ - introduced records pre 1970

True fox-sedge (*Carex vulpina*)
Action plan

1. Current status

1.1 True fox-sedge is a species of wet ditches and pond sides mainly on chalk or limestone, and often grows in standing water. It prefers open conditions and under shade it soon ceases to flower and dwindles to extinction.

1.2 Most of the extant populations for this species are in Kent and Sussex, but it is also found in Gloucestershire and along the River Ray in Oxfordshire. It may also still occur in South Yorkshire (the last record here was made in 1983). However, it is very difficult to distinguish true fox-sedge from false fox-sedge (*C. otrubae*) and the distribution of each species may therefore be somewhat confused. Despite this, it is certain that true fox-sedge has undergone a marked decline since its taxonomic separation from false fox-sedge. True fox-sedge occurs in suitable situations throughout Europe and into Asia.

1.3 In GB this species is now classified as *Vulnerable*. It receives general protection under the Wildlife and Countryside Act 1981.

2. Current factors causing loss or decline

Although not well known, these are thought to include the following:

2.1 Drying of sites due to drought, drainage and water abstraction.

2.2 Wholesale clearance of ditches where it grows.

2.3 Shading of sites due to growth of scrub and other tall vegetation.

3. Current action

3.1 Seed has been collected and used to cultivate plants in private collections where they apparently grow easily and vigorously.

4. Action plan objectives and targets

4.1 Ensure that viable, dynamic populations are maintained on all extant sites.

4.2 Restore populations at five suitable sites by 2003.

4.3 Establish an *ex-situ* programme to protect genetic diversity, create a reserve population and provide experimental material.

5. Proposed action with lead agencies

A survey of all known extant and historic sites should be the first action taken for this species. This will establish its current status and provide information to allow targeting of the other measures recommended. The priorities will include: beneficial management of all extant sites based on a better understanding of the plant's ecological requirements; and protection for each colony from water pollution, damaging drainage activities, inappropriate watercourse management and excessive water abstraction. The re-establishment of new populations should be attempted first by natural regeneration from the seed-bank, followed by reintroductions if necessary.

5.1 Policy and legislation

5.1.1 Consider providing mechanisms, including through relevant agri-environment schemes, to enable the creation of buffer strips alongside key sites (if the results of 5.5.3 show these to be beneficial). (ACTION: EA, EN, MAFF)

5.2 Site safeguard and management

5.2.1 Ensure that key sites for this species receive long-term protection and appropriate management, through SSSI notification if necessary. (ACTION: EN)

5.2.2 On sites where true fox-sedge is thriving, ensure that current management practices are continued. On other sites, where it has declined to just a few clumps, undertake trial management with the aim of enhancing the populations. Scrub should be managed on all sites. (ACTION: EN)

5.2.3 Consider targeting relevant agri-environment schemes to land adjacent to remaining sites for true fox-sedge, seeking to reduce the threat of adverse practices (including herbicide and fertiliser use). (ACTION: EN, MAFF)

5.2.4 Ensure that extant and restored populations for true fox-sedge are not threatened with inappropriate watercourse management. (ACTION: EA, IDBs)

5.2.5 Ensure that Local Environment Agency Plans and Water Level Management Plans take full account of the requirements of this species. In particular, ensure that no further sites for true fox-sedge are lost through increases in levels of water abstraction. (ACTION: EA)

5.3 Species management and protection

5.3.1 Assess the possibility of regenerating plants from the seedbank on historic sites and, if feasible, undertake trial management on five suitable historic sites to achieve this aim. Suitable sites will be those where a long-term management commitment is possible. (ACTION: EN)

5.3.2 Review the success of the experimental management outlined under 5.3.1 in 2003. If regeneration from the seed-bank proves unsuccessful, seek to reintroduce true fox-sedge at five sites based on the findings of 5.5.2. (ACTION: EN)

5.3.3 Collect seed from sites in different parts of the range of this species and deposit in the Millenium Seed Bank at Wakehurst Place (Kew). Plants should also be propagated for reintroductions if necessary. (ACTION: EN, RBG Kew)

5.4 Advisory

5.4.1 Advise all landowners and managers on extant and restored sites of appropriate management for the conservation of this species. (ACTION: EN)

5.4.2 As far as possible, ensure that all relevant agri-environment project officers, relevant drainage engineers and waterways managers are advised of locations of this species, its importance and management needed for its conservation. (ACTION: EN, EA, IDBs, LAs, MAFF)

5.5 Future research and monitoring

5.5.1 Resurvey all known extant and historic sites for this species in order to determine its current distribution and status, and assess possible threats to remaining populations. (ACTION: EN, JNCC)

5.5.2 Undertake detailed monitoring and ecological research on selected viable sites for this species in order to determine more precisely its requirements and the management techniques which should be employed for its conservation. (ACTION: EN, JNCC)

5.5.3 Investigate the impacts of nutrient enrichment and pollution on populations of true fox-sedge and the value of buffer strips for the species. (ACTION: EA, EN, JNCC)

5.6 Communications and publicity

5.6.1 Raise awareness of this vulnerable species amongst the botanical community including advice on how to distinguish true fox-sedge from false fox-sedge. (ACTION: EN)

5.7 Links with other action plans

5.7.1 None proposed.

Carex vulpina

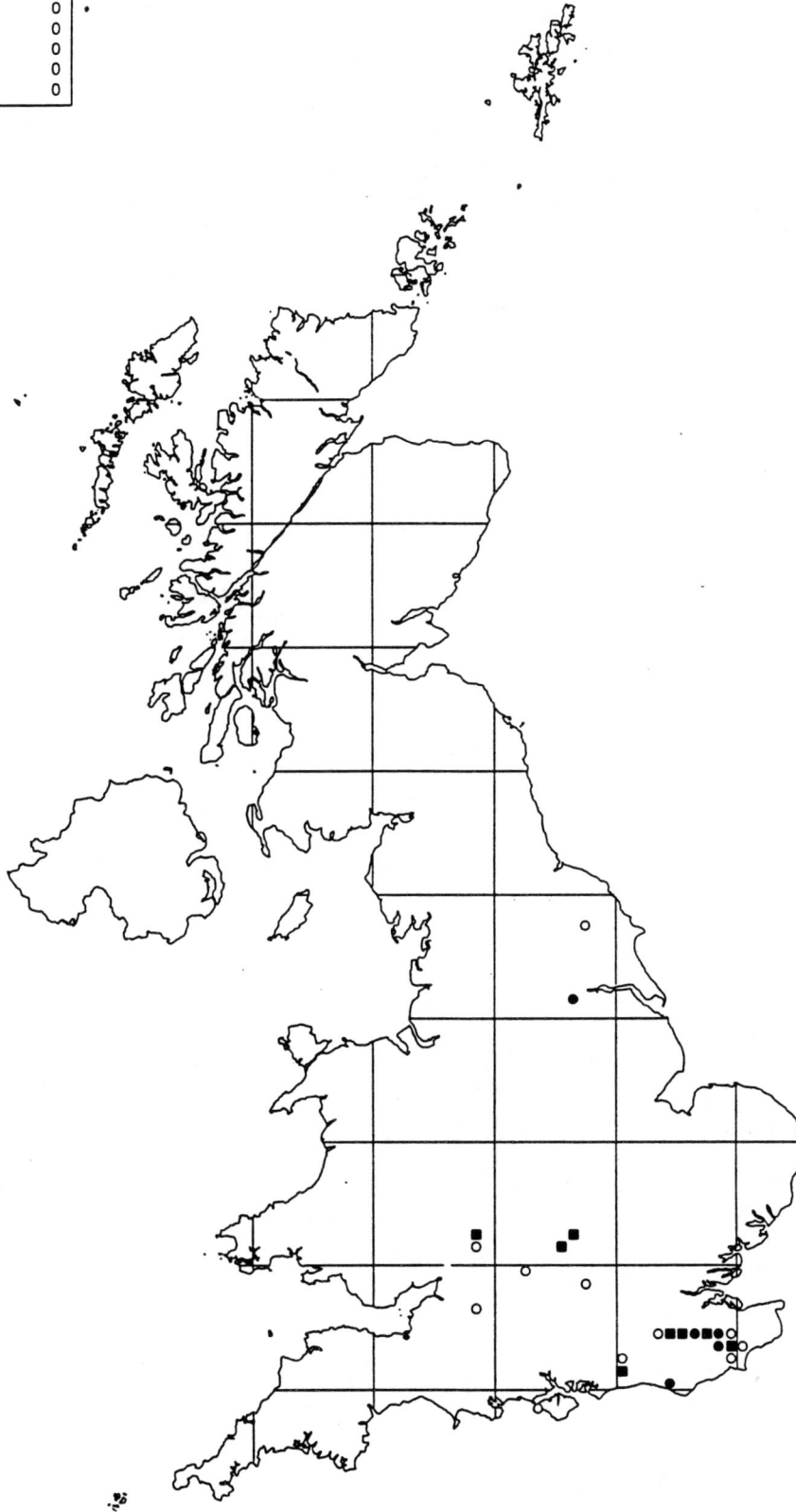

■	8	0
●	5	0
○	11	0
✕	0	0
+	0	0

Distribution of Carex vulpina - true fox-sedge in Britain & N.Ireland, (by 10km square)
Source: British Red Data Book - Vascular plants, 1998, 3rd edition.

■ - records post 1980
● - records 1970 - 1987
○ - records pre 1970
✕ - introduced records post 1970
+ - introduced records pre 1970

147

Cornflower (*Centaurea cyanus*)
Action Plan

1. Current status

1.1 Cornflower is an annual plant of arable fields, often on sandy, acidic soils. Flowers are self-incompatible and are borne between May and August. The seeds, which are believed to remain viable for several years, generally germinate during the following spring with a second flush in late summer. This species was often found in association with corn marigold (*Chrysanthemum segetum*), which also germinates in spring.

1.2 Cornflower once occurred throughout the UK and was a troublesome weed of arable land. Between 1930 and 1960 it was recorded from 264 ten km squares, but by 1985 it had declined to fewer than 50 ten km squares. Today, self-sustaining populations are thought to be confined to only one site in Suffolk, one on the Isle of Wight and one in Lincolnshire. Isolated plants still occur over a large area of the south and east of England and in Wales, although many are due to introductions from wildflower seed mixtures and most persist for no longer than a year. Large numbers sometimes occur when there are deep excavations for roads and pipelines. In Europe as a whole, cornflower is not threatened and is still widely distributed, although it has declined in much of north-west Europe.

1.3 In GB cornflower is now classified as *Endangered*. It receives general protection under the Wildlife and Countryside Act 1981.

2. Current factors causing loss or decline

The following agricultural changes were largely responsible for the decline of cornflower and are now providing constraints on its recovery:

2.1 Increased use of herbicides and fertilisers.

2.2 The development of highly competitive crop varieties.

2.3 The destruction of field-edge refuges.

2.4 The demise of traditional crop rotations.

2.5 The conversion of marginal arable land to pasture.

3. Current action

3.1 Research is ongoing at the Suffolk site to determine the ideal conservation management.

3.2 The Suffolk and Isle of Wight sites are under Countryside Stewardship Scheme agreements.

3.3 Cornflower has been introduced to several trial arable weed conservation plots such as that at Barton Downs (English Nature).

4. Action plan objectives and targets

4.1 Develop and maintain viable populations at all extant native sites where the species is long-established.

4.2 Facilitate the natural colonisation of new sites.

4.3 Regenerate populations of cornflower from the seed-bank at eight historic sites by 2003.

4.4 Establish an *ex-situ* programme to protect genetic diversity, create a reserve population and provide experimental material.

5. Proposed action with lead Agencies

It is important that any action for this species is considered as part of a broader approach aimed at the conservation of all threatened UK arable weeds. The protection and management of extant populations is the priority, but this should be considered in parallel with work aimed at regenerating plants from the seed-bank and with the possible development of national schemes for the beneficial management of important arable habitats (eg the pilot Arable Stewardship Scheme). This will provide opportunities for the long-term expansion of populations into the wider countryside, as will the controlled use of native seed in wildflower mixes. All conservation management should be informed by relevant research where necessary.

5.1 Policy and legislation

5.1.1 Encourage the development of relevant agri-environment schemes, such as the pilot Arable Stewardship Scheme in England, as a potential means of re-establishing cornflower in the countryside. When reviewing such schemes, consider whether changes are needed to increase their potential benefits for this and other threatened arable species. (ACTION: CCW, EN, MAFF, WOAD)

5.1.2 As far as possible, ensure that any seed of cornflower included in wildflower seed mixtures is of native origin. (ACTION: MAFF, WOAD)

5.2 Site safeguard and management

5.2.1 Continue beneficial management at the Suffolk site, implement management at the other three extant sites and refine techniques as the results of research continue to emerge. (ACTION: EN)

5.2.2 Seek to develop a network of suitable habitats within the vicinity of cornflower sites, thereby providing opportunities for its spread. Favourable management will include the relevant options under appropriate agri-environment schemes, eg uncropped headlands. (ACTION: CCW, EN, MAFF, WOAD)

5.3   Species management and protection

5.3.1 Undertake experimental management at eight carefully selected historic sites with the aim of regenerating cornflower from the seed-bank, seeking opportunities through appropriate agri-environment schemes. (ACTION: EN, MAFF)

5.3.2 Collect seed from all extant native sites and any restored sites and deposit in the Millenium Seed Bank at Wakehurst Place (Kew). (ACTION: CCW, EN, RBG Kew)

5.4   Advisory

5.4.1 On sites where cornflower is a significant consideration, advise landowners and managers of the presence and importance of this species, specific management for its conservation, and any potentially damaging actions. Particular attention should be given to optimal cultivation and harvest times. (ACTION: EN)

5.4.2 As far as possible, ensure that all relevant agri-environment project officers are advised of locations of this species, its importance, management requirements and potential threats. (ACTION: EN, MAFF)

5.5   Future research and monitoring

5.5.1 Collate information and resurvey extant and historic sites where necessary in order to gain a more complete understanding of the current distribution and status of cornflower. This will determine the range over which conservation action is appropriate and help to clarify the threats to remaining populations. (ACTION: CCW, EN, JNCC, SNH)

5.5.2 Continue with monitoring and research work on the Suffolk site, and extend to other sites with extant and restored populations with a view to refining conservation management techniques. Where possible, monitoring visits should be combined with meeting landowners to discuss conservation management for the species. (ACTION: EN, JNCC)

5.5.3 Undertake research to determine the selectivity of all graminicides currently in use so as to identify which, if any, are suitable for use in field margins that support cornflower and other threatened arable species. (ACTION: EN, JNCC)

5.6   Communications and publicity

5.6.1 Publicise the plight of this and other threatened arable species. Articles should be written for relevant conservation and farming magazines and newsletters. Botanists should be encouraged to report any new records, eg through Atlas 2000 recording. (ACTION: CCW, EN)

5.6.2 Develop links with European ecologists working to conserve threatened plants of arable habitats. (ACTION: JNCC)

5.6.3 Establish arable conservation display and education centres with the aim of raising public awareness of this threatened group of the UK flora. (ACTION: CCW, EN)

5.7   Links with other action plans

5.7.1 It is likely that implementation of this action plan will benefit other arable species, including *Arabis glabra*, *Bromus interruptus*, *Filago lutescens*, *Filago pyramidata*, *Fumaria occidentalis*, *Fumaria purpurea*, *Galeopsis angustifolia*, *Galium tricornutum*, *Scandix pecten-veneris*, *Silene gallica*, *Torilis arvensis* and *Valerianella rimosa*.

5.7.2 The plan should be considered in conjunction with that for cereal field margins.

Centaurea cyanus

■	43	0
●	82	0
○	376	0
×	71	0
-	37	3

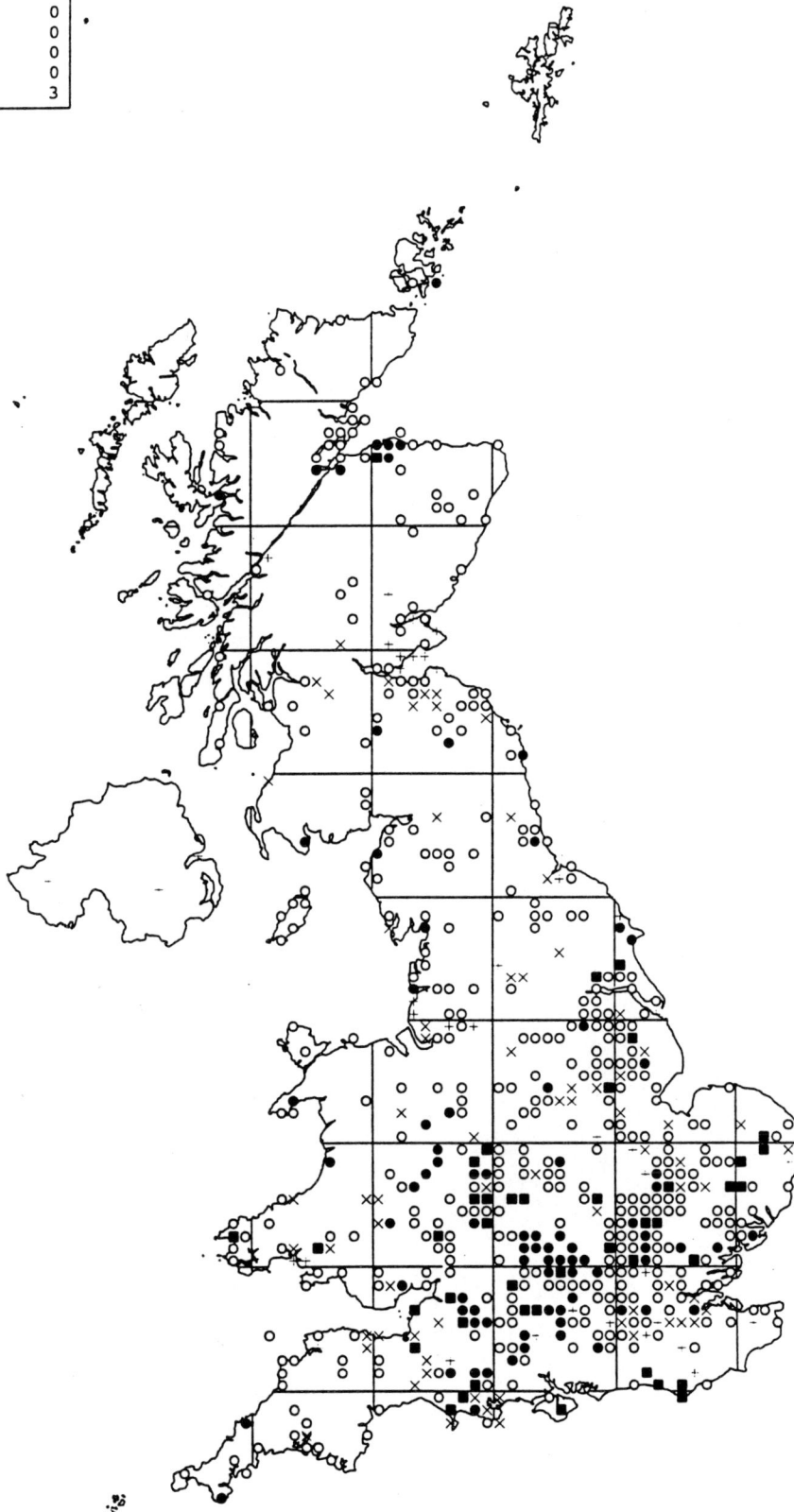

Distribution of Centaurea cyanus - cornflower in Britain & N.Ireland, (by 10km square)
Source: British Red Data Book - Vascular plants, 1998, 3rd edition.

■ - records post 1980
● - records 1970 - 1987
○ - records pre 1970
× - introduced records post 1970
+ - introduced records pre 1970

'Shetland mouse-ear (*Cerastium nigrescens*) Action Plan

1. Current status

1.1 Shetland mouse-ear is found on remarkable natural 'debris' areas formed from the rock serpentinite. It is unclear why these areas have remained 'open' while elsewhere on the serpentinite outcrops a normal process of succession to closed vegetation has occurred. Research suggests that the maintenance of this debris habitat is likely to result from a combination of factors, notably the presence of high concentrations of heavy metals, nutrient imbalance, summer droughts and the particular erosion and weathering characteristics of the serpentinite at the site. The species is closely related to arctic mouse-ear, differing mainly in its dark, almost circular leaves clothed, like the stems, in spreading glandular hairs.

1.2 This species is endemic to Shetland and is naturally restricted to the Keen of Hamar NNR and another smaller debris area also on the island of Unst.

1.3 Shetland mouse-ear is classified as *Vulnerable*. It receives general protection under the Wildlife and Countryside Act 1981.

2. Current factors causing loss or decline

2.1 Part of the Keen of Hamar NNR site was destroyed by agricultural improvement in 1967 and is now good quality grazing pasture.

2.2 Some areas have been damaged by eutrophication resulting from use by grazing animals.

2.3 Developments, such as mining, have damaged parts of these sites.

3. Current action

3.1 A study of the population dynamics of Shetland mouse-ear (and the other rarities of the serpentine debris) has been recently carried out at Stirling University, supported by SNH.

3.2 The Keen of Hamar is a NNR and the other population is also on a site notified as an SSSI and subject to a management agreement.

3.3 Grazing animals have been excluded by agreement from key areas.

3.4 The species has been experimentally introduced to another SSSI on Unst by researchers.

4. Action plan objectives and targets

4.1 Maintain current populations.

4.2 Investigate possibilities for increasing the total population of the species to aid its survival.

5. Proposed action with lead agencies

The main need is for current management to be maintained for extant populations. Population estimates have sometimes been very low indicating that the species might be eliminated by chance events, such as a period of adverse weather conditions. Taking some seed into long-term *ex-situ* storage may provide a safety net if this occurs. Long-term experiments will need to be carried out to see if the areas of Keen of Hamar that have been damaged in the past can be realistically rehabilitated. The progress of the experimental introduction to a new site needs to be followed to assess potential benefits to the survival of the species.

5.1 Policy and legislation

5.1.1 None proposed.

5.2 Site safeguard and management

5.2.1 Maintain current management at existing sites. (ACTION: SNH)

5.2.2 Carry out additional rehabilitation trials on damaged areas if required. (ACTION: SNH)

5.3 Species management and protection

5.3.1 Collect seed samples for storage in the Millenium Seed Bank at Wakehurst Place. Seed should also be made available for reintroductions, if necessary. (ACTION: RBG Kew, SNH)

5.4 Advisory

5.4.1 Inform owners and occupiers of the status of Shetland mouse-ear and notify them of any management of the site that could conflict with the survival of the species. (ACTION: SNH)

5.5 Future research and monitoring

5.5.1 Monitor all populations. (ACTION: SNH)

5.5.2 Report on the feasibility of rehabilitating damaged areas of the Keen of Hamar to allow the restoration of the serpentine plant communities after at least five years monitoring existing rehabilitation experiments. (ACTION: SNH)

5.5.3 Report on the location and extent of other areas of ultramific debris areas on Shetland and the benefits, or otherwise, of introducing the species to individual areas after five years of monitoring the existing introduction experiment. (ACTION: SNH)

5.5.4 Reassess the risk to the species at current sites after at least five years of monitoring existing populations. (ACTION: SNH)

5.6   Communications and publicity

5.6.1 Publicise the international significance of the species to the people of Unst and Shetland. (ACTION: SNH)

5.7   Links with other action plans

5.7.1 None proposed.

Cerastium nigrescens

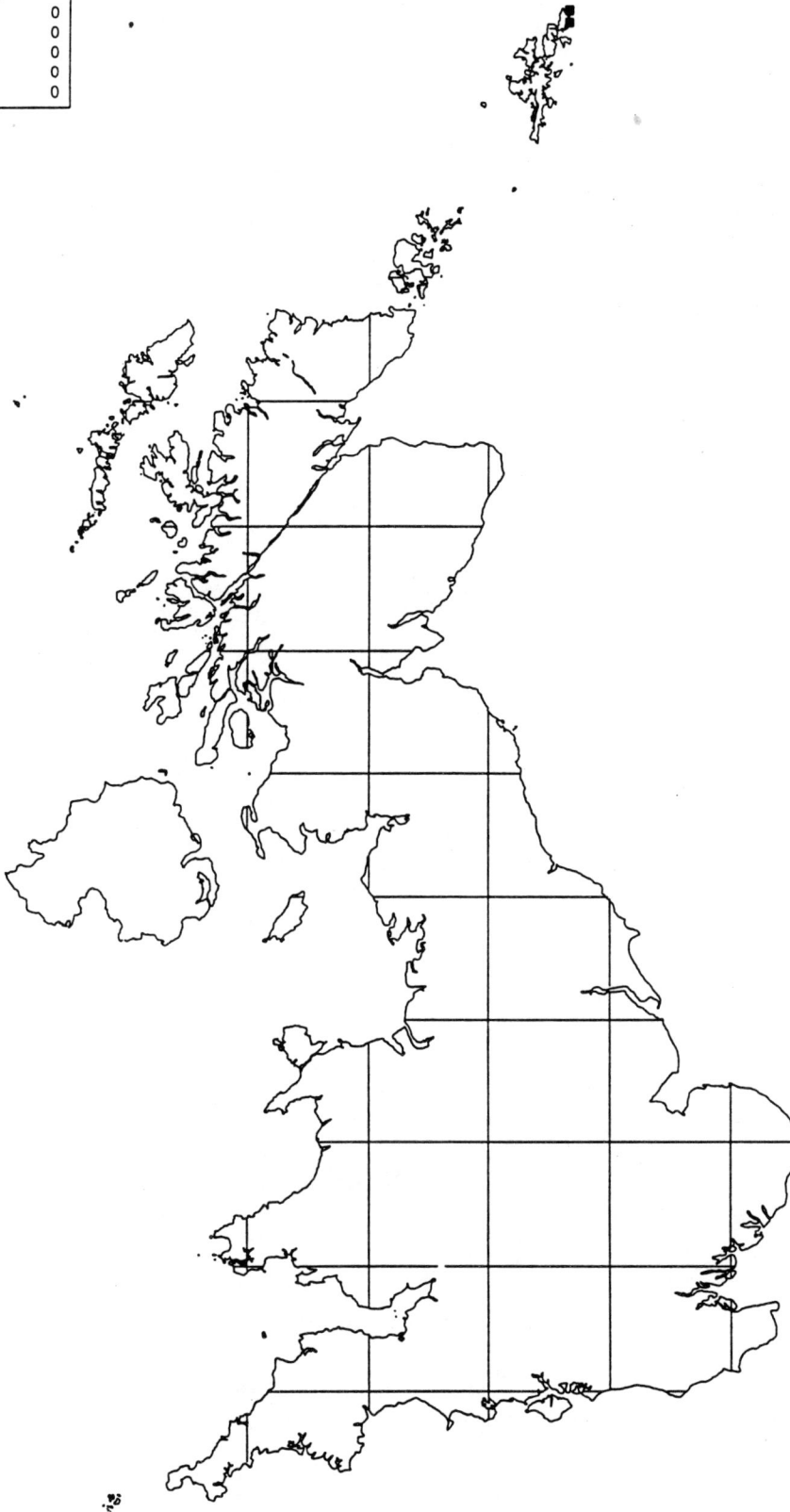

■	2	0
●	0	0
○	0	0
×	0	0
+	0	0

Distribution of Cerastium nigrescens - Shetland mouse-ear in Britain & N.Ireland, (by 10km square).
Source: British Red Data Book - Vascular plants, 1998, 3rd edition.

■ - records post 1980
● - records 1970 - 1987
○ - records pre 1970
× - introduced records post 1970
+ - introduced records pre 1970

Stinking hawk's-beard (*Crepis foetida*)
Action Plan

1. Current status

1.1 Stinking hawk's-beard is an annual or biennial plant which is very rare in Britain, and perhaps always has been. During this century it has only been recorded from a few coastal sites in south-east England, typically on disturbed shingle or chalk. Throughout its range, stinking hawk's-beard always occurs on open, dry, sandy or rocky sites.

1.2 The only records for this species have been from Walmer (Kent, 1901), Eastbourne (Sussex, 1908), Newhaven (Sussex, 1925), Pevensey Bay (Sussex, 1948) and at Dungeness (Kent 1980). It apparently became extinct in England in 1980, when the last plants were recorded at Dungeness. Whilst the presence of a seed-bank here cannot be discounted, there have been no records of truly wild plants since 1980. Elsewhere, it can be found across much of continental Europe, and also in central Asia, but is declining across much of its range.

1.3 In GB stinking hawk's-beard is classified as *Endangered*. It is specially protected under Schedule 8 of the Wildlife and Countryside Act 1981.

2. Current factors causing loss or decline

The reasons for the extinction of stinking hawk's-beard are not clear but the following factors may have been involved:

2.1 Rabbit grazing. Cultivated plants, which behave as biennials and develop a basal rosette of leaves, seem to be highly vulnerable to rabbit grazing, but this does not appear to be the case for plants which grow from seed in the wild. These tend to be small, annual plants which are largely ignored by rabbits. However, they may still be vulnerable at times when other food is unavailable.

2.2 Climatic factors. The species is thought to be susceptible to long periods of wet cold weather which may also explain why it has always been restricted to the south-east of England.

3. Current action

3.1 In 1992, under English Nature's Species Recovery Programme, plants were re-established in two areas on the shingle at Dungeness using local seed which had been stored at Cambridge University Botanic Garden. The reintroduced plants were protected from rabbits using cages and they are now well established. A recent count recorded over 100 plants which were established outside the cages.

3.2 Experimental work is included in the Dungeness re-establishment programme to determine the most suitable substrate for the plant.

3.3 Proposals have been put forward to introduce this species to four further sites (two close to Dungeness, one at Orfordness in Suffolk and another in Hampshire), all four of which are nature reserves. The introductions are planned to take place within the next five years.

3.4 An *ex-situ* seed-bank is held at Wakehurst Place (Kew).

4. Action plan objectives and targets

4.1 Ensure the continued success of the re-establishment programme at Dungeness.

4.2 Reintroduce stinking hawk's-beard to all of its former sites, or introduce it to an equivalent number of alternative sites, by 2003.

4.3 Introduce populations of stinking hawk's-beard at four additional sites in accordance with the proposals under English Nature's Species Recovery Programme. Aim to achieve this by 2003.

5. Proposed action with lead agencies

The action recommended below is intended to support the development and implementation of carefully managed (re)introductions, and to ensure that adequate measures are in place to allow for continued enhancement of the population at Dungeness. Developing a greater understanding of the European status of this species will help inform the work in this action plan.

5.1 Policy and legislation

5.1.1 None proposed.

5.2 Site safeguard and management

5.2.1 Devise and implement measures to control visitors if it is considered that they pose a significant threat to plants at Dungeness and other sites. (ACTION: EN)

5.3 Species management and protection

5.3.1 Assess the feasibility of reintroducing stinking hawk's-beard at the other sites where it was formerly recorded. If they prove unsuitable, introductions should be attempted at alternative sites within the original range of the species. (ACTION: EN, JNCC)

5.3.2 Ensure that current plans to introduce stinking hawk's-beard to four new sites are carried out and populations are established at all sites by 2003. (ACTION: EN)

5.3.3 Continue with the *ex-situ* conservation programme at Wakehurst Place (Kew). (ACTION: EN, RBG Kew)

5.4   Advisory

5.4.1 Where (re)introductions are made, advise all relevant landowners and managers of the importance of the plant, specific management for its conservation, and activities which are potentially damaging to it. (ACTION: EN)

5.5   Future research and monitoring

5.5.1 Continue to monitor colonies at Dungeness for at least another five years. (ACTION: EN)

5.5.2 Monitor newly established populations for at least ten years. Particular attention should be given to recording the damage caused by rabbits. (ACTION: EN)

5.5.3 Make contact with European universities and herbaria and carry out literature searches to increase understanding of the European status of this species. (ACTION: EN, JNCC)

5.6   Communications and publicity

5.6.1 Promote the importance and requirements of this species and other shingle flora in the areas where it occurs. This could be done via local newspapers following successful (re)introductions. (ACTION: EN)

5.7   Links with other action plans

5.7.1 This action plan should be considered in conjunction with those for *Galeopsis angustifolia*, *Limonium binervosum* agg, *Rumex rupestris*, and vegetated shingle.

Crepis foetida

Distribution of Crepis foetida - stinking hawk's-beard in Britain & N.Ireland, (by 10km square)
Source: British Red Data Book - Vascular plants, 1998, 3rd edition.

■ - records post 1980
● - records 1970 - 1987
○ - records pre 1970
× - introduced records post 1970
+ - introduced records pre 1970

159

Deptford pink (*Dianthus armeria*)
Action Plan

1. Current status

1.1 Deptford pink is a plant of dry pastures, disturbed ground, roadsides, field borders and hedgerows. It generally occurs on light, sandy soil often of rather high pH, but is also known on other soils such as at Woodwalton Fen where it grew on peaty soil of pH 4.8. Seed production by Deptford pink is prolific, a normal sized plant producing about 400 seeds. The precise conditions required for germination and establishment are not known, but it is thought to require open conditions for success. However, it is able to compete with taller vegetation once established.

1.2 The range of Deptford pink in Britain lies between north Wales and the south coast of England, with most of its sites occurring in southern England. It has declined severely over the last 60 years, exhibiting one of the most rapid declines of any species in the British flora. Having once been widespread, it was reduced to 34 sites by 1970 and is now known from only 13 to 15 sites. This decline appears to be ongoing and most of the remaining populations are small (1-50 plants), although there are a few sites with hundreds of plants where conditions are suitable. Deptford pink is not threatened in Europe as a whole, where it occurs widely across western and central regions.

1.3 In GB Deptford pink is classified as *Vulnerable*. It is specially protected under Schedule 8 of the the Wildlife and Countryside Act 1981 in respect to England and Wales only.

2. Current factors causing loss or decline

2.1 Conversion of pasture to arable and building land.

2.2 Cessation of grazing.

2.3 Destruction of hedgerows.

2.4 Successional changes leading to loss of the relatively open vegetation structure which Deptford pink is known to require.

3. Current action

3.1 Deptford pink is currently being considered for inclusion on Schedule 8 of the Wildlife and Countryside Act 1981.

4. Action plan objectives and targets

4.1 Maintain the range of Deptford pink in the UK.

4.2 Maintain viable populations at all extant native sites.

4.3 Facilitate natural colonisation of new sites.

4.4 Reinforce three existing native populations by 2003.

4.5 Restore populations at three former native sites by 2008.

4.6 Establish an *ex-situ* programme to protect genetic diversity, create a reserve population and provide experimental material.

5. Proposed action with lead agencies

The priority for conservation action is to continue (or implement) beneficial management for all extant populations. It is also essential that surveys are undertaken to assess the current distribution, status and causes of decline of the species, and autecological studies to refine existing and new site management and protection.

5.1 Policy and legislation

5.1.1 None proposed.

5.2 Site safeguard and management

5.2.1 Consider notifying sites supporting viable, native populations as SSSIs where this is necessary to ensure their long-term protection. (ACTION: CCW, EN)

5.2.2 Consider the need for conservation management at all extant sites. Mechanisms for implementing suitable management may include relevant agri-environment schemes. (ACTION: CCW, EN, MAFF, WOAD)

5.2.3 Ensure that pasture and hedgerow sites are protected from development. (ACTION: CCW, EN, LAs)

5.2.4 When next reviewed, consider targeting Countryside Stewardship and other relevant agri-environment schemes to land adjacent to viable sites for Deptford pink so as to provide opportunities for its population expansion. (ACTION: CCW, EN, MAFF, WOAD)

5.3 Species management and protection

5.3.1 Undertake experimental management on three selected extant sites and three historic sites with the aim of regenerating plants from the seed-bank. (ACTION: CCW, EN)

5.3.2 Assess the feasibility and desirability of reintroducing this species to selected historic sites should regeneration from the seed-bank prove unsuccessful. (ACTION: CCW, EN, JNCC)

5.3.3 Collect seed from a representative number of native sites in different parts of the range of this species and deposit in the Millenium Seed Bank at Wakehurst Place (Kew). Plants should also be propagated for reintroductions if necessary. (ACTION: CCW, EN, RBG Kew)

5.4 Advisory

5.4.1 Ensure that landowners and managers on all remaining sites for Deptford pink are advised of its importance and appropriate management for its conservation. (ACTION: CCW, EN)

5.4.2 As far as possible, ensure that all relevant agri-environment project officers and members of relevant regional agri-environment consultation groups are advised of locations of Deptford pink, its importance, and the need to secure agreements for beneficial land management both within existing sites and in the surrounding areas. (ACTION: CCW, EN, MAFF, WOAD)

5.5 Future research and monitoring

5.5.1 Resurvey all native sites where Deptford pink has been recorded since 1970, and consider a more extensive survey of potential sites, in order to determine its current status, ensure that appropriate management is in place, and identify threats to remaining populations. At least 10 historic sites should also be investigated with a view to clarifying the reasons for the decline of this species. (ACTION: CCW, EN, JNCC)

5.5.2 Undertake research into the autecology of Deptford pink with a view to refining management techniques for its conservation. (ACTION: JNCC)

5.5.3 Devise and implement a monitoring programme for all extant populations. This would need to cover an assessment of population size, current management and potential threats. (ACTION: CCW, EN)

5.6 Communications and publicity

5.6.1 Raise awareness amongst the farming community of formerly widespread, but now rapidly declining species of farmland, such as Deptford pink. An article could be produced for the farming press. (ACTION: CCW, EN)

5.7 Links with other action plans

5.7.1 It is likely that implementation of this action plan will benefit arable species, including *Arabis glabra, Bromus interruptus, Centaurea cyanus, Filago lutescens, Filago pyramidata, Fumaria occidentalis, Fumaria purpurea, Galeopsis angustifolia, Galium tricornutum, Scandix pecten-veneris, Silene gallica, Torilis arvensis* and *Valerianella rimosa*.

5.7.2 The plan should be considered in conjunction with those for cereal field margins, lowland calcareous grassland and lowland dry acid grassland.

162

Dianthus armeria

■	20	0
●	18	0
○	155	0
×	9	0
+	33	0

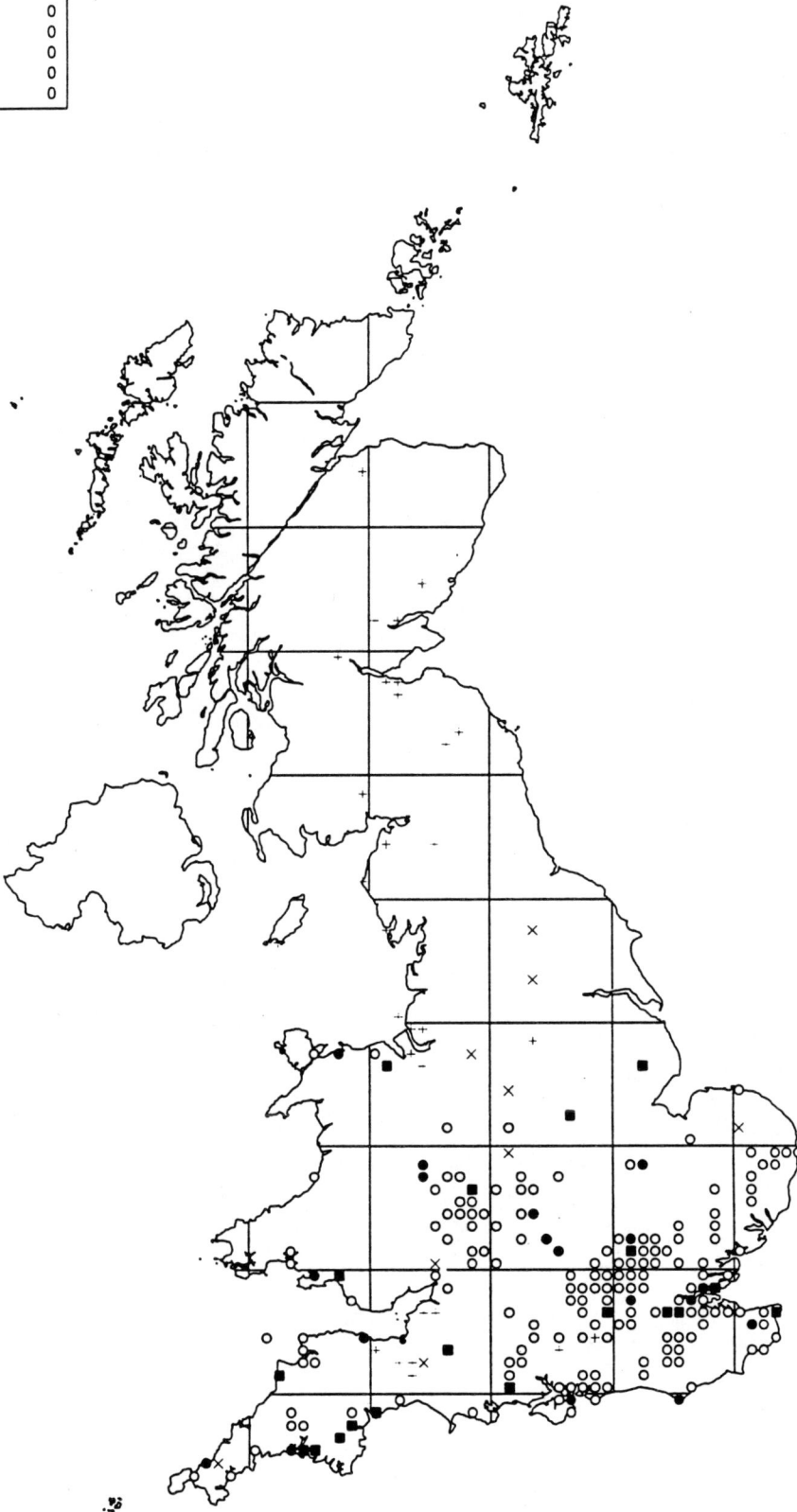

Distribution of Dianthus armeria - Deptford pink in Britain & N.Ireland, (by 10km square).
Source: British Red Data Book - Vascular plants, 1998, 3rd edition.

■ - records post 1980
● - records 1970 - 1987
○ - records pre 1970
× - introduced records post 1970
+ - introduced records pre 1970

163

Red-tipped cudweed (*Filago lutescens*)
Action Plan

1. Current status

1.1 Red-tipped cudweed is a species of light, open soil generally on extensively managed arable land or other disturbed ground including field edges, tracks and sandy commons. It is an annual plant which flowers mainly between July and October. Most seed germination takes place in the autumn, with a second flush in spring. Observations suggest that there is no innate seed dormancy, and it seems unlikely that it has a persistent seed-bank, although this requires further investigation.

1.2 Although once recorded as far north as Yorkshire, the UK range of red-tipped cudweed has always centred around the south-east of England. It has suffered a severe decline over the last 50 years, from 212 sites pre-1930 to just 16 sites today (two of these have not been surveyed since 1994). Its remaining sites are in Hampshire, Surrey, Sussex, Essex, Cambridgeshire and Suffolk, with the largest populations in Surrey. Red-tipped cudweed remains relatively widespread in continental Europe, particularly in central Europe, but appears to be declining throughout its range.

1.3 In GB red-tipped cudweed is classified as *Vulnerable*. It is specially protected under Schedule 8 of the Wildlife and Countryside Act 1981.

2. Current factors causing loss or decline

The following factors were largely responsible for the decline of red-tipped cudweed and are now proving to be constraints on its recovery:

2.1 Increased use of herbicides and fertilisers.

2.2 The development of highly productive crop varieties.

2.3 The destruction of field-margin refuges.

2.4 Earlier summer harvests, destroying plants before they have set seed.

2.5 The demise of traditional crop rotations.

2.6 The conversion of marginal arable land to pasture in traditional areas of mixed farming.

2.7 Metalling and hard-coring of unmade paths and tracks.

2.8 Possibly the decline in stock and rabbit populations on heathlands, leading to the loss of beneficial disturbance.

3. Current action

3.1 Conservation work for this species is ongoing under Plantlife's 'Back from the Brink' project, which is supported by English Nature's Species Recovery Programme. It has included:

3.1.1 A full survey of extinct and existing sites carried out by Plantlife in 1994, determining the distribution and status of the species at that time.

3.1.2 Management of remaining sites carried out, or supervised, by Plantlife, English Nature, Hampshire Wildlife Trust, Sussex Wildlife Trust and RSPB on six existing sites.

3.2 Two sites in Suffolk and one in Surrey are currently protected as SSSIs.

4. Action plan objectives and targets

This action plan is intended to build upon the work proposed under English Nature's Species Recovery Programme by recommending some broader action for the conservation of red-tipped cudweed.

4.1 Maintain viable populations at all extant sites.

4.2 Facilitate natural colonisation of new sites.

4.3 Restore populations of red-tipped cudweed to three suitable historic sites by 2003.

5. Proposed action with lead agencies

It is important that any action for this species is considered as part of a broader approach aimed at the conservation of all threatened UK arable weeds. The protection and management of extant populations is the priority, but this should be considered in parallel with work aimed at regenerating plants from the seed-bank and with the possible development of a national scheme for the beneficial management of important arable habitats (eg the pilot Arable Stewardship Scheme). This will provide opportunities for the long-term expansion of populations into the wider countryside. All conservation management should be informed by relevant research where necessary.

5.1 Policy and legislation

5.1.1 Encourage the development of relevant agri-environment schemes, such as the pilot Arable Stewardship Scheme, as a potential means of re-establishing red-tipped cudweed in the countryside. When reviewing such schemes, consider whether changes are needed to increase their potential benefits for this and other threatened arable species. (ACTION: EN, MAFF)

5.2   Site safeguard and management

5.2.1   Take steps to ensure that sites for red-tipped cudweed which are currently outside SSSIs are protected from damaging activities. If necessary this may include SSSI notification. (ACTION: EN)

5.2.2   Ensure that the management of all sites is beneficial to the conservation of this species. (ACTION: EN)

5.2.3   Seek to develop a network of favourable habitats within the vicinity of red-tipped cudweed sites, thereby providing opportunities for its spread. Suitable management will include the relevant options outlined under the pilot Arable Stewardship Scheme, eg uncropped headlands (cultivated in early autumn). (ACTION: EN, MAFF)

5.3   Species management and protection

5.3.1   Undertake trial management at five carefully selected historic sites with the aim of regenerating red-tipped cudweed from the seed-bank, in the case of arable sites seeking opportunities through appropriate agri-environment schemes. (ACTION: EN)

5.3.2   Assess the feasibility and desirability of undertaking reintroductions at selected sites should attempts to regenerate red-tipped cudweed from the seed-bank prove unsuccessful. (ACTION: EN, JNCC)

5.3.3   Continue with *ex-situ* conservation work as detailed under English Nature's Species Recovery Programme. (ACTION: EN, RBG Kew)

5.4   Advisory

5.4.1   Advise landowners and managers of the presence and importance of red-tipped cudweed, specific management for its conservation and any potentially damaging actions. Particular attention should be given to optimal cultivation and harvest times. (ACTION: EN)

5.4.2   As far as possible, ensure that all relevant agri-environment project officers are advised of locations of this species, its importance, management requirements and potential threats. (ACTION: EN, MAFF)

5.5   Future research and monitoring

5.5.1   Devise and implement a monitoring programme for this species at all sites with extant and restored populations. (ACTION: EN, JNCC)

5.5.2   Undertake research to determine the selectivity of all graminicides currently in use so as to identify which, if any, are suitable for use in field margins that support red-tipped cudweed and other threatened arable species. (ACTION: JNCC)

5.6   Communications and publicity

5.6.1   Publicise the plight of this and other threatened arable species. Articles should be written for relevant conservation and farming magazines and newsletters. Botanists should be encouraged to report any new records, eg through Atlas 2000 recording. (ACTION: EN)

5.6.2   Develop links with European ecologists working to conserve threatened plants of arable habitats. (ACTION: JNCC)

5.6.3   Establish arable conservation display and education centres with the aim of raising public awareness of this threatened group of the UK flora. (ACTION: EN)

5.7   Links with other action plans

5.7.1   It is likely that implementation of this action plan will benefit other arable species, including *Arabis glabra, Bromus interruptus, Centaurea cyanus, Filago pyramidata, Fumaria occidentalis, Fumaria purpurea, Galeopsis angustifolia, Galium tricornutum, Scandix pecten-veneris, Silene gallica, Torilis arvensis* and *Valerianella rimosa.*

5.7.2   The plan should be considered in conjunction with that for cereal field margins.

Filago lutescens

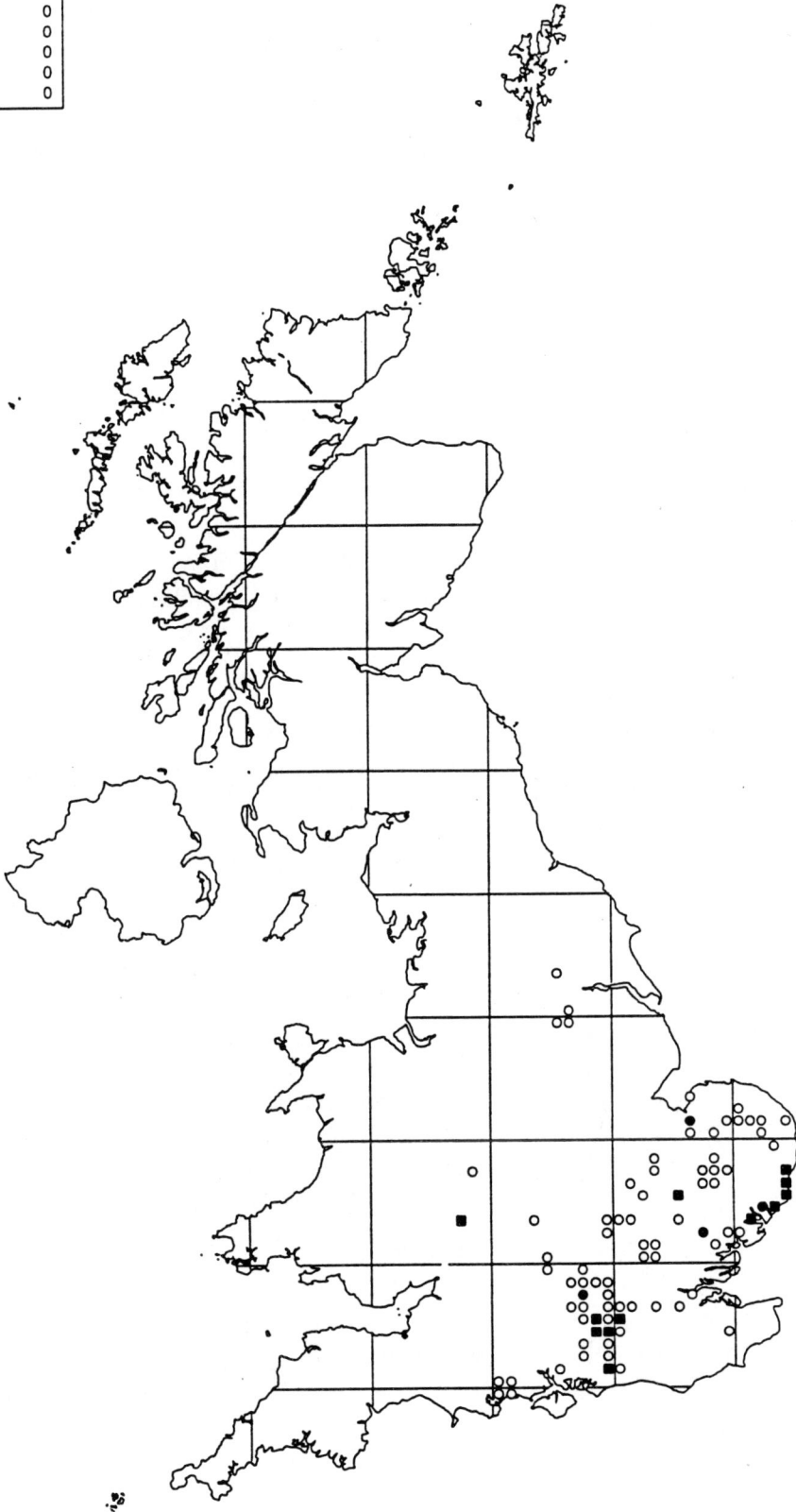

■	12	0
●	4	0
○	69	0
×	0	0
+	0	0

Distribution of Filago lutescens - red-tipped cudweed in Britain & N.Ireland, (by 10km sqaure). Source: British Red Data Book - Vascular plants, 1998, 3rd edition.

■ - records post 1980
● - records 1970 - 1987
○ - records pre 1970
× - introduced records post 1970
+ - introduced records pre 1970

167

Broad-leaved cudweed (*Filago pyramidata*)
Action Plan

1. Current status

1.1 Broad-leaved cudweed is a species associated with arable land and other sites with a long history of disturbance, mainly on chalky and calcareous sandy soils. It has been recorded mostly on marginal farmland which supports only poor, non-competitive, open crops. Flowers are borne mainly between July and September and most seed germination takes place October to December, with a smaller second flush in the spring. Little is known about its seed-bank longevity.

1.2 Most of the sites for this species have been recorded in the south and east of England. It was formerly common on farmland, but has suffered a severe decline over the last 50 years, and now occurs on just three arable sites, with five others on non-arable land. Elsewhere, this species can be found across much of continental Europe, from southern Spain and the Mediterranean, northwards as far as Britain and eastwards to Germany. It also occurs in north Africa and central Asia. In Europe as a whole, this species is not threatened, but it has declined throughout the northern part of its range.

1.3 In GB the species is classified as *Endangered*. It is specially protected under Schedule 8 of the Wildlife and Countryside Act 1981.

2. Current factors causing loss or decline

Many of the agricultural changes which were responsible for the decline of broad-leaved cudweed are now proving to be constraints on its recovery. These include:

2.1 Widespread use of fertilisers and herbicides.

2.2 The development of highly productive crop varieties.

2.3 The destruction of hedge-banks and other field-edge habitats.

2.4 Successional development on sites which are no longer subject to disturbance processes (eg abandoned arable land and sand pits).

2.5 The demise of traditional crop rotations.

3. Current action

3.1 Conservation work for this species is ongoing under Plantlife's 'Back from the Brink' project which is supported by English Nature's Species Recovery Programme. The following action has already been taken:

3.1.1 Surveys carried out by Plantlife, establishing the current UK status and distribution of this species.

3.1.2 Assessments of each extant site, followed by management where perceived to be necessary.

3.1.3 Collection of seed from a number of sites and its deposition at Wakehurst Place (Kew).

3.2 Five sites for this species are protected as SSSIs.

3.3 Monitoring of at least one site is being undertaken by the Wildlife Trusts.

4. Action plan objectives and targets

This action plan is intended to build upon the work proposed under English Nature's Species Recovery Programme, by recommending some broader action for the conservation of broad-leaved cudweed.

4.1 Develop and maintain viable populations at all extant sites.

4.2 Facilitate natural colonisation of new sites.

4.3 Restore populations of broad-leaved cudweed to at least three suitable historic sites by 2003.

5. Proposed action with lead agencies

It is important that any action for this species is considered as part of a broader approach aimed at the conservation of all threatened UK arable weeds. The protection and management of extant populations is the priority, but this should be considered in parallel with work aimed at regenerating plants from the seed-bank and with the possible development of a national scheme for the beneficial management of important arable habitats (eg the pilot Arable Stewardship Scheme). This will provide opportunities for the long-term expansion of populations into the wider countryside. All conservation manage- ment should be informed by relevant research where necessary.

5.1 Policy and legislation

5.1.1 Encourage the development of relevant agri-environment schemes, such as the pilot Arable Stewardship Scheme, as a potential means of re-establishing broad-leaved cudweed in the countryside. When reviewing such schemes, consider whether changes are needed to increase their potential benefits for this and other threatened arable species. (ACTION: EN, MAFF)

5.2 Site safeguard and management

5.2.1 Take steps to ensure that the three sites which currently lie outside SSSIs are protected from damaging activities. If necessary, this may include SSSI notification. (ACTION: EN)

5.2.2 Ensure that all extant sites for broad-leaved cudweed (including railway and quarry sites) receive protection and management which is beneficial to its conservation. (ACTION: EN, LAs)

5.2.3 Seek to develop a network of suitable habitats within the vicinity of broad-leaved cudweed sites, thereby providing opportunities for its spread. Favourable management will include the relevant options outlined under the pilot Arable Stewardship Scheme, eg uncropped headlands (cultivated in early autumn). (ACTION: EN, MAFF)

5.3 Species management and protection

5.3.1 Undertake trial management at three carefully selected historic sites with the aim of regenerating broad-leaved cudweed from the seed-bank. (ACTION: EN)

5.3.2 Assess the feasibility and desirability of undertaking reintroductions at selected sites, should attempts to regenerate broad-leaved cudweed from the seed-bank prove unsuccessful. (ACTION: EN, JNCC)

5.3.3 Continue with *ex-situ* conservation work as proposed under English Nature's Species Recovery Programme. (ACTION: EN, RBG Kew)

5.4 Advisory

5.4.1 Advise landowners and managers of the presence and importance of broad-leaved cudweed, specific management for its conservation, and any potentially damaging actions. Particular attention should be given to optimal cultivation and harvest times. (ACTION: EN)

5.4.2 As far as possible, ensure that all relevant agri-environment project officers are advised of locations of this species, its importance, management requirements and potential threats. (ACTION: EN, MAFF)

5.5 Future research and monitoring

5.5.1 Ensure continued monitoring on all sites with extant or restored populations for at least a further five years. Where possible, monitoring visits should be combined with meeting landowners to discuss conservation management for the species. (ACTION: EN, JNCC)

5.5.2 Undertake research to determine the selectivity of all graminicides currently in use so as to identify which, if any, are suitable for use in field margins that

support this and other threatened arable species. (ACTION: JNCC)

5.6 Communications and publicity

5.6.1 Publicise the plight of this and other threatened arable species. Articles should be written for relevant conservation and farming magazines and newsletters. Botanists should be encouraged to report any new records, eg through Atlas 2000 recording. (ACTION: EN)

5.6.2 Develop links with European ecologists working to conserve threatened plants of arable habitats. (ACTION: JNCC)

5.6.3 Establish arable conservation display and education centres with the aim of raising public awareness of this threatened group of the UK flora. (ACTION: EN)

5.7 Links with other action plans

5.7.1 It is likely that implementation of this action plan will benefit other arable species, including *Arabis glabra, Bromus interruptus, Centaurea cyanus, Filago lutescens, Fumaria purpurea, Fumaria occidentalis, Galeopsis angustifolia, Galium tricornutum, Scandix pecten-veneris, Silene gallica, Torilis arvensis* and *Valerianella rimosa.*

5.7.2 The plan should be considered in conjunction with that for cereal field margins.

Filago pyramidata

■	9	0
●	5	0
○	113	0
×	0	0
–	6	0

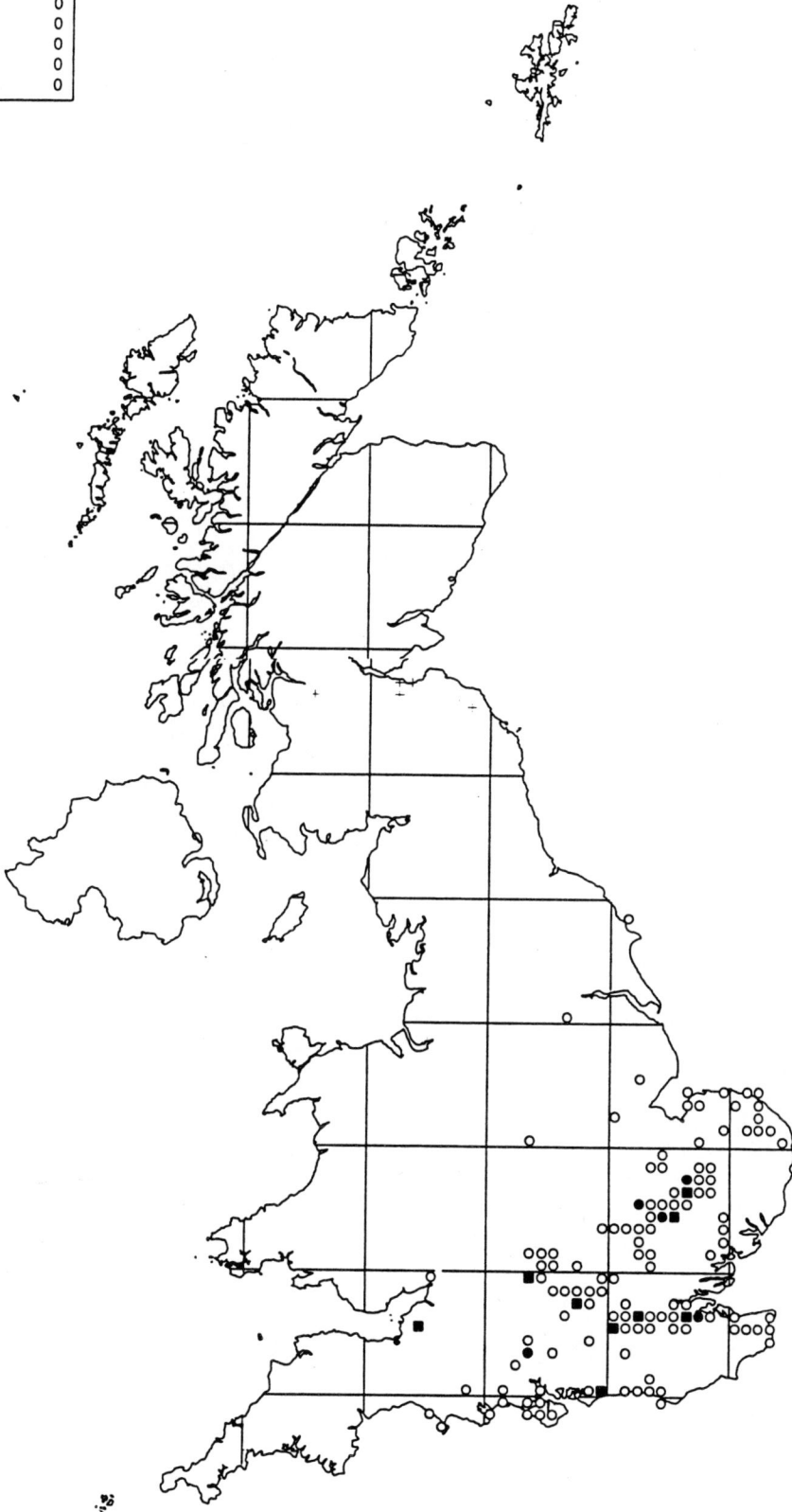

Distribution of Filago pyramidata - broad-leaved cudweed in Britain & N.Ireland, (by 10km square). Source: British Red Data Book - Vascular plants, 1998, 3rd edition.

■ - records post 1980
● - records 1970 - 1987
○ - records pre 1970
× - introduced records post 1970
+ - introduced records pre 1970

Purple ramping-fumitory (*Fumaria purpurea*)
Action Plan

1. Current status

1.1 Purple ramping-fumitory is a species of hedge-banks, arable land, waste ground and occasionally earthy sea-cliffs, favouring sites which have recently been disturbed by animals or farm machinery or habitats opened up by summer drought.

1.2 This species is endemic to Great Britain, Ireland and the Channel Islands and its conservation should therefore be viewed as a high priority. It was not discovered until 1902, and remains easily overlooked by botanists who are not familiar with it. Consequently there is a lack of information on this species, and it is difficult to assess trends in its distribution and reasons for its decline, although changes in agricultural practices over the last 50 years have undoubtedly been significant. Records of purple ramping-fumitory are widely distributed, but are concentrated in western and northern Britain, with stronghold areas in Cornwall and west Lancashire.

1.3 Purple ramping-fumitory is classified as *Nationally Scarce*. It receives general protection under the Wildlife and Countryside Act 1981.

2. Current factors causing loss or decline

Factors causing the decline of this species are poorly understood, but are likely to include:

2.1 Widespread use of herbicides and fertilisers.

2.2 The development of highly productive crop varieties.

2.3 The destruction of hedge-banks and other field-edge habitats.

2.4 The demise of traditional crop rotations.

3. Current action

3.1 None known.

4. Action plan objectives and targets

4.1 Maintain the range and enhance the total population size of this species in the UK.

4.2 Facilitate natural colonisation of new sites and regeneration from the seed-bank at former sites.

4.3 Establish an *ex-situ* programme to protect genetic diversity, create a reserve population and provide experimental material.

5. Proposed action with lead agencies

It is important that any action for this species is considered as part of a broader approach aimed at the conservation of all threatened UK arable weeds. The protection and management of extant populations and a thorough countrywide survey are the priorities. These should be considered in parallel with the possible development of national schemes for the beneficial management of important arable habitats (eg the pilot Arable Stewardship Scheme in England). This will provide opportunities for the long-term expansion of populations into the wider countryside. All conservation management should be informed by relevant research where necessary.

5.1 Policy and legislation

5.1.1 Encourage the development of relevant agri-environment schemes, such as the pilot Arable Stewardship Scheme in England, as a potential means of re-establishing purple ramping-fumitory in the countryside. When reviewing such schemes, consider whether changes are needed to increase their potential benefits for this and other threatened arable species. (ACTION: CCW, EN, MAFF, SNH, SOAEFD, WOAD)

5.2 Site safeguard and management

5.2.1 Promote beneficial management at all extant sites for this species. Particular emphasis should be given to sites where it is associated with species-rich communities. The need for hedge-bottom management should also be assessed. (ACTION: CCW, EN, SNH)

5.2.2 Seek to develop a network of suitable habitats within the natural range of purple ramping-fumitory, thereby providing opportunities for its spread and recolonisation of former sites. Favourable management will include the relevant options under appropriate agri-environment schemes, eg uncropped headlands (cultivated in early to mid March or perhaps earlier in southern areas). (ACTION: CCW, EN, MAFF, SNH, SOAEFD, WOAD)

5.3 Species management and protection

5.3.1 Collect seed from a representative number of sites in various parts of the range of this species and deposit in the Millenium Seed Bank at Wakehurst Place (Kew). (ACTION: CCW, EN, RBG Kew, SNH)

5.4 Advisory

5.4.1 Advise landowners and managers of the presence and importance of purple ramping-fumitory, specific management for its conservation and any potentially damaging actions. Particular attention should be given to optimal cultivation and harvest times. (ACTION: CCW, EN, SNH)

5.4.2 As far as possible, ensure that all relevant agri-environment project officers are advised of locations of this species, its importance, management requirements and potential threats. (ACTION: CCW, EN, MAFF, SNH, SOAEFD, WOAD)

5.5 Future research and monitoring

5.5.1 Collate information and resurvey extant and historic sites where necessary, in order to gain a more complete understanding of the current distribution and status of purple ramping-fumitory, and to assess current site management and threats to remaining populations in arable and non-arable habitats. (ACTION: CCW, EN, JNCC, SNH)

5.5.2 Undertake monitoring on a representative number of extant sites in different parts of the range, with a view to refining conservation management techniques. Where possible, monitoring visits should be combined with meeting landowners to discuss conservation management for the species. (ACTION: CCW, EN, JNCC, SNH)

5.5.3 Undertake research to determine the selectivity of all graminicides currently in use so as to identify which, if any, are suitable for use in field margins that support purple ramping-fumitory and other threatened arable species. (ACTION: JNCC)

5.6 Communications and publicity

5.6.1 Publicise the plight of this and other threatened arable species. Articles should be written for relevant conservation and farming magazines and newsletters. Botanists should be encouraged to report any new records, eg through Atlas 2000 recording. (ACTION: CCW, EN, SNH)

5.6.2 Establish arable conservation display and education centres with the aim of raising public awareness of this threatened group of the UK flora. (ACTION: CCW, EN, SNH)

5.7 Links with other action plans

5.7.1 It is likely that implementation of this action plan will benefit other arable species, including *Arabis glabra, Bromus interruptus, Centaurea cyanus, Filago lutescens, Filago pyramidata, Fumaria occidentalis, Galeopsis angustifolia, Galium tricornutum, Scandix pecten-veneris, Silene gallica, Torilis arvensis* and *Valerianella rimosa*.

5.7.2 The plan should be considered in conjunction with those for cereal field margins, and ancient hedgerows.

Fumaria purpurea

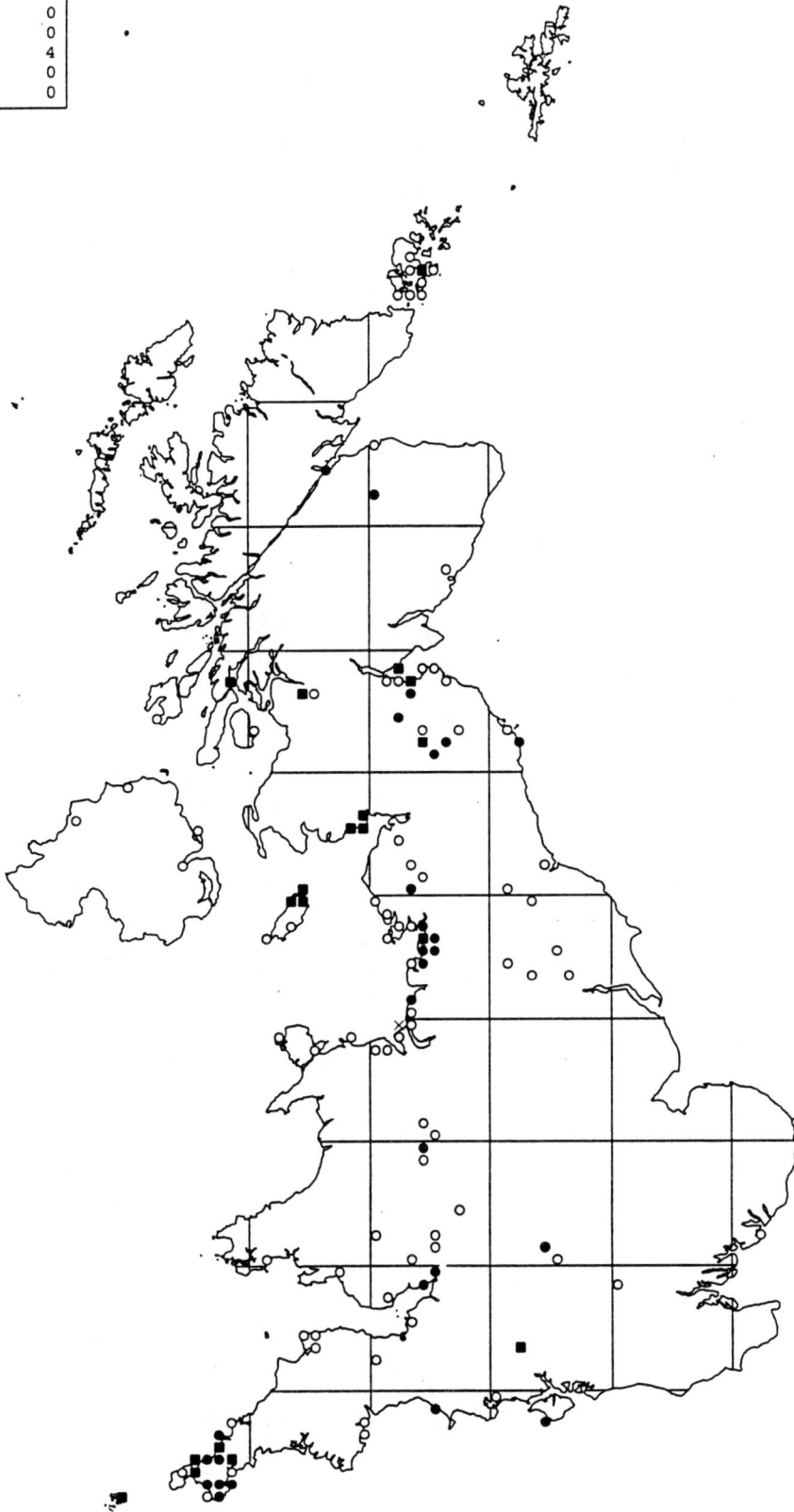

Distribution of Fumaria purpurea - purple ramping-fumitory in Britain & N.Ireland, (by 10km square. Source: British Red Data Book - Vascular plants, 1998, 3rd edition.

■ - records post 1980
● - records 1970 - 1987
O - records pre 1970
✕ - introduced records post 1970
+ - introduced records pre 1970

'Red hemp-nettle (*Galeopsis angustifolia*)
Action Plan

1. Current status

1.1 Red hemp-nettle is a species of arable land, found mostly on calcareous soils but also on coastal sands and shingle in the southern counties of England and Wales. Its distribution is correlated with open vegetation on well drained soils in sunny locations with low rainfall. It is a summer annual which tends to germinate in spring. Consequently, many plants are eradicated during harvest or by early autumn cultivation before they have set seed. It is therefore most frequently encountered in spring-sown crops.

1.2 Red hemp-nettle has shown a severe decline since 1930. It has been recorded from a total of 116 ten km squares since 1970, but has been seen in only 61 of these since 1980. Elsewhere, it is found in western, central and southern Europe, eastwards to Poland and Bulgaria. It is rare in north-western Europe.

1.3 In GB this species is classified as *Nationally Scarce*. It receives general protection under the Wildlife and Countryside Act 1981.

2. Current factors causing loss or decline

2.1 Widespread use of herbicides and fertilisers.

2.2 The development of highly productive crop varieties.

2.3 Destruction of field-edge refuges.

2.4 Autumn cultivation which destroys plants before they have set seed.

2.5 The demise of traditional crop rotations and cultivation on marginal arable land.

2.6 Recreation and tourism on coastal sites may be important factors, but further research is needed to clarify their significance.

3. Current action

3.1 Coastal populations at Snettisham and Dungeness (England) and Gower (Wales) are protected within SSSIs.

4. Action plan objectives and targets

4.1 Maintain the range and enhance the total population size of this species in the UK.

4.2 Facilitate natural colonisation of new sites.

4.3 Restore populations to eight historic sites by 2003.

4.4 Establish an *ex-situ* programme to protect genetic diversity, create a reserve population and provide experimental material.

5. Proposed action with lead agencies

It is important that any action for this species is considered as part of a broader approach aimed at the conservation of all threatened UK arable weeds. The protection and management of extant populations and a thorough countrywide survey should be considered in parallel with work aimed at regenerating plants from the seed-bank and with the possible development of national schemes for the beneficial management of important arable habitats (eg the pilot Arable Stewardship Scheme). This will provide opportunities for the long-term expansion of populations into the wider countryside, as will the controlled use of native seed in wildflower mixes. All conservation management should be informed by relevant research where necessary.

5.1 Policy and legislation

5.1.1 Encourage the development of relevant agri-environment schemes, such as the pilot Arable Stewardship Scheme in England, as a potential means of re-establishing red hemp-nettle in the countryside. When reviewing such schemes, consider whether changes are needed to increase their potential benefits for this and other threatened arable species. (ACTION: CCW, EN, MAFF, WOAD)

5.1.2 As far as possible, ensure that any seed of red hemp-nettle included in wildflower seed mixes is of native origin. (ACTION: MAFF, WOAD)

5.2 Site safeguard and management

5.2.1 Promote beneficial management at all extant sites. Particular attention should be given to viable sites in different parts of its range and to sites where it occurs in a species-rich community. (ACTION: CCW, EN, LAs)

5.2.2 Seek to develop a network of suitable habitats within the vicinity of red hemp-nettle sites, thereby providing opportunities for its spread. Favourable management will include the relevant options outlined under appropriate agri-environment schemes, eg uncropped headlands (cultivated in mid March or possibly earlier in southern regions). (ACTION: CCW, EN, MAFF, WOAD)

5.3 Species management and protection

5.3.1 Undertake trial management at eight suitable historic sites with the aim of regenerating plants from the seed-bank. (ACTION: CCW, EN)

5.3.2 Assess the feasibility and desirability of reintroducing red hemp-nettle at selected sites, should attempts to regenerate it from the seed-bank prove unsuccessful. (ACTION: CCW, EN, JNCC)

5.3.3 Collect seed from a representative number of sites in different parts of the range of this species and deposit in the Millenium Seed Bank at Wakehurst Place (Kew). Plants should also be propagated for reintroductions if necessary. (ACTION: CCW, EN, RBG Kew)

5.4   Advisory

5.4.1 Advise landowners and managers of the presence and importance of red hemp-nettle, specific management for its conservation, and any potentially damaging actions. Particular attention should be given to optimal cultivation and harvest times. (ACTION: CCW, EN)

5.4.2 As far as possible, ensure that all relevant agri-environment project officers are advised of locations of this species, its importance, management requirements and potential threats. (ACTION: CCW, EN, MAFF, WOAD)

5.5   Future research and monitoring

5.5.1 Collate information and survey extant, historic and potential sites in order to gain a more complete understanding of the current distribution and status of red hemp-nettle; to assess current site management and threats to remaining populations; and to determine more precisely the reasons for its decline. (ACTION: CCW, EN, JNCC)

5.5.2 Undertake detailed monitoring on extant and restored sites with a view to refining conservation management techniques. Where possible, monitoring visits should be combined with meeting landowners to discuss conservation management for the species. (ACTION: CCW, EN, JNCC)

5.5.3 Undertake research to determine the selectivity of all graminicides currently in use so as to identify which, if any, are suitable for use in field margins that support this and other threatened arable species. (ACTION: JNCC)

5.6   Communications and publicity

5.6.1 Publicise the plight of this and other threatened arable species. Articles should be written for relevant conservation and farming magazines and newsletters. Botanists should be encouraged to report any new records, eg through Atlas 2000 recording. (ACTION: CCW, EN)

5.6.2 Develop links with European ecologists working to conserve threatened plants of arable habitats. (ACTION: JNCC)

5.6.3 Establish arable conservation display and education centres with the aim of raising public awareness of this threatened group of the UK flora. (ACTION: CCW, EN)

5.7   Links with other action plans

5.7.1 It is likely that implementation of this action plan will benefit other arable species, including *Arabis glabra, Bromus interruptus, Centaurea cyanus, Filago lutescens, Filago pyramidata, Fumaria occidentalis, Fumaria purpurea, Galium tricornutum, Scandix pecten-veneris, Silene gallica, Torilis arvensis* and *Valerianella rimosa.*

5.7.2 The plan should be considered in conjunction with that for cereal field margins.

Galeopsis angustifolia

■	38	0
●	91	0
○	307	0
×	1	0
–	2	0

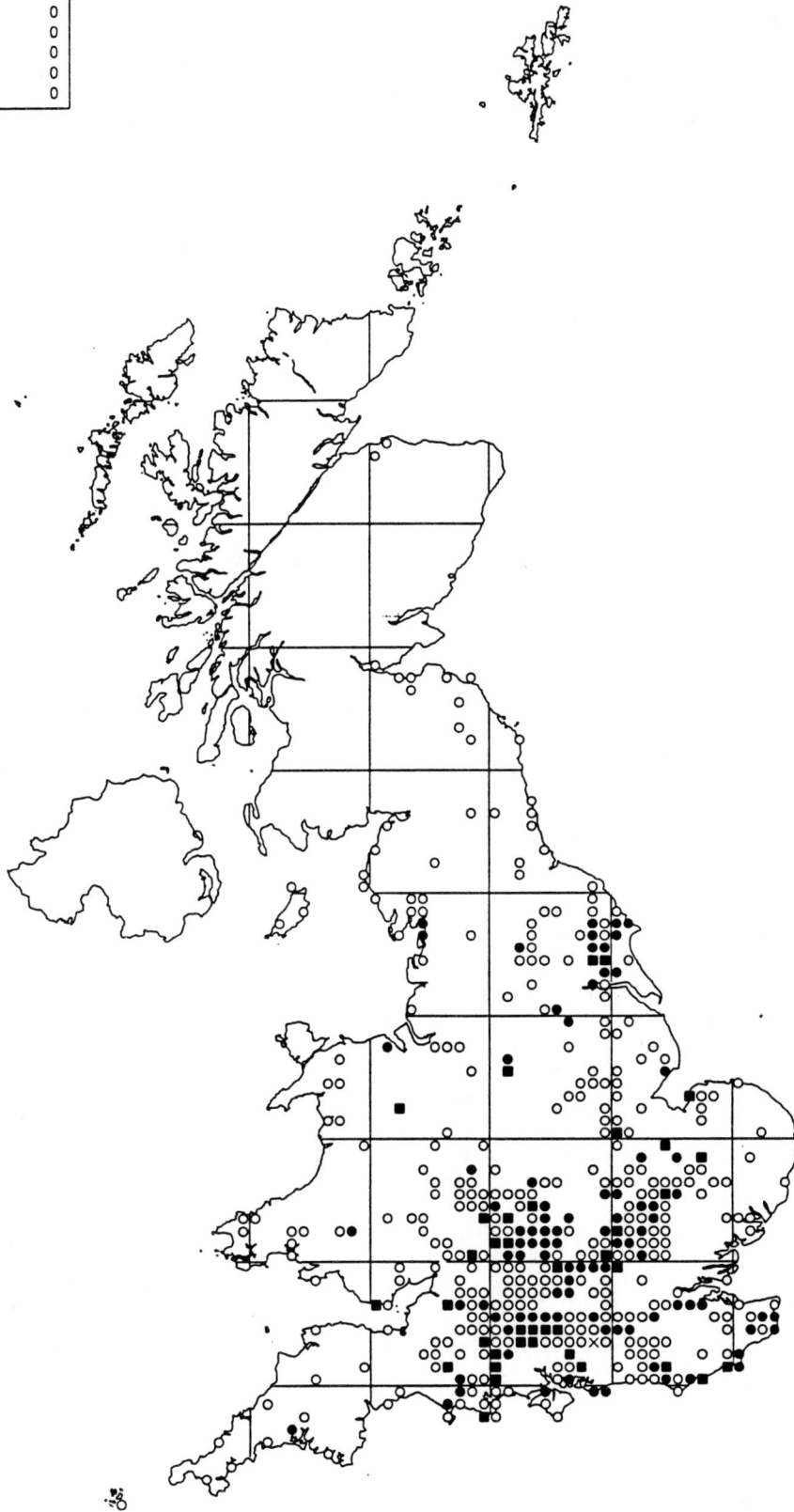

Distribution of Galeopsis angustifolia - red-hemp nettle in Britain & N.Ireland, (by 10km square).
Source: British Red Data Book - Vascular plants, 1998, 3rd edition.

■ - records post 1980
● - records 1970 - 1987
○ - records pre 1970
× - introduced records post 1970
+ - introduced records pre 1970

Corn cleavers (*Galium tricornutum*)
Action Plan

1. Current status

1.1 Corn cleavers is an annual species of arable land, waste ground, hedge-banks and sea-cliffs. Flowers are borne between June and September, with seeds germinating almost exclusively in autumn. It is therefore almost entirely confined to autumn-sown crops.

1.2 Corn cleavers was once a common weed of cereal crops in southern, central and eastern England. However, it has suffered a severe decline this century and is now thought to be restricted to three sites. These are at Rothamsted (in a plot which has never received artificial fertiliser), a field near Oxford (although not seen here since 1985), and a roadside verge in Cambridgeshire. Its decline is associated with the changes in agricultural practice which have taken place this century. This species is not threatened in Europe as a whole, but has become very rare in northern European countries.

1.3 In GB corn cleavers is classified as *Critically Endangered*. It receives general protection under the Wildlife and Countryside Act 1981.

2. Current factors causing loss or decline

The following agricultural changes were largely responsible for the decline of corn cleavers and are now proving to be constraints on its recovery:

2.1 Increased use of herbicides and fertilisers. The higher levels of fertiliser and herbicide applied to winter crops explains why this species has not benefited from the switch to autumn drilling as might otherwise have been expected.

2.2 The development of highly productive crop varieties.

2.3 The destruction of field-edge refuges.

2.4 The demise of traditional crop rotations.

2.5 Successional development on sites which are no longer subject to disturbance processes (eg abandoned arable land).

3. Current action

3.1 Two of the three recent site for this species have received beneficial management for several years.

4. Action plan objectives and targets

4.1 Develop and maintain viable populations at all extant sites.

4.2 Facilitate the colonisation of new sites.

4.3 Restore populations of corn cleavers to eight historic sites by 2003.

4.4 Establish an *ex-situ* programme to protect genetic diversity, create a reserve population and provide experimental material.

5. Proposed action with lead agencies

Because of the extreme rarity of corn cleavers, much of the action recommended here will be targeted at highly localised areas. Beneficial site management is a priority, but this should be combined with attempts to regenerate plants from the seed-bank at former sites. It is also essential that relevant agri-environment schemes are targeted at land adjacent to extant and restored sites so as to provide opportunities for the spread of this species. Survey and monitoring actions will be important for assessing the current status of the species and refining management techniques for it.

5.1 Policy and legislation

5.1.1 Encourage the development of relevant agri-environment schemes, such as the pilot Arable Stewardship Scheme, as a potential means of re-establishing corn cleavers in the countryside. When reviewing such schemes, consider whether changes are needed to increase their potential benefits for this and other threatened arable species. (ACTION: EN, MAFF)

5.2 Site safeguard and management

5.2.1 Ensure that the management of all extant sites for this species is beneficial to its conservation. If necessary consider sites for SSSI notification. (ACTION: EN)

5.2.2 Seek to develop a network of suitable habitats within the vicinity of corn cleavers sites, thereby providing opportunities for its spread. Favourable management will include the relevant options outlined under the pilot Arable Stewardship Scheme, eg uncropped headlands (cultivated in autumn). (ACTION: EN, MAFF)

5.3 Species management and protection

5.3.1 Undertake trial management at eight carefully selected historic sites with the aim of regenerating corn cleavers from the seed-bank. Where regeneration is successful, beneficial management should be implemented immediately. (ACTION: EN, JNCC)

5.3.2 Assess the feasibility and desirability of reintroducing this species at selected historic sites, should regeneration· from the seed-bank prove unsuccessful. (ACTION: EN, JNCC)

5.3.3 Collect seed from all remaining sites for this species, deposit in the Millenium Seed Bank at Wakehurst Place (Kew) and undertake *ex-situ* propagation with a view to improving understanding of its autecology and developing a collection of plants for reintroduction in the wild. (ACTION: EN, RBG Kew)

5.4 Advisory

5.4.1 Advise landowners and managers of the presence and importance of corn cleavers sites, specific management for its conservation and any potentially damaging actions. Particular attention should be given to optimal cultivation and harvest times. (ACTION: EN)

5.4.2 As far as possible ensure that all relevant agri-environment project officers are advised of locations of this species, its importance, management requirements and potential threats. (ACTION: EN, MAFF)

5.5 Future research and monitoring

5.5.1 Survey extant, historic and selected potential sites in order to determine the current status of corn cleavers. (ACTION: EN, JNCC)

5.5.2 Undertake monitoring on all extant and restored sites with a view to refining conservation management techniques. Where possible, monitoring visits should be combined with meeting landowners to discuss conservation management for the species. (ACTION: EN, JNCC)

5.5.3 Undertake research to determine the selectivity of all graminicides currently in use so as to identify which, if any, are suitable for use in field margins that support this species and other threatened arable species. (ACTION: JNCC)

5.6 Communications and publicity

5.6.1 Publicise the plight of this and other threatened arable species. Articles should be written for relevant conservation and farming magazines and newsletters. Botanists should be encouraged to report any new records, eg through Atlas 2000 recording. (ACTION: EN)

5.6.2 Develop links with European ecologists working to conserve threatened plants of arable habitats. (ACTION: JNCC)

5.6.3 Establish arable conservation display and education centres with the aim of raising public awareness of this threatened group of the UK flora. (ACTION: EN)

5.7 Links with other action plans

5.7.1 It is likely that implementation of this action plan will benefit other arable species, including *Arabis glabra, Bromus interruptus, Centaurea cyanus, Filago lutescens, Filago pyramidata, Fumaria occidentalis, Fumaria purpurea, Galeopsis angustifolia, Scandix pecten-veneris, Silene gallica, Torilis arvensis* and *Valerianella rimosa.*

5.7.2 The plan should be considered in conjunction with that for cereal field margins.

Galium tricornutum

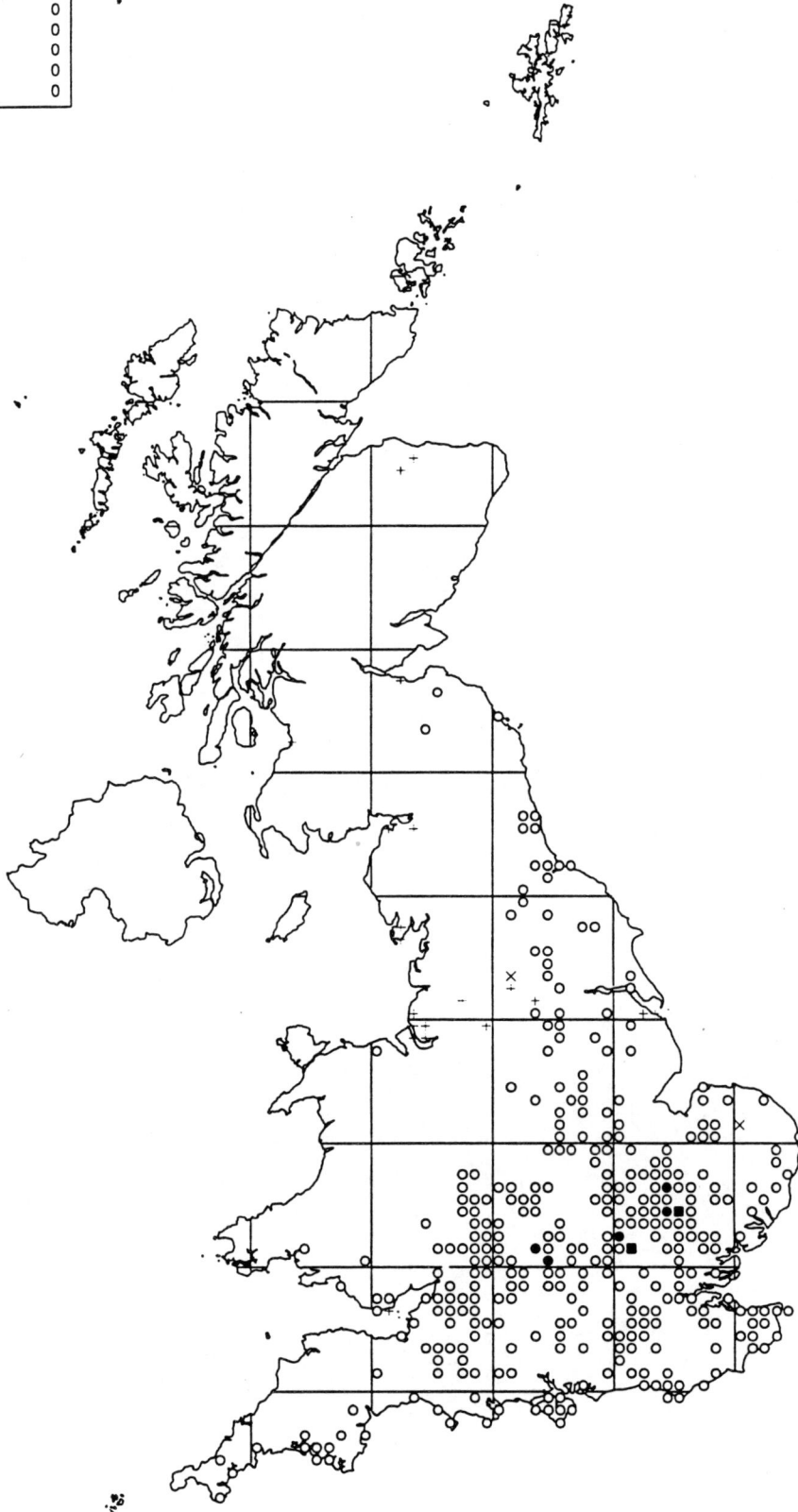

Distribution of Galium tricornutum - corn cleavers in Britain & N.Ireland, (by 10km square). Source: British Red Data Book - Vascular plants, 1998, 3rd edition.

■ - records post 1980
● - records 1970 - 1987
○ - records pre 1970
× - introduced records post 1970
+ - introduced records pre 1970

183

Dune gentian (*Gentianella uliginosa*)
Action Plan

1. Current status

1.1 Dune gentian is an annual species which in the UK grows amongst short vegetation in dune slacks and other dune habitats. It is a small plant which flowers in late summer, with seeds germinating in the autumn or spring. Dune gentian is often found in association with autumn gentian (*G. amarella*), but the level of hybridisation between the two remains unclear.

1.2 The species is endemic to northern and north-western Europe, extending into eastern Russia, and is apparently rare and declining throughout its range. In Britain, material believed to represent dune gentian has been identified from a total of five sites in south Wales and three sites on the Scottish island of Colonsay. Of the four Welsh sites which still support the species, two are NNRs and support large numbers of plants, while the two other sites support much smaller populations. Extinction is thought to have occurred at two Scottish sites. Old records suggest that this species was also once present in Derbyshire and north Devon.

1.3 In GB dune gentian is classified as *Vulnerable*. It is specially protected under Schedule 8 of the Wildlife and Countryside Act 1981.

2. Current factors causing loss or decline

2.1 The loss of vegetation of a suitable structure and successional stage as a result of undergrazing and dune system overstabilisation (a key factor in Wales).

2.2 Overgrazing. Continuous heavy grazing by sheep may have resulted in the loss of dune gentian from two sites on Colonsay. High levels of rabbit grazing may be an important factor in Scotland, although some rabbit grazing is beneficial for this species.

2.3 Hybridisation with autumn gentian may represent a threat to the long-term survival of dune gentian populations.

2.4 The afforestation of two of the Welsh sand dune sites may have resulted in the loss of some populations.

2.5 Landscape and drainage works associated with the construction of a golf course probably had an adverse effect on one of the Welsh populations.

3. Current action

3.1 In 1994, CCW commissioned research into the population genetics of dune gentian in Wales.

3.2 Beneficial grazing has been reinstated at one site in Wales and is continuing at another.

3.3 RBG Edinburgh and SNH have recently commissioned a report on the conservation of dune gentian as part of the Scottish Rare Plant Project.

3.4 During 1996, CCW commissioned a review of the causes and consequences of dune system overstabilisation in Wales.

3.5 All five of the extant and former Welsh sites and two of the three Scottish sites are notified as SSSIs.

4. Action plan objectives and targets

4.1 Develop and maintain viable populations at all extant sites.

4.2 Restore two new viable populations to former sites, one in Wales and one in Scotland, by 2003.

5. Proposed action with lead agencies

Establishment of new populations at sites from which it has been lost should first of all be attempted through appropriate management to encourage regeneration from the seed-bank. If this fails, then reintroduction work should be attempted at suitable sites. Beneficial management regimes at all extant sites for dune gentian must be initiated or continued.

5.1 Policy and legislation

5.1.1 Following further survey and assessment, review the need for protection of this species under Annex II of the EU Habitats and Species Directive. (ACTION: CCW, DETR, EN, JNCC, SNH, SOAEFD)

5.2 Site safeguard and management

5.2.1 Seek to establish suitable grazing and allied management regimes at all former and extant sites. Where grazing is not possible, alternative management practices should be used if appropriate. (ACTION: CCW, SNH)

5.2.2 Ensure that further afforestation proposed in the vicinity of sites for dune gentian avoids any adverse effects to the populations. (ACTION: CCW, FA, FE, SNH)

5.2.3 Consider the management of forest areas adjacent to existing populations and mitigate possible adverse effects. This may include harvesting of some areas at the earliest opportunity. (ACTION: CCW, FA)

5.3 Species management and protection

5.3.1 Undertake trial management at sites in Wales and Scotland from which dune gentian has become extinct, with the aim of regenerating plants from the seed-bank. (ACTION: CCW, SNH)

5.3.2 Consider reintroducing dune gentian to historic sites in Wales and Scotland, should restoration of populations from the seed-bank fail. (ACTION: CCW, RBG Edinburgh, SNH)

5.3.3 Pending the outcome of current work commissioned by RBG Edinburgh, consider the introduction of plants at a suitable Scottish site following appropriate preparatory management. Cultivated material used for this purpose should be derived from plants close to the introduction site. The chosen site should be one at which autumn gentian does not occur and where a long-term management commitment is possible. (ACTION: RBG Edinburgh, SNH)

5.4 Advisory

5.4.1 Ensure that all relevant landowners and managers are aware of the presence and importance of this threatened species. (ACTION: CCW, SNH)

5.5 Future research and monitoring

5.5.1 Collate information and undertake surveys where necessary in order to establish an accurate population size and distribution baseline. (ACTION: CCW, EN, JNCC, SNH)

5.5.2 Monitor extant, restored or (re)introduced populations on a regular basis for at least 10 years. (ACTION: CCW, RBG Edinburgh, SNH)

5.5.3 Undertake surveys of sites in Devon and Derbyshire from which dune gentian has been reported in the past. (ACTION: EN, JNCC)

5.5.4 Commission research into the threats posed to dune gentian by afforestation and overstabilisation of dune systems, and how to mitigate them. (ACTION: CCW, FA, JNCC, RBG Edinburgh, SNH)

5.5.5 Undertake research, in collaboration with European botanists, to examine the taxonomy, seed-bank and germination ecology, and European status of dune gentian. (ACTION: JNCC)

5.6 Communications and publicity

5.6.1 Encourage exchange of information on the ecology of dune gentian and management techniques for its conservation between conservation managers in Wales and Scotland, and the relevant botanical experts. (ACTION: CCW, JNCC, RBG Edinburgh, SNH)

5.6.2 Use the conservation of dune gentian and other rare sand dune species covered by published action plans to illustrate the consequences of dune system overstabilisation for biodiversity. (ACTION: CCW, EN, JNCC, RBG Edinburgh, SNH)

5.7 Links with other action plans

5.7.1 It is likely that implementation of this action plan will benefit fen orchid *Liparis loeselii*.

5.7.2 The plan should be considered in conjunction with that for sand dunes.

Gentianella uliginosa

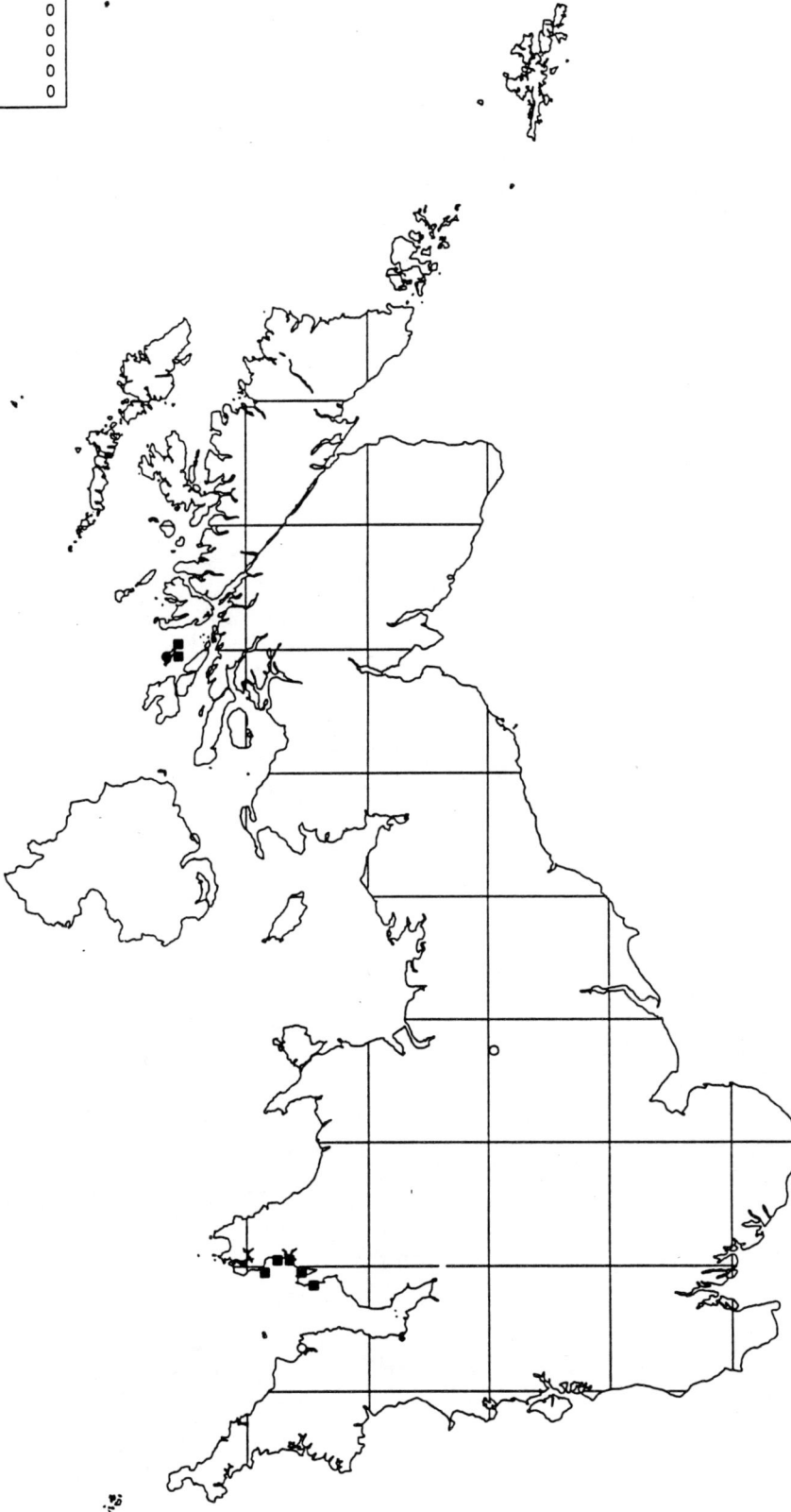

Distribution of Gentianella uliginosa - dune gentian in Britian & N,Ireland, (by 10km square).
Source: British Red Data Book - Vascular plants, 1998, 3rd edition.

■ - records post 1980
● - records 1970 - 1987
○ - records pre 1970
× - introduced records post 1970
+ - introduced records pre 1970

Hawkweeds (*Hieracium* sect *Alpestria*) Action Plan

1. Current status

1.1 This endemic group consists of 14 apomictic species of hawkweed. They are found on coastal rocks, dry heaths, pastures, meadows, streamsides, sea-banks, sea-cliffs and limestone ravines. Most species occur on acid rocks but some are evidently indifferent to base status, whilst *H. difficile* appears calcicolous.

1.2 The species are presently recorded from 18 ten km squares in Shetland. Many of the species are believed to have drastically declined due to recent changes in land use. The only known site of *H. hethlandiae* was destroyed in 1976 by quarrying. Other species (eg *H. difficile*) are also only known from single localities.

1.3 The group is classified as *Vulnerable* in the IUCN red list and three species (*H. attenuatifolium*, *H. northroense* and *H. zetlandicum*) are specially protected under Schedule 8 of the Wildlife and Countryside Act 1981.

2. Current factors causing loss or decline

2.1 Pasture improvement (cultivation and re-seeding, or application of lime and fertilisers).

2.2 Intense grazing which results in removal of flower heads and reduction in successful seed production.

2.3 Other changes in land use, including house building, quarrying and road widening.

3. Current action

3.1 Extensive surveys of Shetland hawkweeds have been carried out Mr J Bevan and by a local botanist, Mr W Scott.

3.2 SNH has monitored populations of scheduled species and W Scott has monitored other species.

3.3 W Scott holds stocks of these species in cultivation.

3.4 Populations of several species are within areas notified as SSSIs.

3.5 *H. hethlandiae* became extinct in the wild in 1976 but plants were successfully reintroduced to a new site by W Scott from 1980 to 1983 and still survive.

4. Action plan objectives and targets

4.1 For each species, ensure the survival of a total of at least 200 plants in at least two wild populations within appropriate habitats, carrying out any necessary reinforcement by 2008.

4.2 Protect the genetic diversity in these species through establishing a seed collection by 2003.

5. Proposed action with lead agencies

The main thrust of this action plan is to ensure the maintenance of existing populations. Grazing is a significant threat to these species and may need reduction at some sites. However, these species might be eliminated from sites with deeper soils by competition from larger plants in the complete absence of grazing. There is a greatly increased risk of loss occurring by chance disasters where species are reduced to a few small sites. Therefore, the actions include prescriptions to increase the number of sites, preferably by reintroduction to historic sites. As these species are apomicts and therefore produce identical genetic copies in their seed without genetic mixing, *ex-situ* conservation can provide a valuable safety net without the usual attendant potential risk of loss of genetic variation through sampling or artificial selection.

5.1 Policy and legislation

5.1.1 Consider the rarest species (*H. hethlandiae*, *H. difficile* and *H. breve*) for protection under Schedule 8 of the Wildlife and Countryside Act 1981 if it appears likely that deliberate action threatens their survival. (ACTION: JNCC, SNH)

5.2 Site safeguard and management

5.2.1 For those species with less than 200 plants in total (identified in 5.5.2), and where monitoring indicates that recruitment is adversely affected by current grazing regimes, attempt to boost recruitment by modifying access by grazing animals. Protection may be either long-term (eg by management agreements to reduce stock numbers at critical periods over many years) or short-term (eg temporary exclosure of grazing from the immediate vicinity of the population) depending on the local need. (ACTION: SNH)

5.3 Species management and protection

5.3.1 Collect seed samples of all species for storage in the Millenium Seed Bank at Wakehurst Place (ensuring that this does not threaten survival or recruitment in the donor populations). Seed can be made available for long-term *ex-situ* collections to reduce the possibility of repeated seed collecting from the wild. (ACTION: RBG Kew, SNH)

5.3.2 Following 5.5.1, collect seed of those species having less than two populations, (ensuring that this does not threaten survival or recruitment in the donor populations) and (re)introduce it to known historic sites which are still suitable for the species (or potentially so), or to suitable new sites. Ensure that any (re)introduction will not threaten the conservation of other species. (ACTION: SNH)

5.4   Advisory

5.4.1   Advise all owners and occupiers and local authorities of the status and significance of these plants and what activities could damage populations, in order to minimise the risk of accidental damage. (ACTION: SNH)

5.5   Future research and monitoring

5.5.1   Reassess the current status of these species in Shetland. Survey should take place at: known population sites (where precise location, population size, successful seed production and potential threats should be assessed); all known past sites (where the potential for restoration should be assessed); and a sample of suitable habitats where the species has previously not been recorded (to assess whether new populations have become established by natural processes). (ACTION: SNH)

5.5.2   Following 5.5.1 identify populations at risk and assess whether there is a requirement for remedial action (5.2.1 and 5.3.2) or further monitoring (5.5.3). (ACTION: SNH)

5.5.3   Monitor the survival of individuals and the success of recruitment annually in threatened populations to assess whether further action is required. (ACTION: SNH)

5.6   Communications and publicity

5.6.1   Communicate the biological interest of this group of plants to as wide an audience as possible while ensuring that the safety of the plants is not compromised. (ACTION: SNH)

5.7   Links with other action plans

5.7.1   None proposed.

Hieracium Sect. Alpestria

Distribution of Hieracium Sect. Alpestria - hawkweeds in Brtain & N.Ireland, (by 10km square).
Source: British Red Data Book - Vascular plants, 1998, 3rd edition.

■ - records post 1980
● - records 1970 - 1987
○ - records pre 1970
✕ - introduced records post 1970
✛ - introduced records pre 1970

191

Pigmy rush (*Juncus pygmaeus*)
Action Plan

1. Current status

1.1 Pigmy rush is a diminutive annual species of seasonally-flooded sandy and peaty places, especially on rutted tracks and gateways. Its survival is dependent upon repeated ground disturbance, typically rutting by vehicles on trackways and, traditionally, poaching by cattle in gateways. Plants germinate in spring with numbers fluctuating markedly each year, depending upon the timing of seasonal changes in water level in its ephemeral habitats.

1.2 In Britain, pigmy rush has only been recorded from the Lizard Peninsula in west Cornwall, but even within this small area it has undergone a severe decline. It is believed to be amongst the most threatened of the Lizard's special plants. It has been recorded from over 20 sites, but is now known at only five, just two of these having large populations. Elsewhere, this species occurs locally in western and southern Europe, northwards to Denmark and also in north-west Africa and Turkey.

1.3 In GB pigmy rush is classified as *Endangered*. It receives general protection under the Wildlife and Countryside Act.

2. Current factors causing loss or decline

2.1 Cessation of use of unmade tracks and gateways where pigmy rush occurs.

2.2 Upgrading and infilling of tracks and gateways where the species occurs. This recently resulted in the loss of the best UK site for the plant.

3. Current action

3.1 All remaining populations of pigmy rush are protected within SSSIs.

3.2 The species occurs in the candidate SAC for Mediterranean temporary pond habitats in the Lizard, Cornwall.

4. Action plan objectives and targets

4.1 Ensure that viable populations are maintained on all extant sites.

4.2 Restore populations to at least five historic sites by 2003.

4.3 Establish an *ex-situ* programme to protect genetic diversity, create a reserve population and provide experimental material.

5. Proposed action with lead agencies

The clear priority for this species is to ensure appropriate management of trackway and gateway sites as it is thought highly probable that this will result in regeneration of the plant from the seed-bank. Further damaging improvements (such as infilling with hard-core and surfacing) to extant and historic sites should be prevented.

5.1 Policy and legislation

5.1.1 None proposed.

5.2 Site safeguard and management

5.2.1 Ensure that appropriate management is in place on all remaining sites. (ACTION: EN)

5.2.2 Promote the uptake of appropriate mechanisms, for example Countryside Stewardship, to encourage the favourable management of historic trackway and gateway sites, and to discourage use of herbicides and fertilisers on land immediately adjacent to extant and restored populations. (ACTION: EN, MAFF)

5.3 Species management and protection

5.3.1 Undertake trial management on at least five suitable historic sites with the aim of regenerating plants from the seed-bank. (ACTION: EN)

5.3.2 Collect seed from all extant sites and deposit in the Millenium Seed Bank at Wakehurst Place (Kew). (ACTION: EN, RBG Kew)

5.4 Advisory

5.4.1 Advise all landowners and managers on extant and restored sites of appropriate management for the conservation of pigmy rush. (ACTION: EN)

5.4.2 As far as possible, ensure that all relevant agri-environment project officers and local authority rights of way officers are advised of locations for this species, its importance and management needed for its conservation. (ACTION: EN, LA, MAFF)

5.5 Future research and monitoring

5.5.1 Resurvey all sites where populations of this plant were found to be extant in the most recent (1994) survey in order to determine the current status of pigmy rush, ensure that appropriate management is in place, and identify potential threats. (ACTION: EN)

5.5.2 Devise and implement a monitoring programme for all extant and restored sites. Where possible, monitoring visits should be combined with meeting landowners to discuss conservation management for the species. (ACTION: EN)

5.5.3 Collate information, and resurvey historic sites where necessary, in order to determine the most suitable sites for restoration management. (ACTION: EN)

5.5.4 Undertake research in order to increase understanding of the biology and ecological requirements of this species and to refine management techniques for its conservation. (ACTION: EN, JNCC)

5.6   Communications and publicity

5.6.1 Raise awareness of the importance of ephemeral and superficially untidy habitats (such as unmade tracks and gateways) and their associated flora. For example an article could be written for farming and conservation magazines/newsletters in Cornwall and for a relevant national conservation publication. (ACTION: EN)

5.7   Links with other action plans

5.7.1 It is likely that implementation of this action plan will benefit *Ranunculus tripartitus*.

5.7.2 The plan should be considered in conjunction with that for lowland heathland.

Juncus pygmaeus

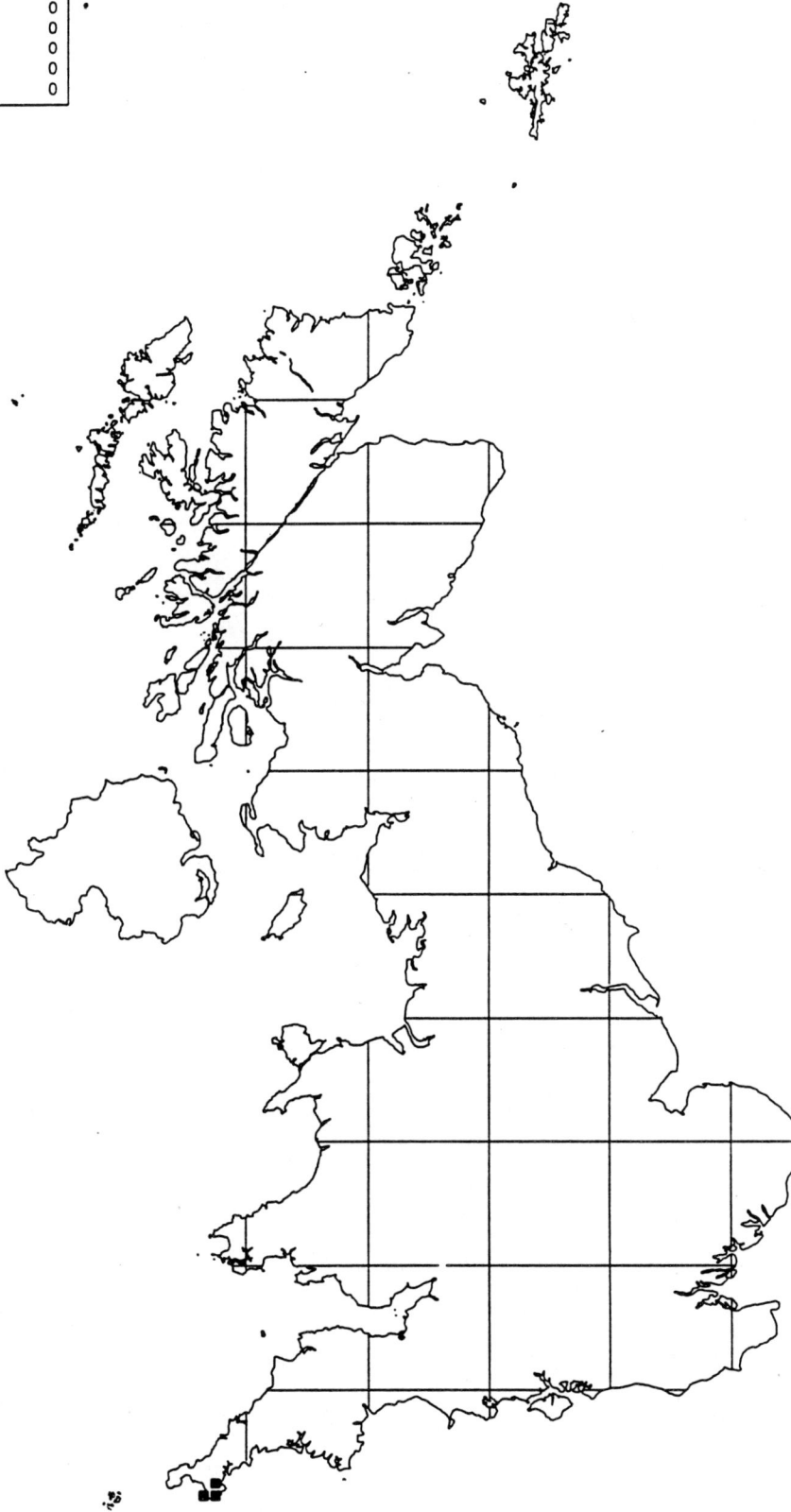

Distribution of Juncus pygmaeus - pygmy rush in Britain & N.Ireland, (by 10km square).
Source: British Red Data Book - Vascular plants, 1998, 3rd edition.

■ - records post 1980
● - records 1970 - 1987
○ - records pre 1970
× - introduced records post 1970
+ - introduced records pre 1970

Cut-grass (*Leersia oryzoides*)
Action Plan

1. Current status

1.1 Cut-grass is a species of wet meadows, ditches, canal- and river-sides. It grows on nutrient-rich mud of acid to neutral pH, often close to the water's edge, and sometimes in cattle-poached ground. Despite being found in a variety of habitats, it has several key ecological requirements including the presence of nutrient-rich mud, stagnant or slow-flowing water. Seasonal inundation and regular disturbance provide the areas of bare mud and open vegetation structure that the species needs.

1.2 Cut-grass has never been widespread in the UK, and since 1985 it has been recorded at only five sites, all of which are in southern England and one of which is a recent reintroduction. It is now thought to be extinct in Dorset. The Amberly Wild Brooks population is the only sizeable one remaining with plants occurring in many ditches over an area of 300 ha. Cut-grass has been recorded throughout Europe from southern Finland to Spain and eastwards to temperate Asia and North America. Whilst it is reported to grow abundantly in some areas, it has decreased markedly in Europe as a whole.

1.3 In Britain cut-grass is classified as *Endangered*. It is specially protected under Schedule 8 of the Wildlife and Countryside Act 1981.

2. Current factors causing loss or decline

2.1 Cessation of traditional watercourse management, including periodic dredging which creates areas of bare mud for colonisation.

2.2 Cessation of grazing which is needed to suppress growth of competitive vegetation. The associated poaching of the ground also provides suitable conditions for germination.

2.3 Restricted availability of wet grassland and swamp habitat as a result of maintaining drainage systems.

2.4 Water pollution may also be a factor, but further research is required to confirm this.

3. Current action

3.1 Populations of cut-grass have been monitored annually for the past 15 years at Amberly Wild Brooks. This work has shown that the plant persists on the banks of managed clean-water ditches which are trampled and grazed by cattle.

3.2 Four of the five extant populations are protected within SSSIs.

3.3 Attempts were made in 1988 and 1990 to re-establish cut-grass in the New Forest.

4. Action plan objectives and targets

4.1 Maintain the range of cut-grass in Britain.

4.2 Enhance its range through the spread of populations from extant sites and through (re)introductions if considered appropriate.

5. Proposed action with lead agencies

Appropriate site management regimes are the key to the successful conservation of cut-grass. Such regimes are already in place on at least three of the four remaining sites so this action plan is mainly intended to facilitate further opportunities for the spread of the species.

5.1 Policy and legislation

5.1.1 None proposed.

5.2 Site safeguard and management

5.2.1 Promote beneficial management of all extant sites through relevant agri-environment schemes. Such management will include grazing and periodic dredging of ditches. (ACTION: EN, MAFF)

5.2.2 Where possible, encourage the creation of suitable habitats for the spread of cut-grass within the vicinity of extant populations. Favourable management will include the relevant options under appropriate agri-environment schemes. (ACTION: EN, MAFF)

5.2.3 Ensure that land drainage work does not take place in the vicinity of extant wet grassland populations. (ACTION: EA, IDBs)

5.2.4 Ensure that watercourse management programmes at sites for cut-grass fully take into account the requirements of the species. (ACTION: EA, IDBs)

5.2.5 Ensure that Local Environment Agency Plans and Water Level Management Plans take full account of the requirements of this species. (ACTION: EA)

5.2.6 Prepare watercourse management plans for all SSSIs with extant populations of cut-grass. (ACTION: EA, EN, IDBs)

5.3 Species management and protection

5.3.1 Assess the possibility of regenerating cut-grass at suitable historic sites and, if appropriate, undertake experimental management to achieve this. If this fails, the feasibility and desirability of reintroducing cut-grass at selected sites should be considered. (ACTION: EN, JNCC)

5.3.2 Collect seed from all extant populations and deposit in the Millenium Seed Bank at Wakehurst Place (Kew). Plants should also be propagated for reintroductions if necessary. (ACTION: EN, RBG Kew)

5.4 Advisory

5.4.1 Ensure that all landowners and managers on extant sites are aware of the presence of this species, its importance and appropriate management for its conservation. (ACTION: EN)

5.4.2 As far as possible, ensure that all relevant agri-environment project officers, relevant drainage engineers and waterways managers are advised of locations of this species and its management requirements. (ACTION: EA, EN, IDBs, LAs, MAFF)

5.5 Future research and monitoring

5.5.1 Resurvey all extant sites in order to determine the current status of cut-grass, check that appropriate management is in place, and identify any potential threats. (ACTION: EN)

5.5.2 Continue to monitor the Amberly Wild Brooks population, and implement monitoring of all other extant populations. (ACTION: EN)

5.5.3 Undertake ecological research with a view to identifying, more precisely, the requirements of cut-grass and refining management techniques for its conservation. Attention should be given to the influence of water pollution on the performance of this species. (ACTION: JNCC)

5.6 Communications and publicity

5.6.1 Develop links with European botanists, particularly those in areas where cut-grass grows abundantly, so as to improve understanding of the biology and ecological requirements of this plant. (ACTION: JNCC)

5.7 Links with other action plans

5.7.1 It is likely that implementation of this action plan will benefit *Potamogeton compressus*.

5.7.2 The plan should be considered in conjunction with that for coastal and floodplain grazing marsh.

Leersia oryzoides

■	5	0
●	0	0
○	17	0
×	0	0
+	0	0

Distribution of Leersia oryzoides - cut-grass in Britain & N.Ireland, (by 10km square).
Source: British Red Data Book - Vascular Plants, 1998, 3rd edition.

■ - records post 1980
● - records 1970 - 1987
○ - records pre 1970
× - introduced records post 1970
+ - introduced records pre 1970

Rock sea lavender (*Limonium* endemic taxa)
Action Plan

1. Current status

1.1 The species of *Limonium* which are endemic to Britain all belong to the *Limonium binervosum* aggregate (rock sea lavenders). The taxonomy of this group was revised in 1986 and nine species and numerous infraspecific taxa are now recognised. Of the nine species, eight are believed to be endemic to Britain, these are *Limonium britannicum, L. dodartiforme, L. loganicum, L. paradoxum, L. parvum, L. procerum, L. recurvum* and *L. transwallianum*. These species grow almost exclusively on rocks and sea-cliffs of a wide range of geological types, although a few have also been recorded from other habitats, for example *L. procerum* on saltmarshes and dune slacks, and *L. dodartiforme* on shingle.

1.2 All known colonies of the endemic rock sea lavenders are confined to the west coasts of England and Wales between Dorset and Cumbria, with different species predominating on different stretches of coast. There is little evidence that these *Limonium* taxa have declined significantly. However, conservation action is proposed because of their endemic status and small population sizes.

1.3 Of the endemic taxa, nine are classified as *Vulnerable* and the other six as *Near Threatened*. They receive general protection under the Wildlife and Countryside Act 1981, although none are specially protected under Schedule 8.

2. Current factors causing loss or decline

2.1 It is possible that trampling of plants by rock climbers and tourists causes localised losses.

2.2 It has been suggested that residual effects of the Sea Empress oil spill may be affecting the performance of *L. parvum* in Pembrokeshire.

3. Current action

3.1 Discussions are ongoing between English Nature and rock climbers in west Cornwall with the aim of minimising the impact of rock climbing on *L. loganicum*.

3.2 Research into the genetics of *L. binervosum* agg is being conducted at Birkbeck College, London.

3.3 All known populations of *L. paradoxum, L. parvum, L. transwallianum, L. dodartiforme, L. logicanum* and *L. recurvum* and some of *L. procerum* and *L. britannicum* lie within SSSIs.

3.4 Colonies of *L. dodartiforme* on shingle are contained within the pSAC of Chesil Beach.

4. Action plan objectives and targets

4.1 Maintain the range of *L. procerum* and *L. britannicum*.

4.2 Maintain the other endemic *Limonium* taxa at all extant sites.

5. Proposed action with lead agencies

Further investigations into the taxonomy, ecology and distribution of the rock sea lavenders are urgently required. Given current understanding of the group the above objectives should address their conservation requirements. It is highly unlikely that this group of plants will require site-based management intervention, although further research should be carried out to confirm this. Measures must be taken to ensure that their habitats are protected from possible threats including pollution and anthropogenic modifications to coastal geomorphology. There is great potential to use some of these taxa to help illustrate the need to review broader coastal management policies such as those for sea defence and oil transportation, in order to conserve coastal biodiversity.

5.1 Policy and legislation

5.1.1 Following further taxonomic clarification reconsider this group of species for addition to Schedule 8 of the Wildlife and Countryside Act 1981. (ACTION: DETR, JNCC)

5.1.2 Consider proposing the British endemic rock sea lavenders for inclusion on Annex II of the EU Habitats and Species Directive. (ACTION: CCW, DETR, EN, JNCC)

5.1.3 Promote management policies which will help maintain the natural geomorphology of the British coastline. This is important for maintaining the shingle habitats for *L. binervosum* agg. (ACTION: EA)

5.1.4 Ensure the identification of Marine Environmental High Risk Areas. The purpose of this action is to help improve the management of oil transportation at sea, and thereby reduce the pollution risk to important coastal sites for *L. binervosum* agg. (ACTION: DETR)

5.2 Site safeguard and management

5.2.1 Ensure that the requirements of the rock sea lavenders are taken into account in habitat management plans for SACs. (ACTION: EN)

5.3   Species management and protection

5.3.1   Promote the development of an *ex-situ* conservation programme for the endemic *Limonium* taxa. (ACTION: CCW, EN, RBG Kew)

5.4   Advisory

5.4.1   Ensure that rock climbing clubs and organisations active on coastal cliffs in Wales and western England are aware of the importance of these plants and advise on particular areas which should be avoided. Priority should be given to sites for *L. loganicum*. (ACTION: CCW, EN)

5.5   Future research and monitoring

5.5.1   Promote continued research into the genetics and taxonomy of *L. binervosum* agg and use the findings to inform future reviews of this action plan. (ACTION: JNCC)

5.5.2   Collate information from relevant experts and re-survey sites where necessary in order to assess the status of populations of *L. binervosum* agg. The species *L. parvum* and *L. loganicum* should both be treated as priorities for further survey with the aim of finding additional sites. (ACTION: CCW, EN, JNCC, SNH)

5.5.3   Investigate current threats to populations including an assessment of the effects of adjacent land uses, eg herbicide drift. (ACTION: CCW, EN, JNCC)

5.5.4   Investigate the approach that has been adopted towards the conservation of *L. binervosum* agg elsewhere in Europe and where appropriate apply the knowledge so gained to the conservation of the group in Britain. (ACTION: JNCC)

5.5.5   Establish good baselines for the monitoring of rock sea-lavenders. (ACTION: CCW, EN, JNCC)

5.5.6   Assess the effects of the Sea Empress oil spill, if any, on populations of *L. parvum*. This species is commonly found growing around the rims of sea-cliff blow-holes and observations suggest that oil residue from the Sea Empress disaster has also accumulated in these areas. (ACTION: CCW)

5.6   Communications and publicity

5.6.1   Assess the need to raise awareness in the tourism sector of the important coastal flora of western Britain, perhaps by writing articles for local tourist guidebooks. (ACTION: CCW, EN, LAs)

5.7   Links with other action plans

5.7.1   This action plan should be considered in conjunction with those for maritime cliffs and vegetated shingle.

Limonium (endemic)

■	15	0
●	2	0
○	0	0
×	0	0
+	0	0

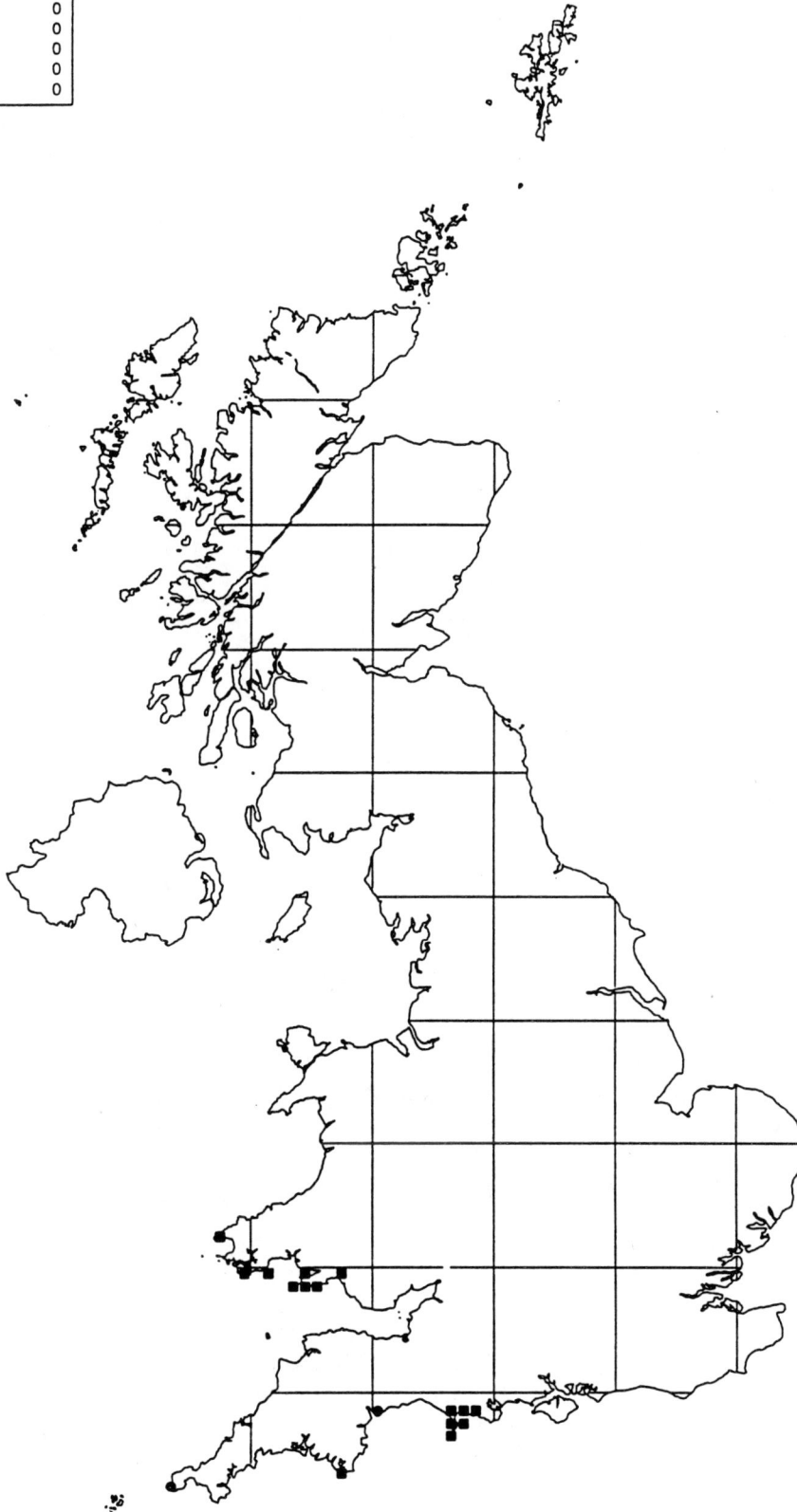

Distribution of Limonium endemic taxa - rock sea lavander in Britain & N.Ireland, (by 10km square). Source: British Red Data Book - Vascular plants, 1998, 3rd edition.

■ - records post 1980
● - records 1970 - 1987
○ - records pre 1970
× - introduced records post 1970
+ - introduced records pre 1970

˙ Marsh clubmoss (*Lycopodiella inundata*)
Action Plan

1. Current status

1.1 Marsh clubmoss is a perennial species of wet heaths, often on bare peaty soil, and occasionally on the margins of lakes and in sand and clay pits, favouring areas which are under water in winter and spring. It often grows in places where human activities provide disturbance and maintain areas of bare, seasonally flooded peat. These include unmade tracks, old peat cuttings and wet areas subjected to poaching by cattle. This species grows at 305 m at Loch Ba in Argyll and up to 190 m in Pembrokeshire, but it is otherwise restricted to lowland sites.

1.2 Marsh clubmoss has undergone a marked decline in the UK although it still holds a high proportion of the European population. Much of the decline was pre-1930, although significant losses have also been recorded in the remaining core areas in the last 20 years. The UK sites remain scattered, from the New Forest to the north coast of Scotland and from west Wales to east Norfolk. There is also one extant site in Northern Ireland. Because marsh clubmoss populations tend to be small and widely scattered, the true extent of its decline may have been masked by the method of recording and mapping plants on a ten km square basis. There have been significant declines within these squares.

1.3 In Britain marsh clubmoss is classified as *Nationally Scarce*. It receives general protection under the Wildlife and Countryside Act 1981, and special protection under Schedule 8 of the Wildlife (NI) Order 1985.

2. Current factors causing loss or decline

2.1 Habitat loss through, for example, building development or improvement of unmade trackways.

2.2 Drainage of habitats.

2.3 Cessation of traditional management practices such as peat cutting and grazing, and the associated successional changes.

2.4 Nitrate and phosphate pollution, and the associated increase in growth of competitive vegetation.

2.5 Atmospheric pollution, including heavy metals, nitrogen and sulphur dioxide may be important factors, although further research is required.

2.6 Afforestation has resulted in the loss of sites in north Wales.

3. Current action

3.1 A recent survey of loch margins in Scotland identified several new sites for this species.

3.2 The North Wales Wildlife Trust made an attempt at relocating plants from one site which was threatened with water level rise, but this was unsuccessful.

3.3 The single site for this species in Northern Ireland is protected within an NNR.

4. Action plan objectives and targets

4.1 Maintain viable populations at all extant sites.

4.2 Enhance population numbers through experimental management at a range of extant sites.

4.3 Restore populations at three suitable historic sites by 2003.

4.4 Assess the feasibility of supporting the conservation of this species through an *ex-situ* programme.

5. Proposed action with lead agencies

This action plan recommends that measures should be implemented to protect all extant sites from damaging developments, and to provide beneficial management wherever possible to regenerate plants from the spore-bank. However, because the reasons for the decline of this species are poorly understood further research, survey and experimental management will be needed to refine the conservation measures proposed. Restoration of populations should be sought through regeneration from the spore-bank before the option of reintroduction is considered.

5.1 Policy and legislation

5.1.1 Assess the scale of protection already afforded to this species by designated sites and consider the need for additional designation or protection on other extant sites. (ACTION: CCW, EN, SNH)

5.1.2 When next reviewed, consider how existing agri-environment schemes could benefit the species, particularly in encouraging extensive land-use practices on land surrounding stronghold sites, and reducing the impact of run-off on water quality. (ACTION: CCW, EN, MAFF, SNH, SOAEFD, WOAD)

5.1.3 In contributing to any review of common land legislation, take into account the requirements of marsh clubmoss and other wet heath species. (ACTION: CCW, EN)

5.2 Site safeguard and management

5.2.1 Where marsh clubmoss falls within SACs, promote favourable wet heath management which will benefit the species. (ACTION: CCW, EN, SNH)

5.2.2 Where indicated as being necessary by 5.5.1, attempt to secure suitable management conditions on threatened sites. (ACTION: CCW, EHS, EN, SNH)

5.3 Species management and protection

5.3.1 Restore marsh clubmoss to three historic sites where conditions still appear to be suitable for the species. Translocation of plant material from extant sites or *ex-situ* sources should only be undertaken if regeneration from the spore-bank or natural recolonisation does not occur. (ACTION: CCW, EHS, EN, SNH)

5.3.2 Assess the feasibility and desirability of establishing an *ex-situ* conservation programme, and implement promptly if appropriate. (ACTION: CCW, EHS, EN, JNCC, SNH)

5.4 Advisory

5.4.1 Ensure that landowners and managers on extant sites are aware of the presence and importance of this species, and are advised on appropriate management. (ACTION: CCW, EHS, EN, SNH)

5.4.2 Advise relevant agri-environment project officers of locations of this species, its importance and management needed for its conservation. (ACTION: CCW, DANI, EHS, EN, MAFF, SNH, SOAEFD, WOAD)

5.5 Future research and monitoring

5.5.1 Collate all known information on extant and former British sites, re-surveying sites where necessary to determine the current distribution and status of this species, assess management regimes and identify current threats. (ACTION: CCW, EHS, EN, FA, JNCC, SNH)

5.5.2 Undertake research into the ecological requirements of this species and the reasons for its decline. Research should include a comparison of survival and performance on sites selected for a range of management conditions in order to inform positive management agreements to maintain and enhance existing populations. (ACTION: CCW, EHS, EN, JNCC, SNH)

5.5.3 Undertake further surveys for the plant, particularly in Scotland and north Wales where new sites may await discovery. (ACTION: CCW, EHS, EN, JNCC, SNH)

5.5.4 Encourage research into the European status of this species. (ACTION: JNCC)

5.6 Communications and publicity

5.6.1 Promote the importance of habitats with fluctuating water levels and high levels of disturbance. An article should be written for appropriate farming and conservation publications. (ACTION: CCW, EHS, EN, SNH)

5.6.2 Encourage botanists to report any records of this species, including ecological information. An article should be written for botanical publications in order to raise awareness of the plant. (ACTION: CCW, EHS, EN, SNH)

5.7 Links with other action plans

5.7.1 It is likely that implementation of this action plan will benefit *Juncus pygmaeus*, *Mentha pulegium*, *Pilularia globulifera* and *Ranunculus tripartitus*.

5.7.2 The plan should be considered in conjunction with those for lowland heathland and purple moorgrass and rush pastures.

Lycopodiella inundata

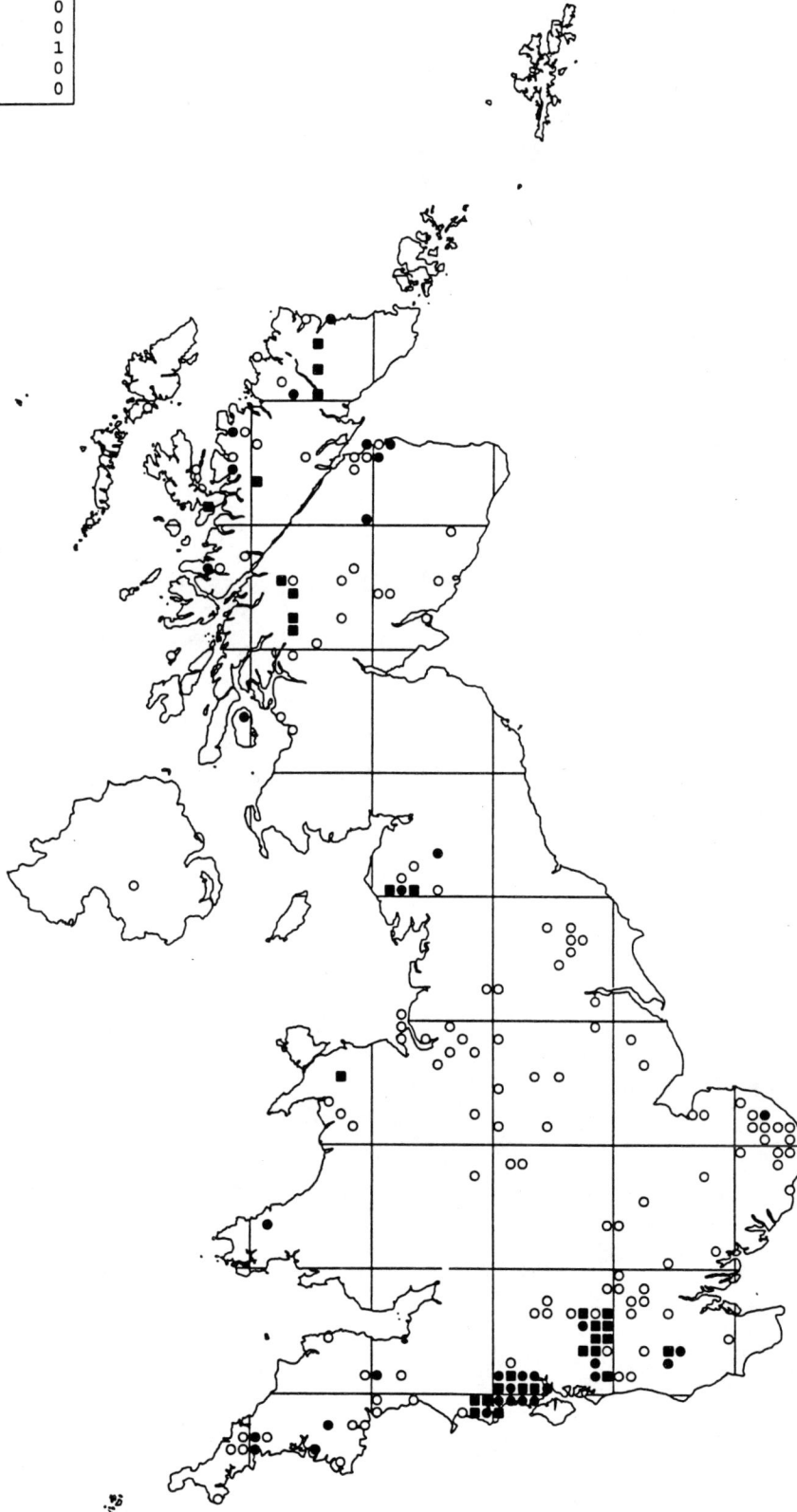

■	30	0
●	34	0
○	121	1
✕	0	0
+	0	0

Distribution of Lycopdiella inundata - marsh clubmoss in Britain & N.Ireland, (by 10km square). Source: British Red Data Book - Vascular plants, 1998, 3rd edition.

■ - records post 1980
● - records 1970 - 1987
○ - records pre 1970
✕ - introduced records post 1970
+ - introduced records pre 1970

Pennyroyal (*Mentha pulegium*)
Action Plan

1. Current status

1.1 Pennyroyal is one of a number of plants associated with seasonally wet habitats which have declined markedly over the last few decades. It is found in very short turf overlying clay and silt on sites that are subjected to grazing, trampling, dunging and general disturbance by livestock or vehicles. These conditions are often associated with traditionally managed lowland village greens, unmetalled trackways and the margins of ponds. Most remaining populations occur where there is rutting and poaching in the absence of hard grazing. The species is a short-lived perennial, that persists only where trampling enables stems to take root in the soil. Although seeds are produced, it is thought that very little recruitment takes place in this way.

1.2 In the UK, pennyroyal is now found in abundance only in the New Forest and on the western shores of Lough Beg in Northern Ireland. It has suffered one of the most severe and widespread declines of any species in the British flora over the last 50 years. Before 1970 it was known from 229 ten km squares, but has been recorded in only 15 of these since 1980. It is widespread in Europe where it is not threatened as a whole, but it is declining in many areas (eg Germany).

1.3 In GB this species is now classified as *Vulnerable*, and is specially protected under Schedule 8 of the Wildlife and Countryside Act 1981 and the Wildlife (NI) Order 1985.

2. Current factors causing loss or decline

2.1 The loss of seasonally wet habitats, either through drainage or excavation to create permanently wet conditions.

2.2 Abandonment or infilling of disturbed habitats favoured by pennyroyal, such as unmade tracks and gateways.

2.3 Cessation of traditional grazing management and subsequent successional changes.

2.4 Habitat destruction by agricultural intensification (such as fertilising or ploughing) and by development.

3. Current action

3.1 All known sites in Northern Ireland are within ASSIs.

3.2 Steps have been taken to ensure the continuation of beneficial pastoral management in the New Forest.

4. Action plan objectives and targets

4.1 Maintain the range of pennyroyal in the UK and establish suitable habitats throughout its historic range.

4.2 Maintain viable populations at all extant sites in the UK.

4.3 Regenerate pennyroyal from the seed-bank on at least five suitable historic sites by 2003.

4.4 Establish an *ex-situ* programme to protect genetic diversity, create a reserve population and provide experimental material.

5. Proposed action with lead agencies

Much of the action recommended here for pennyroyal should be considered as part of a broad range of measures aimed at the conservation of its habitat and the other rare plants associated with it. Accordingly, the most important proposals listed below are those which aim to maintain or restore traditional lowland common management. Survey and assessment of the current status of pennyroyal should be amongst the first actions taken to inform and target the other proposed measures.

5.1 Policy and legislation

5.1.1 Take account of the requirements of pennyroyal when developing new, or reviewing existing, environmental land management schemes that promote the traditional management of lowland commons and village greens. (ACTION: CCW, DANI, DETR, EHS, EN, LAs, MAFF, WOAD)

5.1.2 In contributing to any review of common land legislation, take into account the requirements of pennyroyal and other wet heath species. (ACTION: CCW, EN)

5.2 Site safeguard and management

5.2.1 Seek protection of all extant sites from damaging activities including infilling with hardcore, metalling of trackway sites, drainage and application of agrochemicals. (ACTION: CCW, EHS, EN, FA, FE, MAFF, WOAD)

5.2.2 Ensure the long-term protection and appropriate management of all extant native sites. Where necessary to achieve this, consider notifying sites as SSSIs. (ACTION: CCW, EHS, EN, FA, FE)

5.2.3 Promote the continuation of traditional and beneficial forms of management, such as pony grazing, in the New Forest stronghold area. (ACTION: EN, FA, FE, MAFF)

5.3 Species management and protection

5.3.1 Undertake trial management on at least five suitable historic sites with the aim of regenerating plants from a possible seed-bank. (ACTION: EN)

5.3.2 Assess the feasibility and desirability of reintroducing pennyroyal at suitable historic sites should regeneration from the seed-bank prove unsuccessful. (ACTION: CCW, EHS, EN)

5.3.3 Collect seed from a representative number of sites throughout pennyroyal's range and deposit in the Millenium Seed Bank at Wakehurst Place (Kew). (ACTION: CCW, EHS, EN, RBG Kew)

5.4 Advisory

5.4.1 Ensure that landowners and managers are aware of the presence and importance of this species and are advised on appropriate management. (ACTION: CCW, EHS, EN)

5.4.2 As far as possible, ensure that all relevant agri-environment project officers are advised of locations of this species, its importance and management needed for its conservation. (ACTION: CCW, DANI, EHS, EN, MAFF, WOAD)

5.5 Future research and monitoring

5.5.1 Re-survey all native sites which have not been surveyed in the last three years and where records have been made since 1970, in order to determine the current distribution and status of pennyroyal in the UK, ensure that management at each site is suitable and identify any potential threats. (ACTION: CCW, EHS, EN)

5.5.2 Undertake detailed monitoring and ecological research on three viable sites in different parts of the range of pennyroyal with a view to improving understanding of its requirements and refining management techniques for its conservation. (ACTION: CCW, EHS, EN)

5.5.3 Undertake regular monitoring on sites where populations have been restored. There should be a commitment to do this for at least 10 years. (ACTION: CCW, EHS, EN)

5.5.4 Collate information on the status of pennyroyal throughout Europe. (ACTION: JNCC)

5.6 Communications and publicity

5.6.1 Generally promote the importance of ephemeral, muddy, superficially untidy habitats. Articles could be produced for the media. (ACTION: CCW, EHS, EN)

5.7 Links with other action plans

5.7.1 It is likely that implementation of this action plan will benefit *Pilularia globulifera*, *Lycopodiella inundata*, *Juncus pygmaeus* and *Ranunculus tripartitus*.

5.7.2 The action plan should be considered in conjunction with that for lowland heathland.

Mentha pulegium

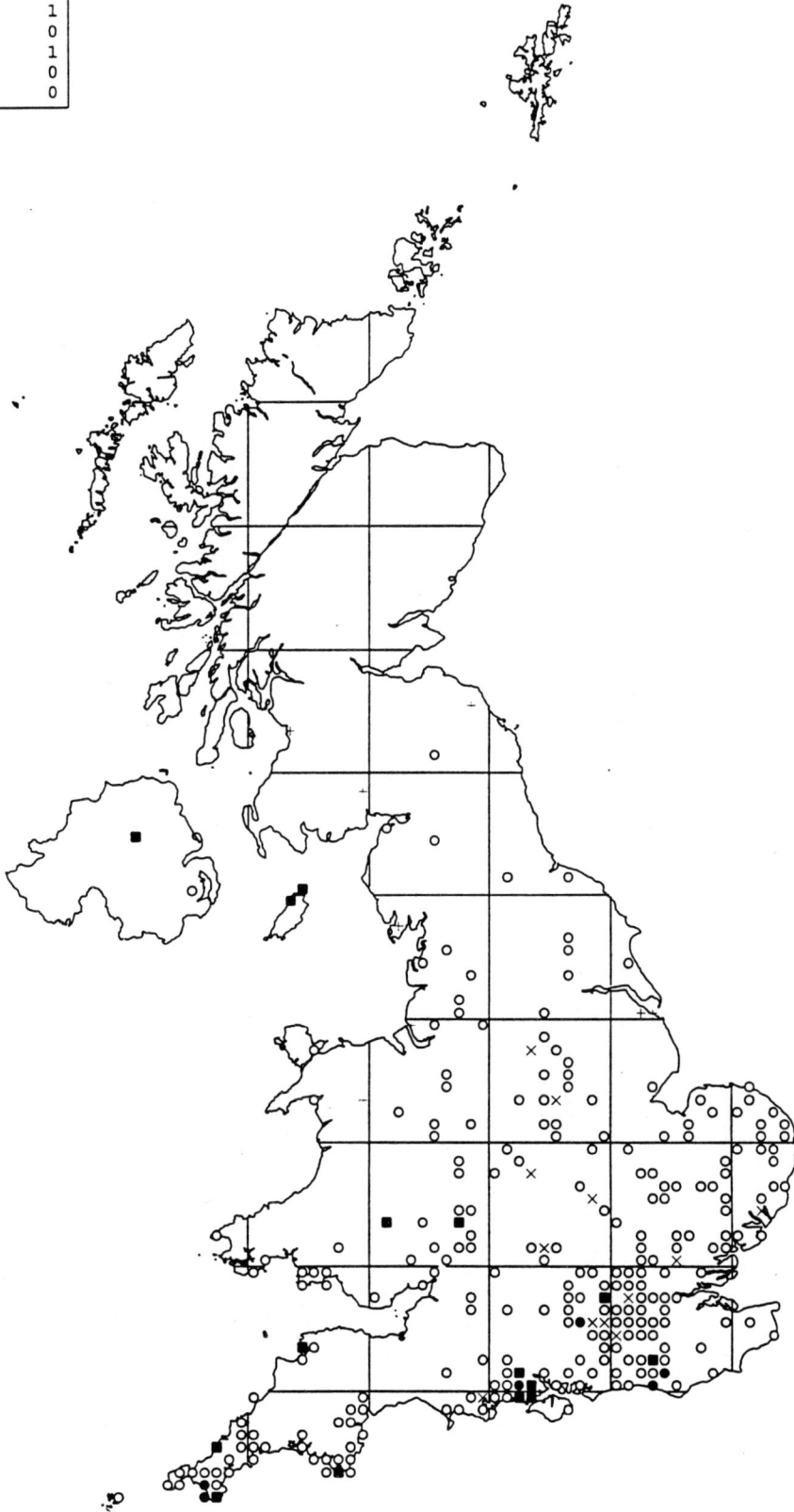

Distribution of Mentha pulegium - pennyroyal in Britain & N,Ireland, (by 10km square).
Source: British Red Data Book - Vascular plants, 1998, 3rd edition.

■ - records post 1980
● - records 1970 - 1987
○ - records pre 1970
× - introduced records post 1970
+ - introduced records pre 1970

211

Pillwort (*Pilularia globulifera*)
Action Plan

1. Current status

1.1 Pillwort is a species of slightly acid to neutral lakes, ponds and marshlands where it grows on bare mud (often a clay or clay-sand substrate) subject to fluctuating water levels. Its former distribution was determined largely by the pattern of beneficial land uses which created the types of habitat in which it thrives. These included cattle ponds, curling ponds and mill ponds. More recently it has been found colonising disused sand pits where it grows in shallow water. It generally favours habitats with some disturbance.

1.2 Pillwort is an internationally threatened species that is declining throughout its range (western Europe). The UK holds a substantial proportion of the world population. Recorded from around 250 ten km squares in the UK over the last 100 years, it has been seen in only 90 of these since 1970. However, it remains scattered throughout the UK, and there are still some substantial populations and several stronghold areas.

1.3 Pillwort is listed on Schedule 8 of the Wildlife (Northern Ireland) Order 1985, but it has not been seen since 1970 and may now be extinct in the province. It receives general protection under the Wildlife and Countryside Act 1981 in the rest of the UK, where it is now classified as *Vulnerable*.

2. Current factors causing loss or decline

2.1 Nitrate/phosphate pollution with the associated increase in pH and the growth of competitive vegetation.

2.2 Abandonment of its main (sometimes artificial) habitats, with lack of disturbance being of particular importance.

2.3 Modification of water bodies for fishing, including permanent flooding, control of water levels and the creation of very steeply sloping banks on some lakes.

2.4 Decline of beneficial land uses, eg curling, grazing, the digging of pits for sand and for paraffin-shale.

2.5 Drainage and ploughing of extant sites.

2.6 Introduction of competitive non-native species of marginal plants. Of particular concern is the invasive Australian swamp stonecrop (*Crassula helmsii*), which has a similar ecology to pillwort.

2.7 Loss of pools created by mineral abstraction to landfill, afforestation and intense recreational uses, eg fisheries. Afforestation has destroyed pillwort habitats at several sites in north Wales.

3. Current action

3.1 As part of Plantlife's 'Back from the Brink' and SNH's Species Action Programme, a pillwort project has been initiated in Scotland. To date this has included site survey and collation of information, and three experimental re-establishments.

3.2 A survey of many of the known sites was undertaken in 1986/87 and further site data were collected during the BSBI Scarce Species Project.

3.3 Transplantation to a former site in Humberside was undertaken by the former NCC, but was unsuccessful, possibly because of high levels of silt suspended in the water.

3.4 Experimental habitat creation work has been undertaken by the Lincolnshire Wildlife Trust.

4. Action plan objectives and targets

4.1 Maintain the range of pillwort and enhance the total UK population.

4.2 Facilitate natural colonisation of new sites.

4.3 Examine the feasibility of re-establishing pillwort at further lost sites where conditions still appear to be favourable.

4.4 Establish an *ex-situ* programme to protect genetic diversity, create a reserve population and provide experimental material.

5. Proposed action with lead agencies

Pillwort is a good coloniser of disturbed, bare habitats. It relies on a vector (eg cattle and ponies) to transfer it to suitable new sites. The thrust of the action recommended here is thus to ensure the continuation or reinstatement of appropriate management both on extant sites and on other suitable sites close by, including the restoration of cattle/pony grazing. Reintroductions as a substitute for traditional vectors should be considered if natural recolonisation fails. Improving understanding of the ecological requirements and life history of this species will serve to identify and refine management techniques for its conservation.

5.1 Policy and legislation

5.1.1 Consider proposing that this species be added to Appendix I of the Bern Convention and Annex IIb of the EU Habitats and Species Directive. (ACTION: DETR, JNCC, SOAEFD)

5.1.2 As far as possible, ensure that the needs of pillwort are considered when reviewing the structure and scope of relevant agri-environment schemes including Countryside Stewardship, the Scottish Countryside Premium Scheme, and in Wales the Tir

Cymen and Habitat Schemes. (ACTION: DANI, MAFF, SOAEFD, WOAD)

5.1.3 Support a review of common land legislation to take into account the requirements of pillwort and other wet heath species. (ACTION: DETR)

5.2 Site safeguard and management.

5.2.1 Where appropriate, promote entry of pillwort sites and on land adjacent to them into relevant agri-environment schemes to encourage sympathetic land management practices which would reduce impacts of enriched run-off. (ACTION: CCW, EHS, EN, MAFF, SNH, SOAEFD, WOAD)

5.2.2 Encourage beneficial site management where a long-term commitment is possible. (ACTION: CCW, EHS, EN, SNH)

5.2.3 Encourage the creation of suitable habitats where opportunities arise in the vicinity of extant sites. Heritage and cultural organisations could consider restoring mill-ponds and curling ponds. Any such schemes should consider the possibility of restoring cattle/pony grazing, or (re)introducing pillwort if natural colonisation fails to occur. (ACTION: Cadw, CCW, EA, EH, EHS, EN, HS, SNH)

5.2.4 Ensure that Local Environment Agency Plans and Water Level Management Plans take full account of the requirements of this species. (ACTION: EA)

5.2.5 Seek to maintain appropriate water level regimes when undertaking or authorising activities at extant sites. (ACTION: EA, IDBs)

5.2.6 Where this species falls within candidate SACs, ensure that management plans take pillwort into account. (ACTION: CCW, EN, SNH)

5.2.7 Consider notifying as SSSIs a representative number of sites with viable populations across the range of this species where this is necessary to ensure their long-term protection. (ACTION: CCW, EHS, EN, SNH)

5.3 Species management and protection

5.3.1 Assess the feasibility and desirability of establishing an *ex-situ* conservation programme and implement promptly if appropriate. (ACTION: EN, RBG Edinburgh, RBG Kew, SNH)

5.3.2 Assess the feasibility and desirability of (re)introducing the species to suitable new and former sites. (ACTION: CCW, EHS, EN, JNCC, SNH)

5.4 Advisory

5.4.1 Ensure that landowners and managers are aware of the presence of pillwort and are advised on appropriate management. Particular attention should be given to owners of land with stronghold populations. (ACTION: CCW, EA, EHS, EN, SNH)

5.4.2 Advise relevant agri-environment project officers of locations of this species, its importance and management needed for its conservation. (ACTION: CCW, DANI, EHS, EN, MAFF, SNH, SOAEFD, WOAD)

5.5 Future research and monitoring

5.5.1 Collate all known information on extant and lost UK sites. (ACTION: JNCC)

5.5.2 Re-survey all known sites to assess the changes that have occurred since the early 1980s and to identify potential threats. Priority should be given to isolated sites in the lowlands. (ACTION: CCW, EHS, EN, SNH)

5.5.3 Continue with research into techniques for *ex-situ* conservation (eg cryopreservation). (ACTION: JNCC, RBG Edinburgh, RBG Kew)

5.5.4 Investigate the effects of competitive non-native marginal plants, eg Australian swamp stonecrop, on pillwort populations. (ACTION: CCW, EHS, EN, JNCC, SNH)

5.6 Communications and publicity

5.6.1 Promote the importance of habitats with fluctuating water levels and high levels of disturbance. Articles could be written for appropriate county wildlife trust magazines and other relevant farming and conservation publications. (ACTION: CCW, EHS, EN, SNH)

5.7 Links with other action plans

5.7.1 It is likely that implementation of this action plan will benefit *Juncus pygmaeus*, *Lycopodiella inundata*, *Mentha pulegium* and *Ranunculus tripartitus*.

5.7.2 The plan should be considered in conjunction with those for lowland heathland and aquifer-fed fluctuating water bodies.

Pilularia globulifera

■	55	0
●	38	0
O	165	4
×	0	0
+	0	0

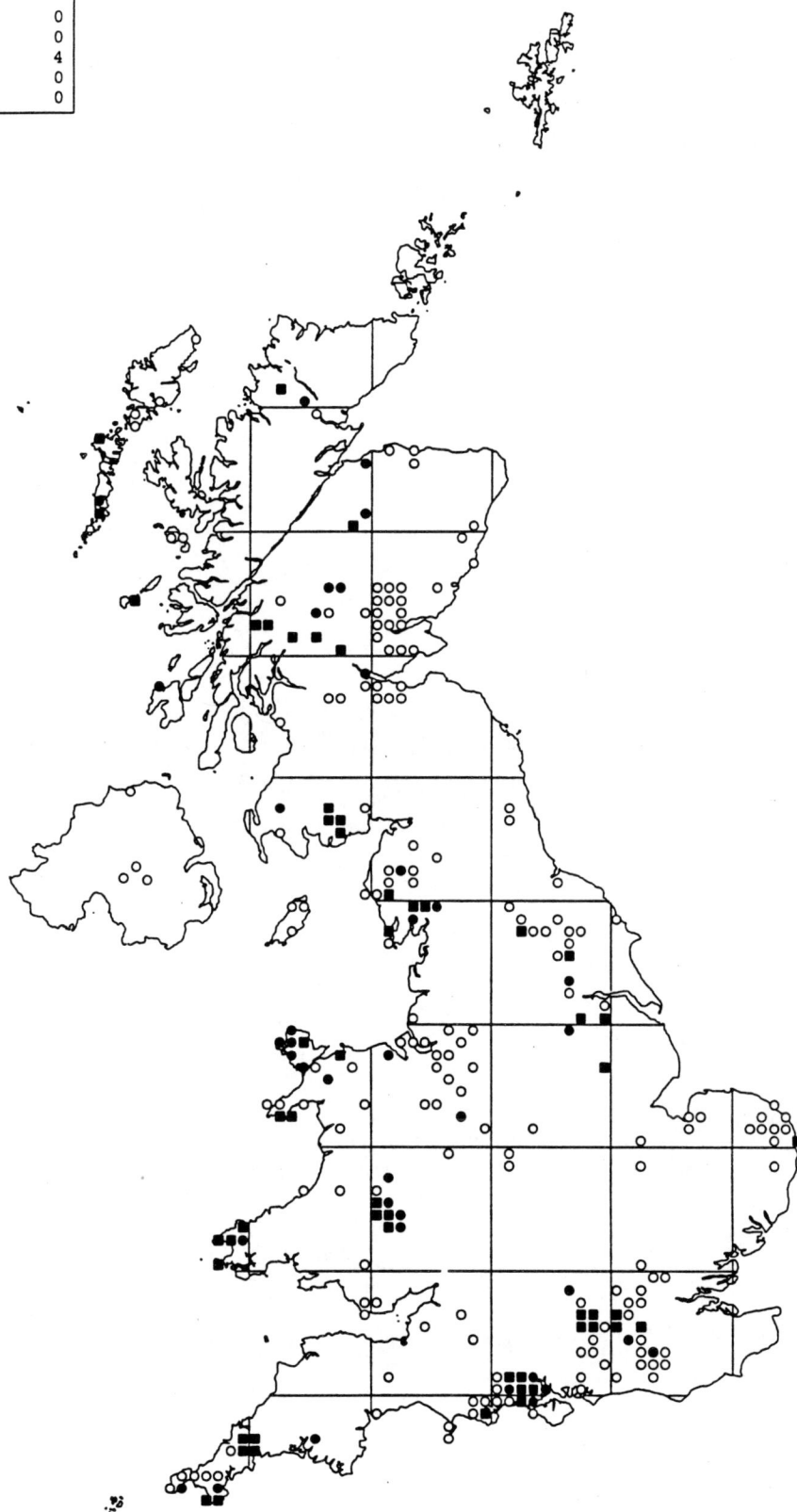

Distribution of Pilularia globulifera - pillwort in Britain & N.Ireland, (by 10km square).
Source: Red Data Book - Vascular plants, 1998, 3rd edition.

■ - records post 1980
● - records 1970 - 1987
O - records pre 1970
× - introduced records post 1970
+ - introduced records pre 1970

215

Grass-wrack pondweed (*Potamogeton compressus*)
Action Plan

1. Current status

1.1 Grass-wrack pondweed is a species of still or slow flowing, calcareous, mesotrophic water and it has been recorded from rivers, canals, ox-bows, drainage ditches and lowland lakes. Flowers and fruits are produced rather sparingly, with plants in grazing marsh ditches perhaps producing more than those in other habitats. New plants are generally formed from turions (reduced branches) which begin to develop in late June.

1.2 The distribution of this species is concentrated in central England, the Welsh borders and the Norfolk coast, but it has also been recorded from Scotland and is widespread elsewhere in Europe. It has been in decline for a long period in Britain.

1.3 In GB this species is now classified as *Nationally Scarce*. It receives general protection under the Wildlife and Countryside Act 1981.

2. Current factors causing loss or decline

2.1 Eutrophication of its aquatic habitats.

2.2 Neglect and drying out of canals and ditches.

2.3 Increase in pleasure boat traffic and associated disturbance and pollution.

3. Current action

3.1 Off-line reserves have been created beside the Montgomery Canal (eastern Wales) for this and other species. However, the value of this measure in the long term is as yet unclear.

4. Action plan objectives and targets

4.1 Maintain the range and enhance the total population size of grass-wrack pondweed in the UK.

4.2 Facilitate colonisation of new sites.

5. Proposed action with lead agencies

The successful conservation of grass-wrack pondweed will rely upon the implementation of a range of broad-based measures. The principal needs are to improve water quality at its remaining sites, prevent further losses as a result of erosion from boat-traffic, ensure that its needs are considered in the production and implementation of relevant water level management plans, and assess ways of establishing new populations. Work to increase understanding of the autecology and distribution of this species is also needed.

5.1 Policy and legislation

5.1.1 Consider how relevant agri-environment schemes could benefit grass-wrack pondweed. (ACTION: MAFF, SOAEFD, WOAD)

5.1.2 Ensure that the requirements of this species are considered during the production of relevant Local Environment Agency Plans and examine applicability of catchment plans to Scotland. (ACTION: EA, SEPA, SNH)

5.2 Site safeguard and management

5.2.1 Consider the value of buffer strips and other measures alongside watercourses in reducing the impacts of nutrient enrichment and pollution on key populations of grass-wrack pondweed. These measures are likely to be most valuable in Broadland, where grass-wrack pondweed grows in drainage ditches that are highly vulnerable to eutrophication. (ACTION: Broads Authority, CCW, EA, EN, MAFF, SNH, SOAEFD, WOAD)

5.2.2 As far as possible, ensure that no further sites for grass-wrack pondweed are lost through water abstraction, land drainage or inappropriate watercourse management. (ACTION: EA, IDBs)

5.2.3 Devise and implement measures to restrict boat traffic speed in areas where grass-wrack pondweed occurs. Provide off-line refuges where appropriate. (ACTION: British Waterways, Broads Authority, EA)

5.2.4 Ensure that the requirements of grass-wrack pondweed are considered during canal restoration work. (ACTION: British Waterways)

5.3 Species management and protection

5.3.1 Assess the feasibility and desirability of re-establishing grass-wrack pondweed at suitable sites from which it has been lost. (ACTION: CCW, EN, JNCC, SNH)

5.4 Advisory

5.4.1 Advise landowners and managers who manage waters containing grass-wrack pondweed of its presence, importance and appropriate management for its conservation. (ACTION: CCW, EA, EN, SEPA, SNH)

5.4.2 As far as possible, ensure that all agri-environment project officers and members of appropriate liaison groups and partner organisations are advised of locations of this species, its importance and appropriate management for its conservation.

(ACTION: CCW, EN, MAFF, SNH, SOAEFD, WOAD)

5.5   Future research and monitoring

5.5.1 Collate information, and resurvey sites where necessary to determine the current distribution and status of grass-wrack pondweed in Britain. (ACTION: CCW, EN, JNCC, SNH)

5.5.2 Undertake detailed ecological recording at selected viable sites with a view to improving understanding of the requirements of grass-wrack pondweed and refining techniques for its conservation. (ACTION: JNCC)

5.5.3 Where possible, undertake monitoring to determine the effectiveness of the relevant agri-environment schemes in improving water quality and in assisting with the conservation of threatened aquatic plants such as grass-wrack pondweed. Use the results to aid the review process of various schemes. (ACTION: EA, JNCC, MAFF, SOAEFD, WOAD)

5.5.4 Investigate the impact of boat traffic speed on grass-wrack pondweed populations. (ACTION: British Waterways, Broads Authority, EA)

5.6   Communications and publicity

5.6.1 Raise awareness amongst boating groups of the presence and importance of grass-wrack pondweed. (ACTION: CCW, EN, SNH)

5.7   Links with other action plans

5.7.1 It is likely that implementation of this action plan will benefit *Leersia oryzoides* and *Luronium natans*.

5.7.2 The plan should be considered in conjunction with that for coastal and floodplain grazing marshes.

Potamogeton compressus

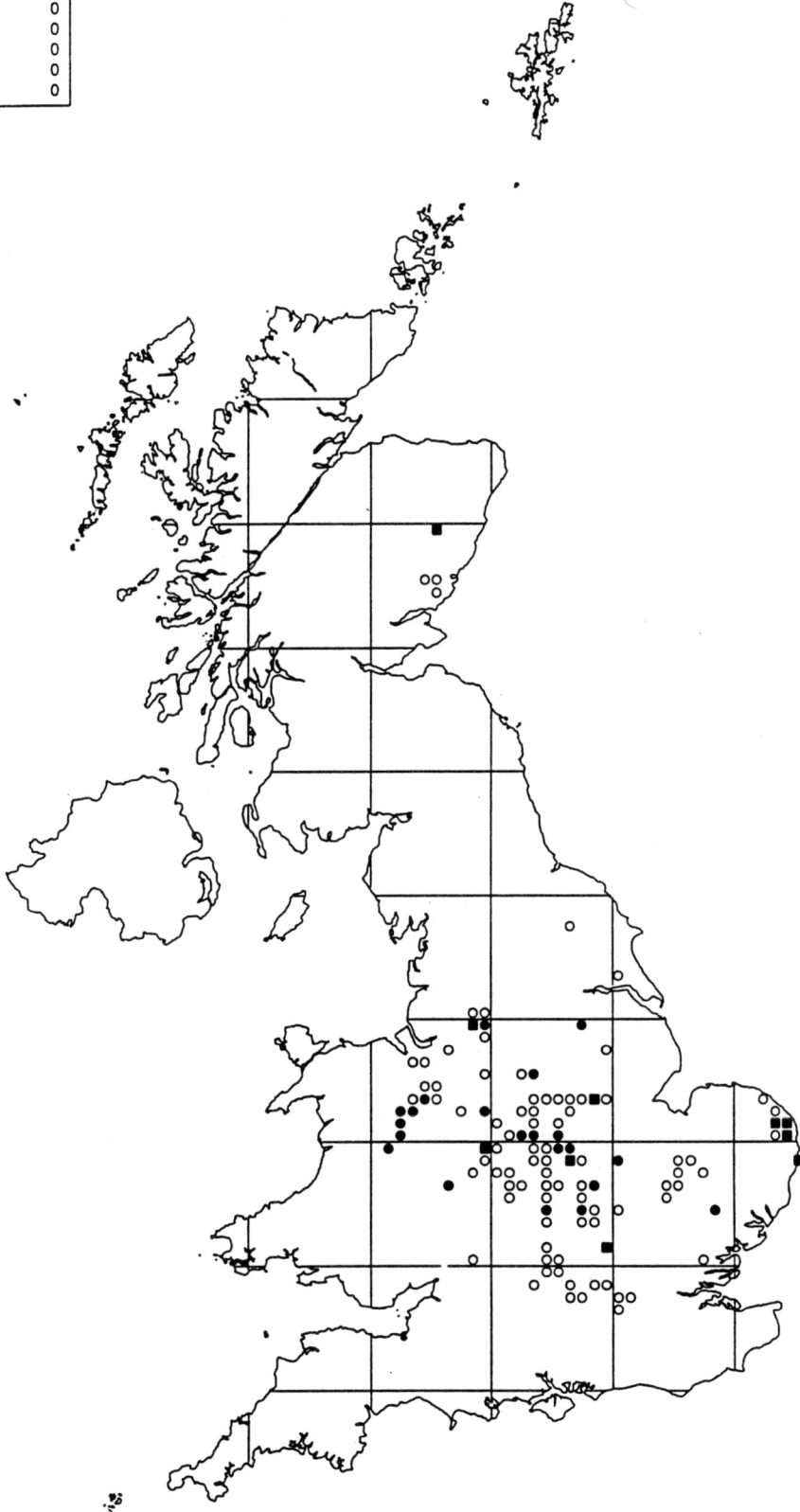

■	10	0
●	21	0
○	82	0
×	0	0
−	0	0

Distribution of Potamogeton compressus - grass-wracked pondweed in Britain & N.Ireland, (by 10km square). Source: British Red Data Book - Vascular plants, 1998, 3rd edition.

■ - records post 1980
● - records 1970 - 1987
○ - records pre 1970
✕ - introduced records post 1970
✛ - introduced records pre 1970

Woolly willow *(Salix lanata)*
Action Plan

1. Current status

1.1 Woolly willow is one of a number of bushy willows found only in mountain areas. In other parts of the world these willows form high altitude scrub above the tree line but in Britain are usually present only as relict scattered bushes found on ledges inaccessible to grazing animals, on cliffs and in stream gorges. The woolly willow is further restricted by its requirement for calcareous soils.

1.2 Vegetation mapping of all upland SSSI in Scotland suggests that 2000 ha of land was occupied by willow scrub with woolly willow before the vegetation was modified by the influence of man. It now occurs in only 12 locations in Scotland. All but one of these populations are very small (less than 100 plants) and four are of single individuals. Willows have separate sexes and so these single bushes are now incapable of regenerating without artificial help. At least two recorded populations have died out since 1950. The species is restricted to Arctic and sub-Arctic Eurasia and in the UK is confined to Scotland.

1.3 In GB woolly willow is classified as *Vulnerable*. It receives general protection under the Wildlife and Countryside Act 1981.

2. Current factors causing loss or decline

2.1 Grazing has removed montane willows from accessible ground and restricts the woolly willow to small niches on very steep areas where it is more vulnerable to chance events such as erosion, rock falls and snow avalanches.

2.2 Lack of recruitment is likely to be a factor in the survival of all the very small populations while the isolated single sex populations are now clearly incapable of sexual regeneration since they are beyond the range of pollen transport.

3. Current action

3.1 All but two populations are within SSSIs and five are within SACs identified for sub-arctic willow scrub (although two of these populations are single plants).

3.2 The significance of this species has been made known to some landowners and in some cases there is an expressed intention to reduce the numbers of red deer (to improve the quality of deer stocks).

3.3 Plants from Breadalbane sites have been raised from cuttings and seed to reinforce populations on Ben Lawers NNR.

3.4 Exclosures have been erected around the largest remaining population and on Ben Lawers to enable

spread of the species to ground less vulnerable to catastrophic impacts (see 2.1).

3.5 This species is an important component of sub-Arctic willow scrub, an EC Habitats and Species Directive Annex 1 habitat.

4. Action plan objectives and targets

4.1 Ensure that all existing (1997) populations are successfully regenerating by 2003.

4.2 Ensure that each population will consist of at least 50 plants (or the sustainable maximum for the site) by 2008.

4.3 Reintroduce the species to two former sites by 2003.

5. Proposed action with lead agencies

Like other tree-line species, the woolly willow is part of an element of biodiversity that is vulnerable to current land use in the British uplands. The proposed actions are mainly related to making the current relict populations self-sustaining by restoring active regeneration to increase their size. Since many of the populations are reduced to few plants (sometimes of one sex only), there is an urgent need to carry out reinforcements. Grazing will need to be reduced at most sites, and schemes for this should be designed to allow the willow to re-invade ground adjacent to existing sites. In these less precipitous areas, the species will be less vulnerable to mortality from catastrophic impacts.

5.1 Policy and legislation

5.1.1 Investigate the possibility of benefiting the woolly willow through a programme of restoring natural tree-line communities in selected areas of Britain's mountains, as an element of forestry policy. (ACTION: FA)

5.2 Site safeguard and management

5.2.1 Where the survival or regeneration potential of surviving bushes is threatened by grazing, reduce grazing intensity by managing stocking levels or by the use of exclosures, ensuring that this does not significantly threaten other important elements of the biodiversity of the area. (ACTION: SNH)

5.2.2 Attempt to enlarge very small populations by favourable habitat management or by use of exclosures, again ensuring that this does not significantly threaten other elements of biodiversity. Wherever possible extend the population to ground less vulnerable to damage from catastrophic impacts. (ACTION: SNH)

5.3   Species management and protection

5.3.1   In those populations where natural sexual regeneration is prevented by lack of numbers, or by the absence of one sex, attempt to improve recruitment by establishing new bushes. Seek to increase genetic diversity initially by using wild-collected seed rather than vegetative material. (ACTION: SNH)

5.3.2   Reintroduce two extinct populations to former sites following the recommendations of 5.5.4. (ACTION: SNH)

5.4   Advisory

5.4.1   Advise all owners and occupiers of land with woolly willow populations of their presence, significance and management requirements.   (ACTION: SNH)

5.5   Future research and monitoring

5.5.1   Complete status assessment at all known sites by recording the location and sex of all surviving bushes. (ACTION: SNH)

5.5.2   Monitor the survival, incidence of grazing and seed production of all bushes. (ACTION: SNH)

5.5.3   Investigate genetic variation within and between populations to inform translocation measures. (ACTION: SNH)

5.5.4   Investigate the feasibility of restoring populations to former sites by collating past records, checking that the species is not still present, assessing the presence and extent of suitable habitat, and considering any modifications required to current management for the establishment of the willow. Consideration should also be given to possible damage to other elements of biodiversity if management is modified, and willingness of the landowners to permit the action. (ACTION: SNH)

5.6   Communications and publicity

5.6.1   Use the woolly willow as an example to demonstrate the effects of current land use of upland areas in Britain, and the necessary remedial management to maintain those elements of biodiversity which are threatened by current practices. (ACTION: SNH)

5.7   Links with other action plans

5.7.1   None proposed.

Salix lanata

■	10	0
●	3	0
○	1	0
×	0	0
+	0	0

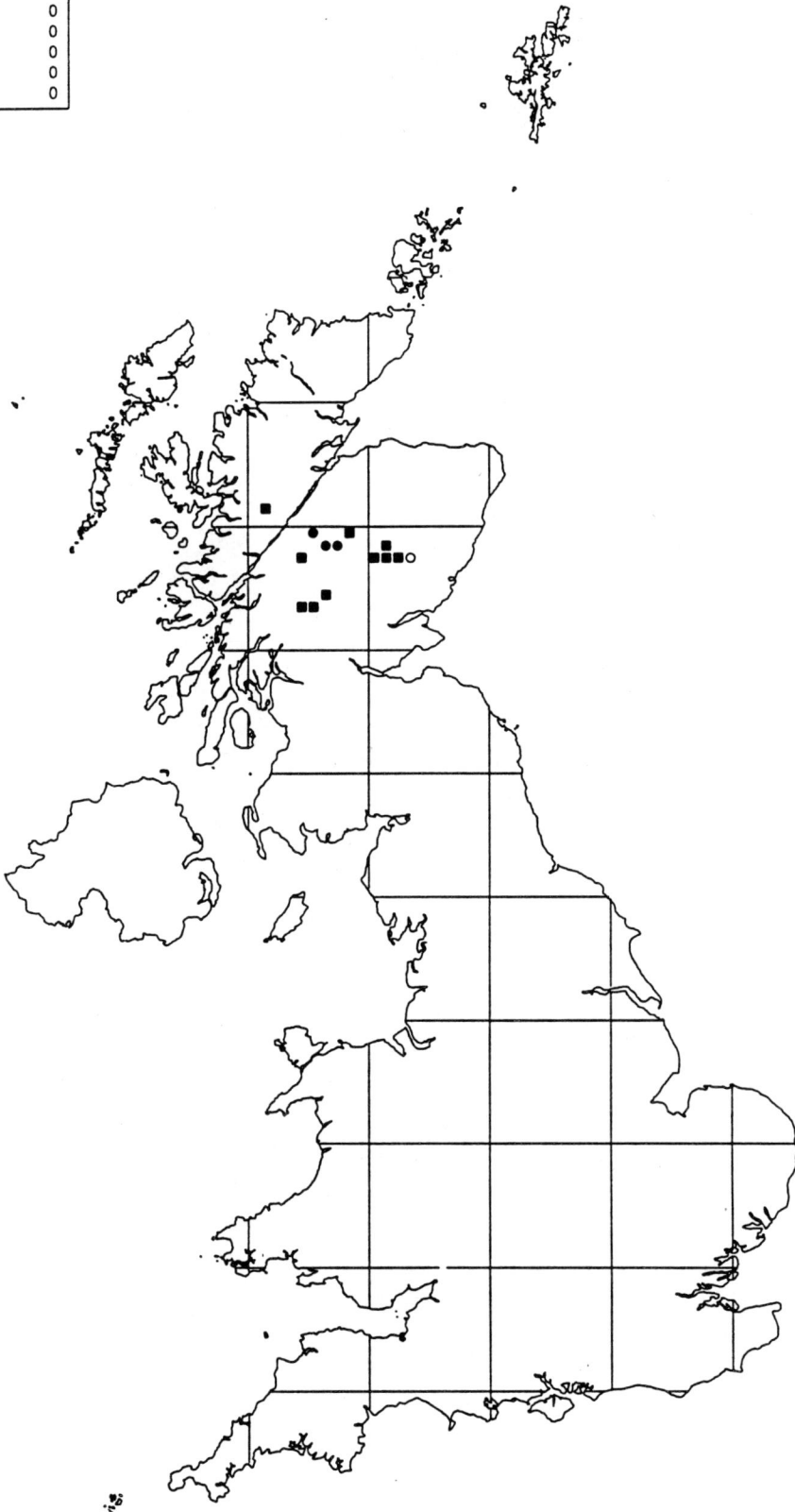

Distribution of Salix lanata - wooly willow in Britain & N.Ireland, (by 10km square).
Source: British Red Data Book - Vascular plants, 1998, 3rd edition.

■ - records post 1980
● - records 1970 - 1987
○ - records pre 1970
× - introduced records post 1970
+ - introduced records pre 1970

Shepherd's needle (*Scandix pecten-veneris*)
Action Plan

1. Current status

1.1 Shepherd's needle is a species of arable land and waste places. It favours heavy calcareous clay soils which are dry in summer and is also known to occur on disturbed coastal sites, perhaps indicating its original niche prior to its expansion into arable habitats. It is an annual species which mainly germinates between October and early November, with a smaller second flush in the spring. It has a very low level of seed dormancy which renders it particularly vulnerable to periods of inappropriate management.

1.2 Shepherd's needle was once widespread, being recorded from sites scattered throughout the UK. However, it has been declining severely for over 50 years and is now almost entirely restricted to southern and eastern England. It remains frequent in a small area of Suffolk, and where it does occur, it can be in very dense stands. The European distribution of shepherd's needle is centred mainly on the Mediterranean, extending westwards to the UK and northwards to Denmark. It has declined considerably throughout north-western and eastern Europe.

1.3 In GB this species is classified as *Nationally Scarce*. It receives general protection under the Wildlife and Countryside Act 1981.

2. Current factors causing loss or decline

2.1 Increased use of herbicides and fertilisers.

2.2 The development of highly competitive crop varieties.

2.3 The destruction of field-edge refuges.

2.4 The demise of traditional crop rotations and cultivation on marginal arable land.

3. Current action

3.1 Shepherd's needle is included within the Game Conservancy Trust's (1994) advisory booklet on arable wildflower management.

4. Action plan objectives and targets

4.1 Maintain the range and enhance the total population size of shepherd's needle in the UK.

4.2 Facilitate the colonisation of new sites.

4.3 Establish an *ex-situ* programme to protect genetic diversity, create a reserve population and provide experimental material.

5. Proposed action with lead agencies

It is important that any action for this species is considered as part of a broader approach aimed at the conservation of all threatened UK arable weeds. The protection and management of extant populations, and a thorough countrywide survey, are the priorities. These should be considered in parallel with the possible development of national schemes for the beneficial management of important arable habitats (eg the pilot Arable Stewardship Scheme). This will provide opportunities for the long-term expansion of populations into the wider countryside. The possibility of restoring populations to historic sites should be investigated, and all conservation management should be informed by relevant research where necessary.

5.1 Policy and legislation

5.1.1 Encourage the development of relevant agri-environment schemes, such as the pilot Arable Stewardship Scheme in England, as a potential means of re-establishing shepherd's needle in the countryside. When reviewing such schemes, consider whether changes are needed to increase their potential benefits for this and other threatened arable species. (ACTION: CCW, EN, MAFF, WOAD)

5.2 Site safeguard and management

5.2.1 Promote beneficial management at all extant sites. Particular attention should be given to viable sites in different parts of its range and to sites where it occurs in a species-rich community. (ACTION: EN)

5.2.2 Seek to develop a network of suitable habitats within the vicinity of shepherd's needle sites, thereby providing opportunities for its spread. Favourable management will include the relevant options outlined under appropriate agri-environment schemes, eg uncropped headlands (cultivated between mid October and early November). (ACTION: CCW, EN, MAFF, WOAD)

5.3 Species management and protection

5.3.1 Assess the feasibility of regenerating this species from the seed-bank, or if this fails carrying out reintroductions, on selected historic sites. (ACTION: EN, JNCC)

5.3.2 Collect seed from a representative number of extant sites throughout the range of this species and deposit in the Millenium Seed Bank at Wakehurst Place (Kew). (ACTION: CCW, EN, RBG Kew)

5.4 Advisory

5.4.1 Advise landowners and managers of the presence and importance of shepherd's needle, specific management for its conservation, and any potentially damaging activities. Particular attention should be given to optimal cultivation and harvest times. (ACTION: CCW, EN)

5.4.2 As far as possible, ensure that all relevant agri-environment project officers are advised of locations of this species, its importance, management requirements and potential threats. (ACTION: EN, MAFF)

5.5 Future research and monitoring

5.5.1 Collate information and resurvey extant and historic sites where necessary in order to gain a more complete understanding of the current distribution and status of shepherd's needle. This will determine the range over which conservation action is appropriate and help to clarify the threats to remaining populations. (ACTION: CCW, EN, JNCC)

5.5.2 Undertake monitoring of a representative number of extant populations, with a view to refining conservation management techniques. Where possible, monitoring visits should be combined with meeting landowners to discuss conservation management for the species. (ACTION: EN, JNCC)

5.5.3 Undertake research to determine the selectivity of all graminicides currently in use so as to identify which, if any, are suitable for use in field margins that support this and other threatened arable species. (ACTION: JNCC)

5.6 Communications and publicity

5.6.1 Publicise the plight of this and other threatened arable species. Articles should be written for relevant conservation and farming magazines and newsletters. Botanists should be encouraged to report any new records, eg through Atlas 2000 recording. (ACTION: CCW, EN)

5.6.2 Develop links with European ecologists working to conserve threatened plants of arable habitats. (ACTION: JNCC)

5.6.3 Establish arable conservation display and education centres with the aim of raising public awareness of this threatened group of the UK flora. (ACTION: CCW, EN)

5.7 Links with other action plans

5.7.1 It is likely that implementation of this action plan will benefit other arable species, including *Arabis glabra, Bromus interruptus, Centaurea cyanus, Filago lutescens, Filago pyramidata, Fumaria occidentalis, Fumaria purpurea, Galeopsis angustifolia, Galium tricornutum, Silene gallica, Torilis arvensis* and *Valerianella rimosa.*

5.7.2 The plan should be considered in conjunction with that for cereal field margins.

Scandix pecten-veneris

■	59	0
●	74	0
○	540	2
×	5	0
+	7	0

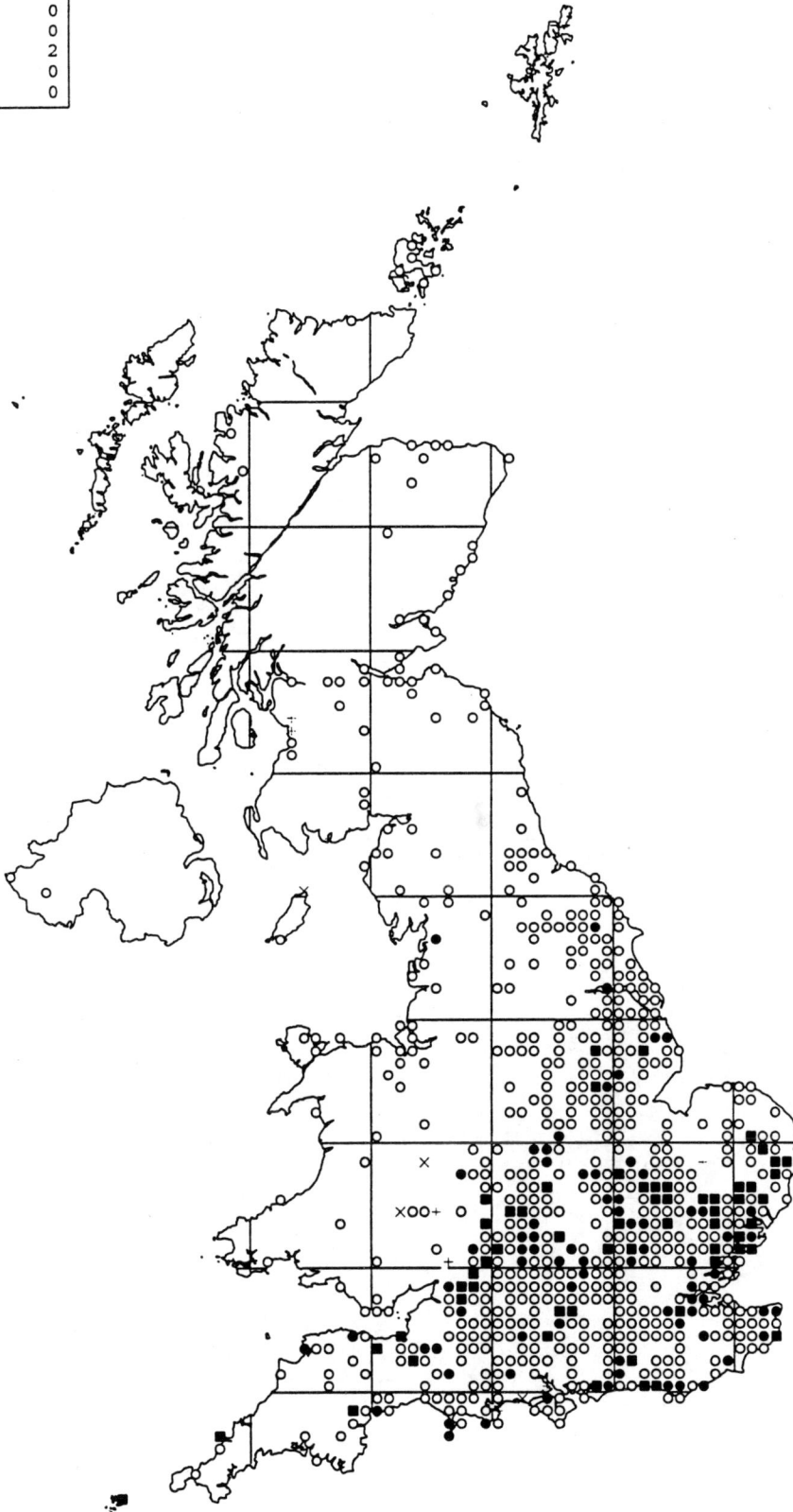

Distribution of Scandix pecten-veneris - shepherd's needle in Britain & N.Ireland, (by 10km square). Source: British Red Data Book - Vascular plants, 1998, 3rd edition.

■ - records post 1980
● - records 1970 - 1987
○ - records pre 1970
× - introduced records post 1970
+ - introduced records pre 1970

227

Triangular club-rush (*Schoenoplectus triqueter*)
Action Plan

1. Current status

1.1 Triangular club-rush is a perennial species which grows on mud-banks along the lower reaches of tidal rivers. At low tide these mud-banks are often exposed, but the plants may become completely submerged by the highest tides. It is tolerant of brackish conditions, but may prefer freshwater seepage around its roots.

1.2 This species has been recorded from a number of sites in southern England, including the Rivers Tamar (Devon and Cornwall), Arun (West Sussex), Medway (Kent) and Thames (Greater London). However, it has suffered a dramatic decline and is now restricted to one clump on the River Tamar in Devon. Indications are that this individual is flowering poorly and erratically. It is thought that triangular club-rush is a relatively mobile species, but in Britain the rate of colonisation of new sites has failed to keep pace with habitat destruction. The species is widespread outside Britain, occurring across central and southern Europe, and extending into western Asia and North Africa.

1.3 In GB the species is classified as *Critically Endangered*. It is specially protected under Schedule 8 of the Wildlife and Countryside Act 1981.

2. Current factors causing loss or decline

2.1 Engineering work on river embankments has reduced the amount of suitable habitat available for recovery, and may have been implicated in the loss of some populations in the past.

2.2 Other suggested factors are speculative, but include water pollution, erosion of river banks due to wash from boat traffic, and climatic influences.

2.3 It is possible that hybridisation has contributed to the decline of this species. Hybrids with grey club-rush (*S. tabernaemontani*) occur on the Rivers Tamar, Arun and Medway. Similarly, hybrids with common club-rush (*S. lacustris*) have also been recorded on the Rivers Tamar and Thames.

3. Current action

3.1 Surveys for the plant were undertaken on the River Tamar in 1985, 1989, 1994 and 1996; the River Arun in 1987; and the River Medway in 1987 and 1996.

3.2 Plants are kept in cultivation at Wakehurst Place (Kew).

3.3 Habitat studies of the Irish population have been undertaken by the Environment Agency.

4. Action plan objectives and targets

4.1 Restore a viable, dynamic population of triangular club-rush on the River Tamar by supplementing the last remaining clump of the species.

4.2 Restore viable, dynamic populations throughout the former range of the species, giving priority to the Rivers Arun and Medway.

4.3 Establish an *ex-situ* programme to protect genetic diversity, create a reserve population and provide experimental material.

5. Proposed action with lead agencies

The objectives for triangular club-rush will best be met by undertaking research into its ecological requirements and the reasons for decline, and using this information to help conduct a programme of experimental re-establishments and site management work.

5.1 Policy and legislation

5.1.1 None proposed.

5.2 Site safeguard and management

5.2.1 Where possible, minimise hard engineering of river channels along which this plant has been recorded, and continue to develop alternative river management techniques including the restoration of floodplains for flood control. This action applies to the Rivers Arun, Medway and Tamar in particular. (ACTION: EA, LAs)

5.2.2 Ensure that future habitat management within the River Tamar SAC is appropriate to the needs of triangular club-rush. (ACTION: EN)

5.2.3 Assess the possibility of creating suitable habitat for the plant in the vicinity of the last remaining clump. (ACTION: EN)

5.3 Species management and protection

5.3.1 If considered feasible based on the results of the research actions outlined below, undertake experimental reintroductions on at least five suitable sites on the Rivers Arun and Medway using seeds and rhizome fragments from plants cultivated at RBG Kew. Reintroductions should be tried in a range of circumstances including different inundation regimes, substrate types and vegetation types so as to determine the optimum conditions. (ACTION: EN)

5.4   Advisory

5.4.1   None proposed.

5.5   Future research and monitoring

5.5.1   Undertake a survey of the Rivers Tamar, Medway and Arun to look for any unrecorded clumps of triangular club-rush and to identify any suitable sites for reintroduction of the plant. (ACTION: EN)

5.5.2   Undertake annual monitoring of the last remaining extant population and of any newly re-established populations. (ACTION: EN)

5.5.3   Assess the feasibility and desirability of deflecting the eroding force of the river away from the single extant population on the River Tamar. (ACTION: EA, EN)

5.5.4   Carry out a full autecological assessment of this species with a view to refining conservation action. The assessment should include an investigation of the reasons for its decline, and should identify any threats including boat traffic, water pollution, successional changes, adjacent land-use practices, and climate change. (ACTION: EN, JNCC)

5.5.5   Investigate seed production in triangular club-rush. Seed production in remaining plants is known to be poor, but it would be helpful to find out if this has always been the case. A survey of herbarium specimens may give useful information, as would observations on the performance of plants being held in cultivation. (ACTION: EN, JNCC)

5.5.6   Consider investigating the impacts of nutrient enrichment and pollution on populations of triangular club-rush and consider the value of buffer strips alongside main water courses in the vicinity of key sites. (ACTION: EA, EN, MAFF)

5.6   Communications and publicity

5.6.1   Develop links with botanists in Ireland and elsewhere within the European range of this species, in order to understand, more precisely, its biology and preferred conditions. (ACTION: JNCC)

5.7   Links with other action plans

5.7.1   None proposed.

Schoenoplectus triqueter

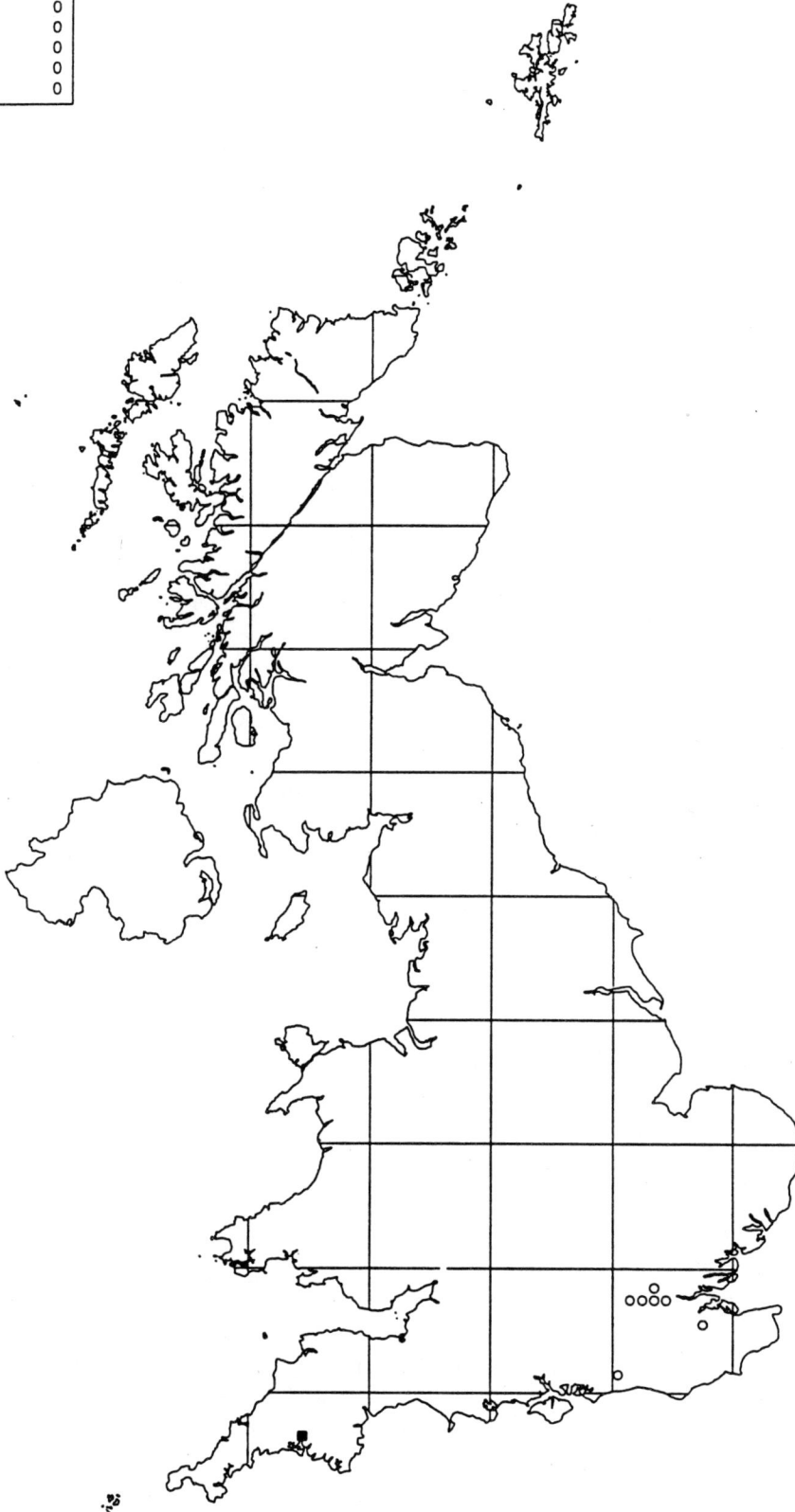

Distribution of Schoenoplectus triqueter - triangular club rush in Britain & N.Ireland, (by 10km square).
Source: British Red Data Book - Vascular Plants, 1998, 3rd edition.

■ - records post 1980
● - records 1970 - 1987
○ - records pre 1970
× - introduced records post 1970
+ - introduced records pre 1970

231

Perennial knawel (*Scleranthus perennis* ssp *prostratus*)
Action Plan

1. Current status

1.1 The endemic subspecies of perennial knawel is a biennial or short-lived perennial of semi-open, very short grassy heaths, compacted tracks and abandoned arable land, generally on acidic, sandy soil. It is a poor competitor, and open soil is required for seedling establishment. Flowers may appear at any time during the year, but are mainly produced between June and September.

1.2 This has never been a widespread plant and it has suffered a marked decline over the last 50 years. It is now restricted to the southern part of Breckland and has become extinct in Norfolk. There are three extant sites remaining and only one of these supports large numbers of plants.

1.3 This endemic subspecies of perennial knawel is classified as *Endangered* and is given special protection under Schedule 8 of the Wildlife and Countryside Act 1981.

2. Current factors causing loss or decline

The factors listed below were associated with the decline of this species and are now constraints on its recovery:

2.1 Increased use of herbicides and fertilisers.

2.2 The destruction of field-margin refuges.

2.3 The abandonment of marginal arable land and heathland.

2.4 Afforestation of former sites and potential sites for colonisation.

2.5 Deterioration of former and potential sites due to inappropriate grazing.

2.6 Loss of sites to building developments.

3. Current action

3.1 This species is currently included in English Nature's Species Recovery Programme and the following actions have been undertaken to date:

3.1.1 Management of all remaining sites for this species, including grazing and periodic rotovation.

3.1.2 Plants are being introduced to three new sites. Drought and rabbit damage have caused some losses, but the introduction programme is continuing.

3.1.3 Establishment of a seed collection at RBG Kew. Plants are also being propagated *ex-situ* in a private collection for use in future reintroductions.

3.1.4 Regular monitoring of all extant and restored sites.

3.2 All three extant populations are protected within SSSIs.

4. Action plan objectives and targets

This action plan is intended to build upon work proposed under English Nature's Species Recovery Programme by recommending some broader action for the conservation of this endemic subspecies of perennial knawel.

4.1 Restore and maintain viable populations at all extant sites.

4.2 Establish populations at three new sites by 2003.

4.3 Facilitate natural colonisation of further sites.

5. Proposed action with lead agencies

The site-based work for this species should be considered in parallel with broader improvements to Breckland conservation management, in order to increase the possibility that this taxon will develop self-sustaining populations. Conservation techniques for this taxon need to be refined, and awareness of its decline and rarity raised, in order to improve its conservation.

5.1 Policy and legislation

5.1.1 Ensure that the requirements of this taxon and other elements of the Breckland flora are fully considered when deciding on future forestry management and expansion near to extant sites. (ACTION: EN, FA, FE)

5.1.2 Take account of the requirements of this taxon when reviewing the Breckland ESA scheme. (ACTION: EN, MAFF)

5.2 Site safeguard and management

5.2.1 Ensure that all extant and restored sites receive management which is beneficial to the conservation of this Breckland subspecies of perennial knawel as detailed under the Species Recovery Programme. (ACTION: EN)

5.2.2 Seek to develop a network of suitable habitats within the vicinity of extant populations which will provide opportunities for the spread of this taxon. Favourable management could include options under the Breckland ESA. (ACTION: EN, MAFF)

5.2.3 Ensure that all extant and restored sites are protected from housing development and damaging agricultural operations. (ACTION: EN, LAs)

5.3   Species management and protection

5.3.1   Continue with work detailed under the Species Recovery Programme for this taxon. (ACTION: EN)

5.4   Advisory

5.4.1   On extant and restored sites for perennial knawel in Breckland, advise landowners and managers of its importance and appropriate management for its conservation. (ACTION: EN)

5.4.2   Advise the Breckland ESA project officer and members of the regional agri-environment consultation group of locations for this taxon, its importance and management needed for its conservation, including the need to create suitable habitat within the vicinity of extant and restored sites where opportunities arise. (ACTION: EN, MAFF)

5.5   Future research and monitoring

5.5.1   Continue with regular monitoring of extant and restored sites as detailed under the Species Recovery Programme. During these monitoring visits the opportunity should be taken to advise landowners and managers on appropriate management. (ACTION: EN)

5.5.2   Investigate the autecology of this subspecies with a view to informing restoration management. Priorities should include seed-bank dynamics and the optimal timing for, and methods of, ground disturbance. (ACTION: EN, JNCC)

5.6   Communications and publicity

5.6.1   Raise awareness among local people of the importance of this endemic taxon and other rare species of the Breckland flora, the reasons for their decline, and action needed to secure their recovery. (ACTION: EN)

5.7   Links with other action plans

5.7.1   Implementation of this action plan has potential benefits for *Arabis glabra* and *Bromus interruptus*.

5.7.2   The plan should be considered in conjunction with that for lowland dry acid grassland.

Scleranthus perennis subsp.prostratus

■	3	0
●	0	0
○	7	0
×	0	0
+	0	0

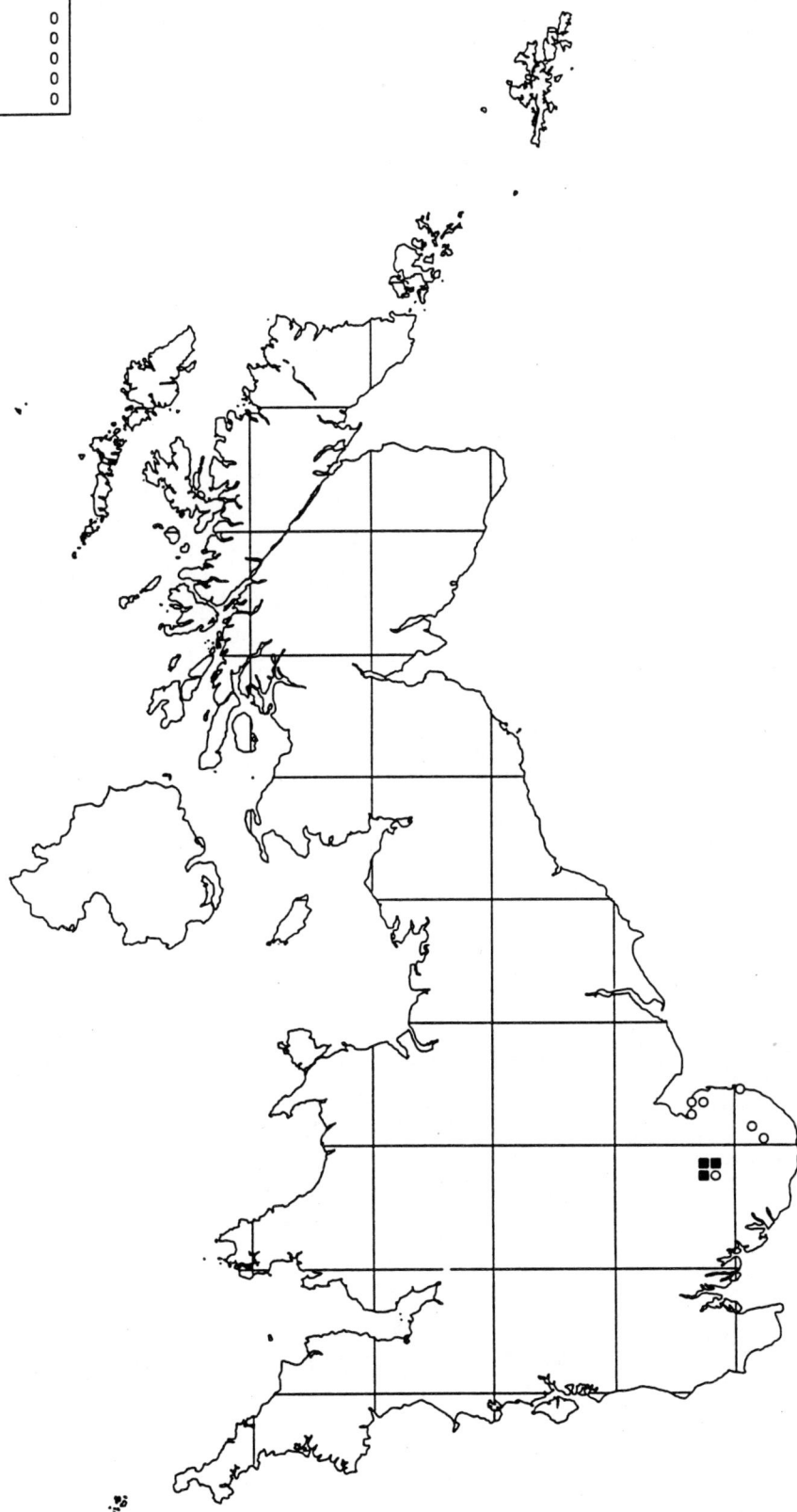

Distribution of Scleranthus perennis subsp.prostratus - perennial knawel in Britain & N.Ireland, (by 10km square). Source: British Red Data Book - Vascular plants, 1998, 3rd edition.

■ - records post 1980
● - records 1970 - 1987
○ - records pre 1970
× - introduced records post 1970
+ - introduced records pre 1970

Small-flowered catchfly (*Silene gallica*) Action Plan

1. Current status

1.1 Small-flowered catchfly is a species of arable land, waste ground and sandy seashores. It is a winter annual, mainly germinating in autumn but also capable of doing so in spring. It is therefore found in both spring and winter crops.

1.2 This species was once widespread in the UK and has been recorded in 283 ten km squares as far north as central Scotland. However, it has undergone a very rapid decline and is now concentrated in southern and western England and Wales, and most of its remaining sites are in coastal areas. Its decline has been associated with agricultural changes, but has been compounded by its vulnerability to harsh winters (seedlings cannot tolerate temperatures of less than -10° C). The loss of repeated introductions from uncleaned European seed may have given the appearance of an even more catastrophic decline. Small-flowered catchfly is widespread in central and southern Europe. It is not threatened in Europe as a whole, but has virtually disappeared from northern Europe.

1.3 In GB small-flowered catchfly is classified as *Nationally Scarce*. It receives general protection under the Wildlife and Countryside Act 1981.

2. Current factors causing loss or decline

2.1 Increased use of herbicides and fertilisers. The higher levels of fertiliser and herbicide applied to winter crops explains why this species has not benefited from the switch to autumn drilling as might otherwise have been expected.

2.2 The development of highly productive crop varieties.

2.3 The destruction of field-edge refuges.

2.4 The conversion of marginal arable land to pasture.

2.5 Early harvests (ie around mid-July) which can destroy plants before seed has been set.

2.6 The demise of traditional crop rotations.

2.7 Tourist developments on coastal sites, which may be an important threat and have been responsible for the loss of a notable Welsh site.

3. Current action

3.1 None known.

4. Action plan objectives and targets

4.1 Maintain the range and enhance the total population size of small-flowered catchfly in the UK.

4.2 Facilitate natural colonisation of new sites.

4.3 Restore populations to eight suitable historic sites by 2003.

4.4 Establish an *ex-situ* programme to protect genetic diversity, create a reserve population and provide experimental material.

5. Proposed action with lead agencies

It is important that any action for this species is considered as part of a broader approach aimed at the conservation of all threatened UK arable weeds. The protection and management of extant populations, and a thorough countrywide survey, are the priorities. These should be considered in parallel with work aimed at regenerating plants from the seed-bank and with the possible development of a national scheme for the beneficial management of important arable habitats (eg the pilot Arable Stewardship Scheme). This will provide opportunities for the long-term expansion of populations into the wider countryside, as will the controlled use of native seed in wildflower mixes. All conservation management should be informed by relevant research where necessary, particularly into the threats to remaining populations in both arable and non-arable habitats.

5.1 Policy and legislation

5.1.1 Encourage the development of relevant agri-environment schemes, such as the pilot Arable Stewardship Scheme in England, as a potential means of re-establishing small-flowered catchfly in the countryside. When reviewing such schemes, consider whether changes are needed to increase their potential benefits for this and other threatened arable species. (ACTION: EN, MAFF)

5.2 Site safeguard and management

5.2.1 Promote beneficial management at all extant arable and coastal sites. Particular emphasis should be given to populations which are associated with species-rich communities. (ACTION: CCW, EN, LAs)

5.2.2 Seek to develop a network of suitable habitats within the vicinity of small-flowered catchfly sites, thereby providing opportunities for its spread. Favourable management will include the relevant options outlined under the pilot Arable Stewardship Scheme, eg uncropped headlands (cultivated in autumn). (ACTION: CCW, EN, MAFF)

5.3 Species management and protection

5.3.1 Undertake trial management at eight carefully selected historic sites with the aim of regenerating small-flowered catchfly from the seed-bank. (ACTION: EN, JNCC)

5.3.2 Assess the feasibility and desirability of reintroducing small-flowered catchfly to selected sites should attempts to regenerate it from the seed-bank prove unsuccessful. (ACTION: EN, JNCC)

5.3.3 Collect seed from a representative number of extant populations in different parts of the range of this species and deposit at Wakehurst Place (Kew). Plants should also be propagated for reintroductions if necessary. (ACTION: CCW, EN, RBG Kew)

5.4 Advisory

5.4.1 Advise landowners and managers of the presence and importance of small-flowered catchfly, specific management for its conservation, and any potentially damaging actions. Particular attention should be given to optimal cultivation and harvest times. (ACTION: CCW, EN)

5.4.2 As far as possible, ensure that all relevant agri-environment project officers are advised of locations of this species, its importance, management requirements and potential threats. (ACTION: CCW, EN, MAFF)

5.5 Future research and monitoring

5.5.1 Collate information and resurvey extant and historic sites where necessary in order to gain a more complete understanding of the current distribution and status of small-flowered catchfly, and to assess current site management and threats to remaining populations. (ACTION: CCW, EN, JNCC)

5.5.2 Undertake monitoring on a representative number of extant sites and all restored sites, with a view to refining conservation management techniques. Where possible, monitoring visits should be combined with meeting landowners to discuss conservation management for the species. (ACTION: CCW, EN, JNCC)

5.5.3 Undertake research to determine the selectivity of all graminicides currently in use so as to identify which, if any, are suitable for use in field margins that support this and other threatened arable species. (ACTION: JNCC)

5.6 Communications and publicity

5.6.1 Publicise the plight of this and other threatened arable species. Articles should be written for relevant conservation and farming magazines and newsletters. Botanists should be encouraged to report any new records. (ACTION: EN)

5.6.2 Develop links with European ecologists working to conserve threatened plants of arable habitats. (ACTION: JNCC)

5.6.3 Establish arable conservation display and education centres with the aim of raising public awareness of this threatened group of the UK flora. (ACTION: EN)

5.7 Links with other action plans

5.7.1 It is likely that implementation of this action plan will benefit other arable species, including *Arabis glabra, Bromus interruptus, Centaurea cyanus, Filago lutescens, Filago pyramidata, Fumaria occidentalis, Fumaria purpurea, Galeopsis angustifolia, Galium tricornutum, Scandix pecten-veneris, Torilis arvensis* and *Valerianella rimosa*.

5.7.2 The plan should be considered in conjunction with those for cereal field margins and vegetated shingle.

238

Silene gallica

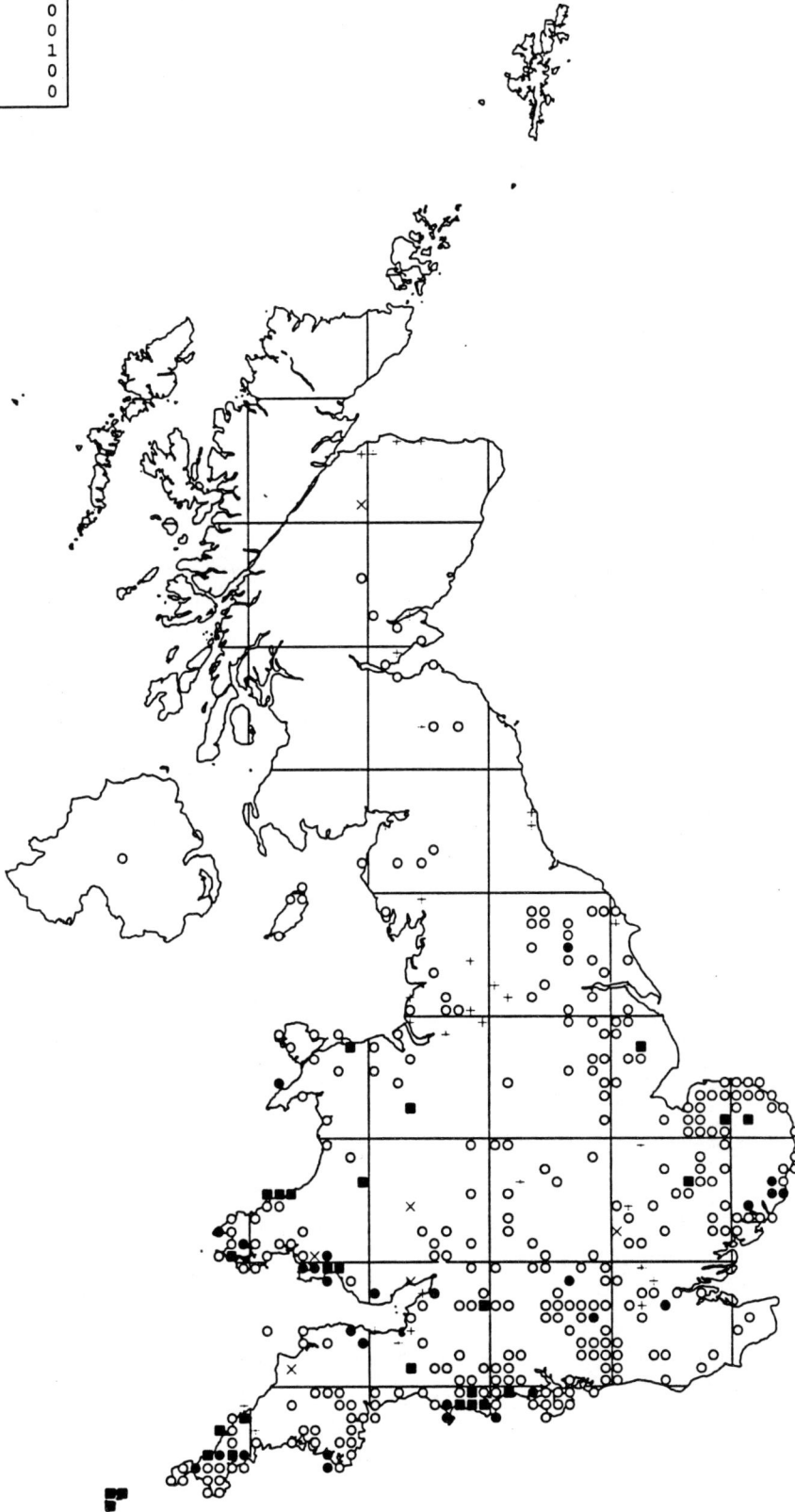

**Distribution of Silene gallica - small-flowered catchfly in Britain & N.Ireland, (by 10km square).
Source: British Red Data Book - Vascular plants, 1998, 3rd edition.**

■ - records post 1980
● - records 1970 - 1987
○ - records pre 1970
× - introduced records post 1970
+ - introduced records pre 1970

239

· Greater water-parsnip (*Sium latifolium*)
Action Plan

1. Current status

1.1 Greater water-parsnip is a species of wet ditches and tall-herb fens and swamps. It grows in shallow, still or slow-moving water that is alkaline and rich in nitrogen, and is generally found on peat or alluvial soil. It is able to tolerate vigorous growth of other emergents such as common reed (*Phragmites australis*) or reed-mace (*Typha* spp) but is excluded by growth of carr. Greater water-parsnip is intolerant of extended periods of heavy grazing or frequent cutting. It thrives in ditches where water is kept open by occasional clearance with a bucket excavator or scythe.

1.2 In the past greater water-parsnip was most commonly found on rafts of semi-floating vegetation at the margins of lakes and large rivers. However, following the drainage and reclamation of fens in the UK, it is now most often found in drainage ditches in the south and east of England. It continues to thrive in the Lough Erne system of Northern Ireland. It is widespread in Europe, but very rare near the Mediterranean.

1.3 In GB greater water-parsnip is classified as *Nationally Scarce* but its population is not as large as this classification might imply. It receives general protection under the Wildlife and Countryside Act 1981.

2. Current factors causing loss or decline

2.1 Frequent cleaning and over-engineering of ditches.

2.2 Drainage of sites.

2.3 Exposure to prolonged heavy grazing.

2.4 Dereliction of ditches leading to reed and scrub invasion.

3. Current action

3.1 A large proportion of the Northern Ireland population is protected by ASSI/SAC/SPA status (Upper Lough Erne).

3.2 In the Somerset Levels, greater water-parsnip has been recorded in six SSSIs in the last 15 years.

4. Action plan objectives and targets

4.1 Maintain the range of greater water-parsnip in the UK.

4.2 Ensure that viable populations are maintained at all extant sites.

4.3 Regenerate plants from the seed-bank on five suitable historic sites in England by 2003.

4.4 Provide opportunities for the spread of greater water-parsnip from extant sites.

5. Proposed action with lead agencies

The successful conservation of this species will demand both site-based work and broader policy action. The priorities are the establishment of beneficial management regimes at extant sites, in conjunction with the promotion of appropriate river management and suitable agricultural practices on land adjacent to extant sites. Work is needed to ascertain the current distribution and status of the species, and to increase understanding and awareness of its ecological requirements.

5.1 Policy and legislation

5.1.1 Promote the restoration of more natural river dynamics on lowland rivers in Britain, including the restoration of alluvial floodplains, in order to create permanent or semi-permanent water habitats for this species. (ACTION: EA)

5.2 Site safeguard and management

5.2.1 When next reviewed, consider targeting Countryside Stewardship and other relevant agri-environment schemes to land adjacent to extant sites for greater water-parsnip in order to create suitable conditions for population expansion. (ACTION: EN, MAFF)

5.2.2 Ensure that Local Environment Agency Plans and Water Level Management Plans take full account of the requirements of this species. (ACTION: EA)

5.2.3 Where possible, seek beneficial management for this species at extant sites. Ditches should not be cleaned out too regularly and sites should not be heavily grazed. (ACTION: EA, EN, IDBs, MAFF)

5.2.4 Consider stronghold sites for notification as SSSIs where this is necessary to ensure their long-term protection from damaging activities. (ACTION: EN)

5.3 Species management and protection

5.3.1 Undertake management on five suitable historic sites with the aim of regenerating plants from the seed-bank. (ACTION: EN)

5.3.2 Assess the feasibility and desirability of reintroducing this species to suitable historic sites should regeneration from the seed-bank prove unsuccessful. (ACTION: EN, JNCC)

5.3.3 Collect seed from a representative number of sites in different parts of the range of this species and deposit in the Millenium Seed Bank at Wakehurst Place (Kew). (ACTION: EN, RBG Kew)

5.4   Advisory

5.4.1 Ensure that all landowners and managers of extant sites are aware of the management requirements of this plant. (ACTION: EN)

5.4.2 As far as possible, ensure that all relevant agri-environment project officers and members of regional agri-environment consultation groups are advised of locations of this species, its importance and management needed for its conservation. They should also be advised of the need to develop beneficial management practices on sites adjacent to existing populations so as to facilitate the spread of greater water-parsnip. (ACTION: EN, MAFF)

5.5   Future research and monitoring

5.5.1 Collate information and re-survey sites where necessary in order to determine the current distribution and status of greater water-parsnip in Britain, and assess threats to remaining populations. (ACTION: EN, JNCC)

5.5.2 Undertake autecological research and detailed monitoring on three viable sites in order to increase knowledge of the ecological requirements of greater water-parsnip and refine management techniques for its conservation. (ACTION: EN, JNCC)

5.6   Communications and publicity

5.6.1 Use the conservation of greater water-parsnip to help illustrate the need to develop natural river and flood dynamics for biodiversity. A short statement on the requirements of this species should be prepared and circulated amongst relevant groups, including river managers. (ACTION: EA, IDBs, JNCC)

5.7   Links with other action plans

5.7.1 This action plan should be considered in conjunction with those for fens, coastal and floodplain grazing marshes and reedbeds.

Sium latifolium

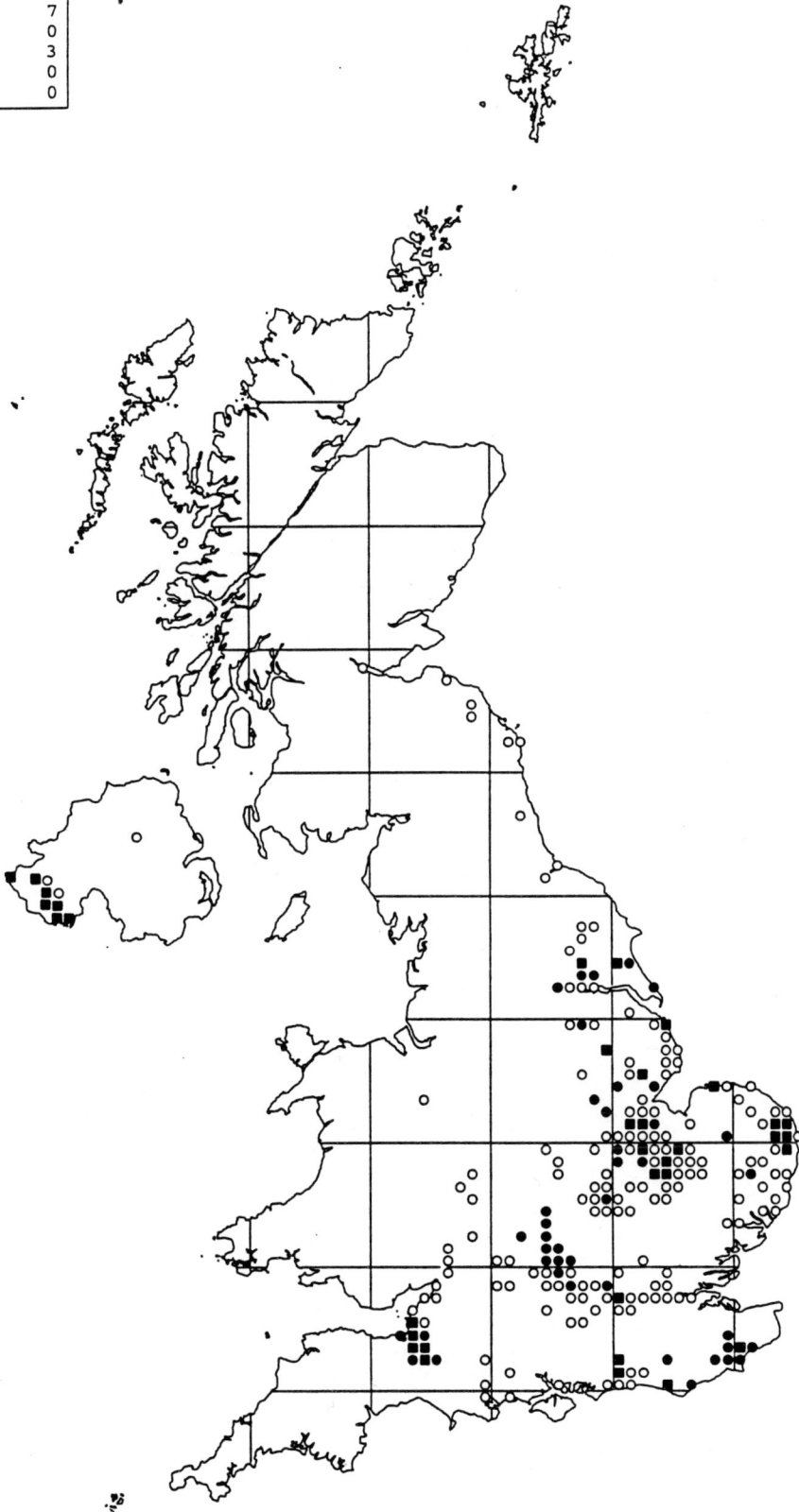

■	28	7
●	41	0
○	149	3
×	0	0
+	0	0

Distribution of Sium latifolium - greater-water parsnip in Britain & N.Ireland, (by 10km square).
Source: British Red Data Book - Vascular plants, 1998, 3rd edition.

■ - records post 1980
● - records 1970 - 1987
○ - records pre 1970
× - introduced records post 1970
+ - introduced records pre 1970

Ley's whitebeam (*Sorbus leyana*)
Action Plan

1. Current status

1.1 Ley's whitebeam is an apomictic microspecies (a taxon arising through the asexual development of the maternal germ cells in the absence of fertilisation) and is thought to be derived from mountain ash (*S. aucuparia*) and rock whitebeam (*S. rupicola*). It is a distinctive large deciduous shrub or small tree which flowers in late May and early June. Fruits form in September, but are generally rather few in number. Germination of seed is also poor, with complete failure in some years. It is believed to be a light-demanding species which is probably unable to colonise densely shaded sites. It is also thought to be highly palatable to grazing stock at the seedling and sapling stage. Together with the apparent drought tolerance of mature trees, these factors probably explain its restriction to cliff habitats.

1.2 Ley's whitebeam is endemic to south Wales, where it is known from only two localities on steep limestone cliffs. At one site 13 trees were recorded in 1983, mostly on partly wooded cliffs, while at the other three native trees have been reported, together with four trees which have become established from nursery grown saplings planted in 1962. Thus the total known wild population consists of a likely maximum of 16 established trees.

1.3 Ley's whitebeam is now classified as *Critically Endangered*. It receives general protection under the Wildlife and Countryside Act 1981.

2. Current factors causing loss or decline

2.1 A number of ecological factors are thought to be involved in restricting the populations of Ley's whitebeam, including grazing, disease, competition with introduced trees and shrubs, and seed productivity, which is probably low due to small population size and poor breeding success. Further research is required to unravel their relative importance.

2.2 Afforestation activities in the past may have destroyed potential colonisation sites.

2.3 Its preferred habitat of limestone cliff crevices and ledges is also scarce.

3. Current action

3.1 The two known sites for this species are protected as SSSIs.

3.2 Six nursery-grown saplings were planted at one of its sites by the Forestry Commission in 1962; four of these were still present in March 1996.

3.3 A specimen has been planted at the Forest Enterprise Garw Nant Visitor Centre.

3.4 A workshop was held at Wakehurst Place in April 1996 on the conservation status of whitebeams in the UK and a report is being produced.

3.5 *Ex-situ* populations are present in botanic gardens across the UK (including Westonbirt, Cambridge University and Ness Gardens).

4. Action plan objectives and targets

4.1 Maintain and, where possible, enhance populations of Ley's whitebeam at its extant sites.

4.2 By 2003, identify two sites which would be suitable for the introduction of cultivated material should the wild populations be lost.

5. Proposed action with lead agencies

This taxon has always been rare and its restriction to just two sites renders it highly vulnerable to localised catastrophes. The priorities for it are therefore: to ensure that sites are protected and suitably managed; and to make provision for the establishment of further populations at sites within its likely natural range using cultivated material should this prove necessary. It will be necessary to increase understanding of the ecological requirements of this taxon, identify threats to existing populations and monitor patterns of recruitment.

5.1 Policy and legislation

5.1.1 Consider the inclusion of this taxon on Schedule 8 of the Wildlife and Countryside Act 1981, at the earliest possible opportunity. (ACTION: CCW, JNCC)

5.2 Site safeguard and management

5.2.1 Following the research outlined in 5.5.3, assess the need for site management at extant sites in order to create favourable conditions for growth and recruitment. If a management programme is considered necessary, it should be implemented by 2003. (ACTION: CCW, FE)

5.2.2 Seek opportunities for the creation of suitable habitats for Ley's whitebeam within currently afforested areas. (ACTION: CCW, FE)

5.3 Species management and protection

5.3.1 Coordinate existing programmes for the *ex-situ* conservation of Ley's whitebeam and seek to involve Wakehurst Place and the new National Botanic Garden of Wales. The material cultivated for any future introduction schemes should be genetically representative, as identified by the research outlined under 5.5.4. Priority should also be given to the maintenance of *ex-situ* populations of budded material and, if possible, seed from all existing wild individuals. (ACTION: CCW)

5.3.2 Undertake a survey to identify suitable sites away from (but close to) native localities where cultivated seedlings of Ley's whitebeam could be introduced in the event of wild populations being lost (although sites with *S. minima* or *S. anglica* should be avoided). This work should also serve to identify potential sites for natural recruitment. (ACTION: CCW)

5.4 Advisory

5.4.1 Advise landowners and managers of sites supporting native populations (and sites proposed for introduction), the importance of this taxon and any activities which may be damaging to it. (ACTION: CCW)

5.5 Future research and monitoring

5.5.1 Survey the two known sites for this species and map all surviving trees and any seedlings found. The sites should then be monitored frequently for at least 10 years and the need to protect individual seedlings reviewed at each visit. (ACTION: CCW)

5.5.2 Make a demographic assessment of each population, and use the findings to inform site and species management. (ACTION: CCW)

5.5.3 Assess potential factors which may be limiting the population size, including the effects of disease, herbivores and the spread of non-native trees, with a view to developing a beneficial management programme for both sites. (ACTION: CCW, FE)

5.5.4 Consider a genetic screening programme to add to existing data on intra- and inter-population genetic variation. (ACTION: CCW)

5.6 Communications and publicity

5.6.1 Promote the development of existing visitor interpretation about endemic whitebeams at the Garw Nant Centre and seek to establish a similar educational resource at the new Welsh National Botanic Garden. (ACTION: CCW, FE)

5.7 Links with other action plans

5.7.1 This action plan should be considered in conjunction with those for upland mixed ash woodland and lowland calcareous grassland.

Sorbus leyana

■	2	0
●	0	0
○	0	0
×	0	0
–	0	0

Distribution of Sorbus leyana - Ley's whitebeam in Britain & N.Ireland, (by 10km square).
Source: British Red Data Book - Vascular plants, 1998, 3rd edition.

■ - records post 1980
● - records 1970 - 1987
○ - records pre 1970
× - introduced records post 1970
+ - introduced records pre 1970

247

Cotswold pennycress (*Thlaspi perfoliatum*)
Action Plan

1. Current status

1.1 Cotswold pennycress is an annual member of the cabbage family. It is a small, spring-flowering plant particularly characteristic of oolitic limestone in the Cotswolds where it has been recorded growing amongst open vegetation on pastures, screes, walls, tracks and quarries. It has low powers of dispersal, and requires ground disturbance near to fruiting plants in order to create the conditions required for germination and reduce subsequent competition from other vegetation.

1.2 Cotswold pennycress is rare in Britain, and probably always has been. It occurs as a native plant at eight sites in the Cotswolds in Oxfordshire and Gloucestershire, but has also become established at other sites within this area and outside, often being introduced with oolite ballast or blown along railway lines by trains. Elsewhere, it has been recorded across southern Europe, and northwards to Belgium and central Germany. It is not threatened in Europe as a whole.

1.3 In GB Cotswold pennycress is classified as *Vulnerable*. It is specially protected under Schedule 8 of the Wildlife and Countryside Act 1981.

2. Current factors causing loss or decline

2.1 Removal of hedges, walls and associated banks.

2.2 Ploughing and levelling of sites.

2.3 Increased use of herbicides and fertilisers.

2.4 Neglect of marginal land leading to sward closure and scrub invasion.

3. Current action

3.1 Conservation work for this species is ongoing under Plantlife's 'Back from the Brink' project which is supported by English Nature's Species Recovery Programme. The following action has already been taken:

3.1.1 Plantlife conducted a survey of all extant sites and recent historical sites in 1992. The Ashmolean Natural History Society surveyed sites in Oxfordshire. Data gathered from these surveys enabled Plantlife to assess possible sites for reintroductions.

3.1.2 Plantlife has undertaken or overseen management work at four sites with native populations of this species.

4. Action plan objectives and targets

This action plan is intended to build upon the work proposed under English Nature's Species Recovery Programme, and also to promote some broader action for the conservation of Cotswold pennycress.

4.1 Restore and maintain viable populations at all sites with native, extant populations.

4.2 Regenerate plants from the seed-bank on three suitable historic sites in the native range by 2003.

5. Proposed action with lead agencies

Many of the remaining populations for this species which are considered to be truly native are ecologically isolated. It is important that they are fully protected and beneficially managed, and that measures are taken where possible to facilitate their spread. However, because of their isolation and the risk of this species becoming completely confined to these areas, it seems appropriate to recognise the importance of other sites with non-native populations (particularly those where the plant is long established) within its native range. The management of truly native sites should therefore be considered in parallel with that of railway and quarry sites.

5.1 Policy and legislation

5.1.1 Ensure that the requirements of Cotswold pennycress are considered during future reviews of the Cotswold Hills ESA scheme. (ACTION: MAFF)

5.2 Site safeguard and management

5.2.1 Consider notifying as SSSIs, native sites with viable populations of this species where this is necessary to ensure their long-term protection. (ACTION: EN)

5.2.2 Seek to maintain or reinstate grazing management on pasture habitats through the most appropriate mechanism (eg SSSI management agreements, Countryside Stewardship, Cotswold Hills ESA scheme). (ACTION: EN, MAFF)

5.2.3 Undertake management of quarry and railway sites including scrub clearance and ground disturbance where necessary. (ACTION: EN)

5.2.4 Consider the requirements of this species when assessing the future of old quarry workings and when considering applications for further mineral extraction. (ACTION: EN, LAs)

5.3 Species management and protection

5.3.1 Undertake trial management at three historic, native sites with the aim of regenerating plants from the seed-bank. (ACTION: EN)

5.4   Advisory

5.4.1 Advise landowners of the importance of this species, appropriate management for its conservation, and activities which might be damaging to it. (ACTION: EN)

5.4.2 Advise project officers of the Cotswold Hills ESA scheme of the presence and importance of Cotswold pennycress within their area, and guide them on management regimes for the conservation of this plant. (ACTION: EN, MAFF)

5.4.3 Ensure that railway track maintenance and contract staff are aware of the presence of this species and are advised of its conservation needs. (ACTION: EN)

5.5   Future research and monitoring

5.5.1 Continue the monitoring programme at all extant sites as established by Plantlife. Where possible, monitoring visits should be combined with meeting landowners to discuss conservation management for the species. (ACTION: EN).

5.5.2 Assess ways in which the conservation requirements of Cotswold pennycress may be integrated with quarrying policy in the Cotswolds. (ACTION: EN, LAs)

5.6   Communications and publicity

5.6.1 Raise the level of awareness of the importance of this species and its conservation requirements in local communities in the Cotswolds. (ACTION: EN)

5.7   Links with other action plans

5.7.1 None proposed.

Thlaspi perfoliatum

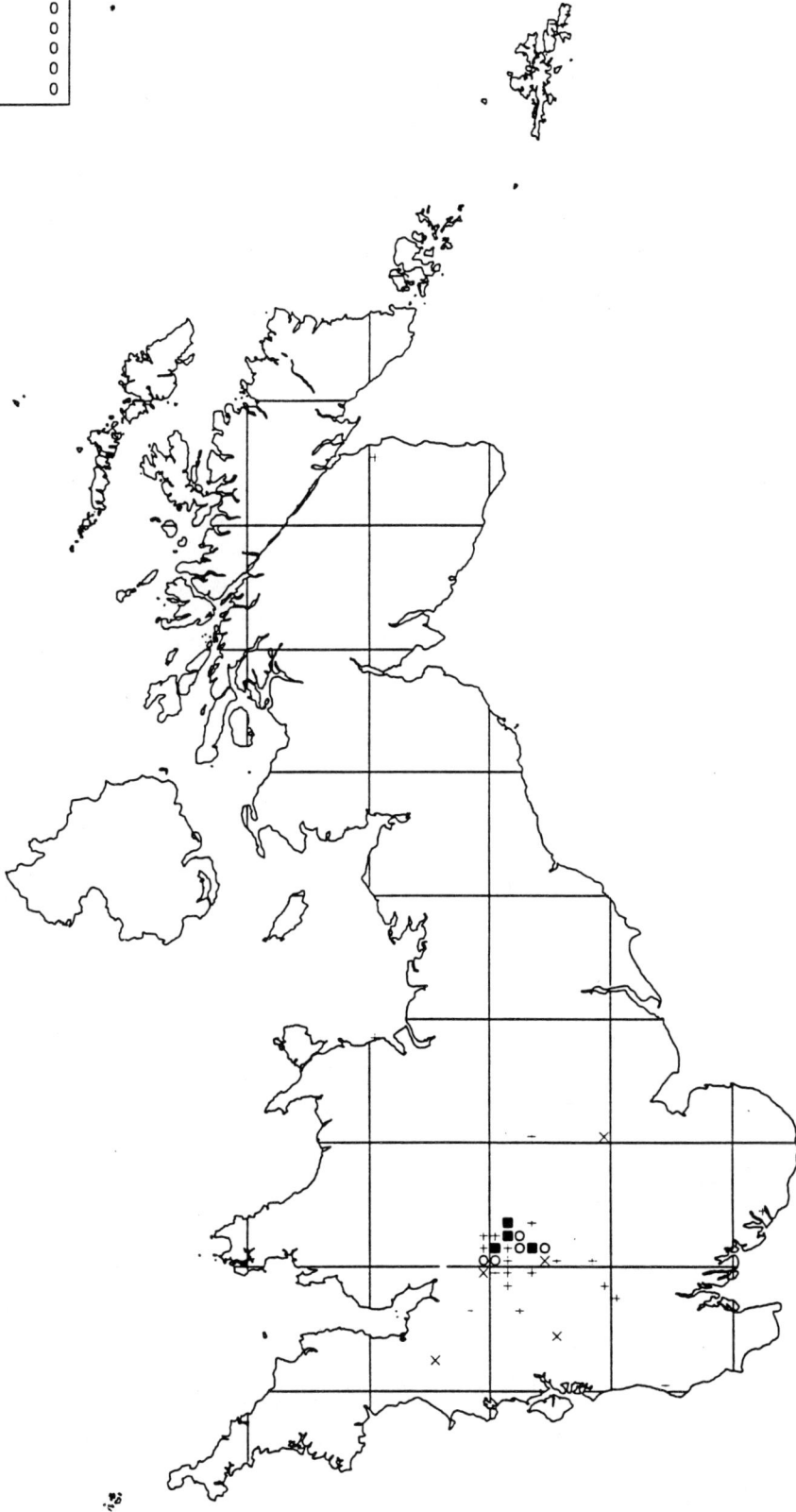

■	4	0
●	0	0
○	5	0
×	5	0
+	22	0

Distribution of Thlaspi perfoliatum - Cotswold pennycress in Britain & N.Ireland, (by 10km square). Source: British Red Data Book - Vascular plants, 1998, 3rd edition.

■ - records post 1980
● - records 1970 - 1987
○ - records pre 1970
× - introduced records post 1970
+ - introduced records pre 1970

251

Spreading hedge-parsley (*Torilis arvensis*)
Action Plan

1. Current status

1.1 Spreading hedge-parsley is a species of arable land, most frequently found on heavy calcareous soils, almost exclusively in autumn-sown cereal crops but occasionally on road and railway verges. It is an annual plant, or rarely a biennial, and relies on animals to act as a vector for dispersal. Most seeds germinate in autumn; a small amount do so in spring. Germination is intermittent and seed is thought to remain dormant in the soil for several years.

1.2 Spreading hedge-parsley has declined rapidly in the UK from 136 ten km squares between 1930 and 1960, to just 82 since 1970 and perhaps less than 20 since 1986. This species is found throughout western, southern and central Europe and south-western Asia, but is declining and threatened in most countries in north-western Europe.

1.3 In GB the species is classified as *Nationally Scarce*. It receives general protection under the Wildlife and Countryside Act 1981.

2. Current factors causing loss or decline

Several features associated with agricultural change over the last 50 years have been responsible for the decline of spreading hedge-parsley and are now providing constraints on its recovery. These include:

2.1 Increased use of herbicides and fertilisers.

2.2 The development of highly competitive crop varieties.

2.3 The destruction of field-edge habitats.

2.4 The decline of the practice of folding sheep on arable land which has meant that sheep no longer act as a vector for the dispersal of seeds.

2.5 The decline of traditional crop rotations.

3. Current action

3.1 This species is present on an SSSI in Somerset.

3.2 There are voluntary management agreements at two of its sites in Hampshire and one in Hertfordshire.

4. Action plan objectives and targets

4.1 Maintain viable populations at all extant sites.

4.2 Facilitate natural colonisation of new sites.

4.3 Restore populations of spreading hedge-parsley to eight suitable historic sites by 2003.

4.4 Establish an *ex-situ* programme to protect genetic diversity, create a reserve population and provide experimental material.

5. Proposed action with lead agencies

It is important that any action for this species is considered as part of a broader approach aimed at the conservation of all threatened UK arable weeds. The protection and management of extant populations and a thorough countrywide survey are the priorities. These should be considered in parallel with work aimed at regenerating plants from the seed-bank and with the possible development of a national scheme for the beneficial management of important arable habitats (eg the pilot Arable Stewardship Scheme). This will provide opportunities for the long-term expansion of populations into the wider countryside. All conservation management should be informed by relevant research where necessary.

5.1 Policy and legislation

5.1.1 Encourage the development of relevant agri-environment schemes, such as the pilot Arable Stewardship Scheme in England, as a potential means of re-establishing spreading hedge-parsley in the countryside. When reviewing such schemes, consider whether changes are needed to increase their potential benefits for this and other threatened arable species. (ACTION: EN, MAFF)

5.2 Site safeguard and management

5.2.1 Ensure that the management of all remaining sites for this species is beneficial to its conservation. (ACTION: EN)

5.2.2 Seek to develop a network of suitable habitats within the vicinity of spreading hedge-parsley sites, thereby providing opportunities for its spread. Favourable management will include the relevant options outlined under the pilot Arable Stewardship Scheme, eg uncropped headlands (cultivated between mid October and early November). (ACTION: EN, MAFF)

5.3 Species management and protection

5.3.1 Undertake trial management on eight selected historic sites with the aim of regenerating populations of spreading hedge-parsley from the seed-bank. (ACTION: EN)

5.3.2 Assess the feasibility and desirability of reintroducing populations of spreading hedge-parsley should regeneration from the seed-bank prove unsuccessful. (ACTION: EN, JNCC)

5.3.3 Collect seed from plants on a representative number of sites in different parts of its range in the UK and deposit in the Millenium Seed Bank at Wakehurst Place (Kew). Plants should also be propagated for reintroductions if necessary. (ACTION: EN, RBG Kew)

5.4 Advisory

5.4.1 Advise landowners and managers of the presence and importance of key spreading hedge-parsley sites, specific management for its conservation, and any potentially damaging actions. Particular attention should be given to optimal cultivation and harvest times. (ACTION: EN)

5.4.2 As far as possible, ensure that all relevant agri-environment project officers are advised of locations of this species, its importance, management requirements and potential threats. (ACTION: EN, MAFF)

5.5 Future research and monitoring

5.5.1 Collate information and resurvey extant sites where necessary to gain a more complete understanding of the current distribution and status of spreading hedge-parsley. This will determine the range over which conservation action is appropriate and help to clarify the threats to remaining populations. (ACTION: CCW, EN, JNCC).

5.5.2 Undertake monitoring on a representative number of extant sites with a view to refining conservation management techniques. Where possible, monitoring visits should be combined with meeting landowners to discuss conservation management for the species. (ACTION: EN, JNCC)

5.5.3 Undertake research to determine the selectivity of all graminicides currently in use so as to identify which, if any, are suitable for use in field margins that support this and other threatened arable species. (ACTION: JNCC)

5.6 Communications and publicity

5.6.1 Publicise the plight of this and other threatened arable species. Articles should be written for relevant conservation and farming magazines and newsletters. Botanists should be encouraged to report any new records, eg through Atlas 2000 recording. (ACTION: EN)

5.6.2 Develop links with European ecologists working to conserve threatened plants of arable habitats. (ACTION: JNCC)

5.6.3 Establish arable conservation display and education centres with the aim of raising public awareness of this threatened group of the UK flora. (ACTION: EN)

5.7 Links with other action plans

5.7.1 It is likely that implementation of this action plan will benefit other arable species, including *Arabis glabra, Bromus interruptus, Centaurea cyanus, Filago lutescens, Filago pyramidata, Fumaria occidentalis, Fumaria purpurea, Galeopsis angustifolia, Galium tricornutum, Scandix pecten-veneris, Silene gallica* and *Valerianella rimosa.*

5.7.2 The plan should be considered in conjunction with that for cereal field margins.

Torilis arvensis

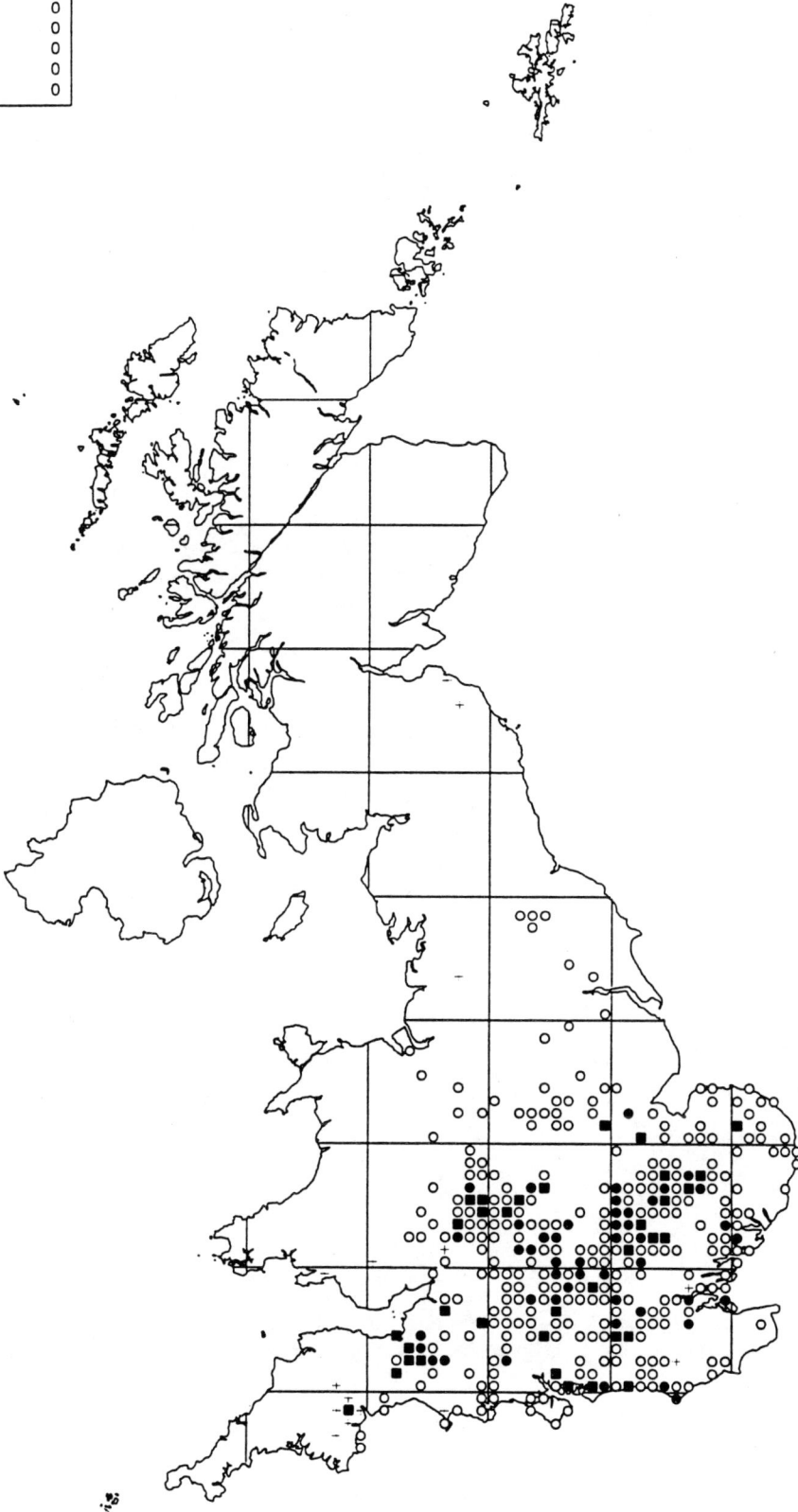

■	35	0
●	47	0
○	252	0
×	0	0
+	16	0

Distribution of Torilis arvensis - spreading hedge-parsley in Britain & N.Ireland, (by 10km square).
Source: British Red Data Book - Vascular plants, 1998, 3rd edition.

■ - records post 1980
● - records 1970 - 1987
○ - records pre 1970
× - introduced records post 1970
+ - introduced records pre 1970

255

Broad-fruited corn-salad (*Valerianella rimosa*)
Action Plan

1. Current status

1.1 Broad-fruited corn-salad is a plant of arable fields and other open habitats on chalk and limestone. It is an annual which germinates in late autumn, with a smaller flush in spring. Plants flower from late June to late July (sometimes August), with most seed being produced by August. Little is known about the dormancy characteristics of the seed.

1.2 Broad-fruited corn-salad was formerly recorded from southern England northwards as far as central Scotland, and also in Wales and Ireland. However, it was not as widespread as many other arable weeds, being recorded from only 43 ten km squares between 1930 and 1960. It has declined rapidly over the last 50 years and there may now be only two reliable sites in the UK (in Somerset and Gloucestershire), although there have also been recent records from Devon and Hampshire. Broad-fruited corn-salad has a predominantly southern-continental distribution in Europe. It has declined throughout much of the northern part of its range, but is not threatened in Europe as a whole.

1.3 In GB the species is classified as *Critically Endangered*. It receives general protection under the Wildlife and Countryside Act 1981.

2. Current factors causing loss or decline

Several features associated with the intensification of agriculture over the last 50 years have been responsible for the decline of broad-fruited corn-salad and are now proving to be constraints on its recovery. These include:

2.1 Increased use of herbicides and fertilisers.

2.2 The development of highly competitive crop varieties.

2.3 The destruction of field-edge refuges.

2.4 Early crop harvests (ie around mid-July).

2.5 The demise of traditional crop rotations.

2.6 Abandonment of marginal farmland and associated loss of ground disturbance.

3. Current action

3.1 One of the two sites is an SSSI and management is directed towards the conservation of broad-fruited corn-salad and other rare arable plants.

4. Action plan objectives and targets

4.1 Establish and maintain viable populations at all extant sites.

4.2 Facilitate natural colonisation of new sites.

4.3 Restore populations of broad-fruited corn-salad to eight suitable historic sites by 2003.

4.4 Establish an *ex-situ* programme to protect genetic diversity, create a reserve population and provide experimental material.

5. Proposed action with lead agencies

Because of the extreme rarity of this species, much of the action recommended here will be targeted to highly localised areas. Beneficial site management is a priority, but this should be combined with attempts to regenerate plants at former sites. It is also essential that, where possible, relevant agri-environment schemes are targeted to land adjacent to extant and restored sites so as to provide opportunities for the spread of this species.

5.1 Policy and legislation

5.1.1 Consider this species for inclusion on Schedule 8 of the Wildlife and Countryside Act 1981. (ACTION: DETR, JNCC)

5.1.2 Encourage the development of relevant agri-environment schemes, such as the pilot Arable Stewardship Scheme, as a potential means of re-establishing broad-fruited corn-salad in the countryside. When reviewing such schemes, consider whether changes are needed to increase their potential benefits for this and other threatened arable species. (ACTION: EN, MAFF)

5.2 Site safeguard and management

5.2.1 Ensure beneficial management at both key sites and refine techniques used as the results of research continue to emerge. (ACTION: EN)

5.2.2 Seek to develop a network of suitable habitats within the vicinity of broad-fruited corn-salad sites, thereby providing opportunities for its spread. Favourable management will include the relevant options outlined under the pilot Arable Stewardship Scheme, eg uncropped headlands (cultivated in autumn). (ACTION: EN, MAFF)

5.3 Species management and protection

5.3.1 Undertake trial management on at least eight sites where this species has recently been recorded with the aim of regenerating plants from the seed-bank. (ACTION: EN)

5.3.2 Assess the feasibility and desirability of reintroducing broad-fruited corn-salad at selected sites should regeneration from the seed-bank prove unsuccessful. (ACTION: EN, JNCC)

5.3.3 Collect seed from all extant sites and any restored sites and deposit in the Millenium Seed Bank at Wakehurst Place (Kew). Plants should be propagated for reintroductions if necessary. (ACTION: EN, RBG Kew)

5.4 Advisory

5.4.1 Advise landowners and managers of the presence and importance of broad-fruited corn-salad, specific management for its conservation, and any potentially damaging actions. (ACTION: EN)

5.4.2 As far as possible ensure that all relevant agri-environment project officers are advised of locations of this species, its importance, management requirements and potential threats. (ACTION: EN, MAFF)

5.5 Future research and monitoring

5.5.1 Collate information and resurvey extant and historic sites where necessary to gain a more complete understanding of the current distribution and status of broad-fruited corn-salad. This will determine the range over which conservation action is appropriate and help to clarify the threats to remaining populations. (ACTION: CCW, EN, JNCC).

5.5.2 Undertake regular monitoring at the main extant sites, and extend to any successfully restored sites, with a view to refining conservation management techniques. Where possible, monitoring visits should be combined with meeting landowners to discuss conservation management for the species. (ACTION: EN, JNCC)

5.5.3 Undertake research to determine the selectivity of all graminicides currently in use so as to identify which, if any, are suitable for use in field margins that support this and other threatened arable weed species. (ACTION: JNCC)

5.6 Communications and publicity

5.6.1 Publicise the plight of this and other threatened arable species. Articles should be written for relevant conservation and farming magazines and newsletters. Botanists should be encouraged to report any new records and be made aware of the characteristics that distinguish it from the more common narrow-fruited corn-salad (*V. dentata*). (ACTION: CCW, EN)

5.6.2 Develop links with European ecologists working to conserve threatened plants of arable habitats. (ACTION: JNCC)

5.6.3 Establish arable conservation display and education centres with the aim of raising public awareness of this threatened group of the UK flora. (ACTION: EN)

5.7 Links with other action plans

5.7.1 It is likely that implementation of this action plan will benefit other arable species, including *Arabis glabra, Bromus interruptus, Centaurea cyanus, Filago lutescens, Filago pyramidata, Fumaria occidentalis, Fumaria purpurea, Galeopsis angustifolia, Galium tricornutum, Scandix pecten-veneris, Silene gallica* and *Torilis arvensis.*

5.7.2 The plan should be considered in conjunction with that for cereal field margins.

Valerianella rimosa

■	4	0
●	9	0
○	104	0
✕	1	0
+	0	0

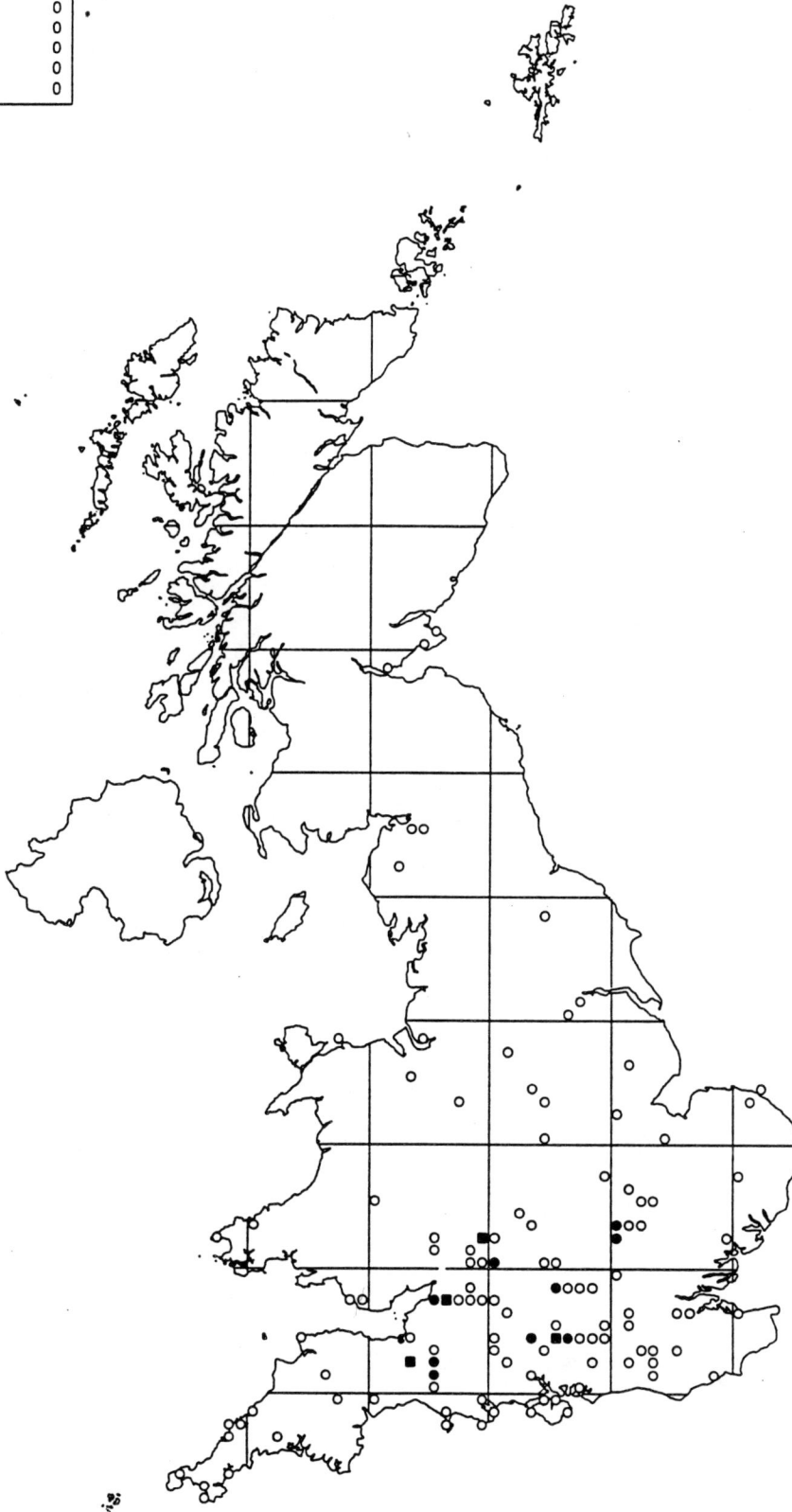

Distribution of Valerianella rimosa - broad-fruited corn-salad in Britain & N.Ireland, (by 10km square). Source: British Red Data Book - Vascular plants, 1998, 3rd edition.

■ - records post 1980
● - records 1970 - 1987
○ - records pre 1970
✕ - introduced records post 1970
+ - introduced records pre 1970

Oblong woodsia (*Woodsia ilvensis*)
Action Plan

1. Current status

1.1 Oblong woodsia is a small, tufted fern found in Britain in tree-less, rock habitats above 350 m, mainly on cliffs and crags but occasionally on stable screes. In other parts of the world it grows on similar habitats although these are usually in the woodland zone and sometimes in lowland and even coastal areas.

1.2 Currently there are fewer than 100 plants known in the UK, distributed between 11 sites (6 in Scotland, 1 in England and 4 in Wales), and 5 broad localities (Highland, Tayside, Dumfries, Cumbria and Gwynedd). The plant was eliminated from at least eight sites in Cumbria, Durham and Dumfries when fern collecting was popular during the Victorian era. Today, all colonies are declining or are at best stable, and all except the colony in Cumbria (around 80 plants) are extremely small (only 1-7 plants). Despite the availability of apparently suitable habitats, there is no evidence of regeneration, recruitment, or spread at any site in Britain. Oblong woodsia is widespread in the boreal regions of North America and Europe/Asia but rare in Europe south of Scandinavia.

1.3 In GB oblong woodsia is classified as *Endangered*. It is specially protected under Schedule 8 of the Wildlife and Countryside Act 1981.

2. Current factors causing loss or decline

2.1 British populations, being at the edge of the range, may be particularly vulnerable to recent climatic changes. Prolonged summer drought has been seen to cause frond desiccation and spore abortion.

2.2 It is assumed that the oblong woodsia, like other very rare ferns with small populations, is still at some risk from collectors.

2.3 There is no evidence of recruitment at British populations of this species but the factors responsible for this are not yet clear. It has been speculated that the climate at its sites may now be unsuitable or that collecting may have affected the genetic variation in the species.

3. Current action

3.1 Oblong woodsia is included in SNH's Species Action Programme and is to be included in EN's Species Recovery Programme.

3.2 All colonies are within SSSIs; three are within NNRs.

3.3 Spores were collected, under license, from most sites in 1996 and placed in a spore-bank at RBG Edinburgh. Attempts are being made to establish *ex-situ* collections of sporophytes from these spores.

3.4 Two sporophytes have been collected under licence from EN for growing at the RBG Edinburgh.

3.5 The ecology and reproductive biology of oblong woodsia is being investigated by RBG Edinburgh and the University of Edinburgh.

4. Action plan objectives and targets

4.1 Maintain populations at all remaining sites.

4.2 Reverse decline of three populations by 2008.

4.3 Restore populations at three former sites by 2003.

5. Proposed action with lead agencies

Continued research into the factors causing decline and preventing recruitment is urgently needed to identify practical solutions for remedial management. Almost all surviving populations are very small and declines are continuing, so there is a clear short-term need to supplement the most threatened populations to permit their survival. An attempt also needs to be made to restore populations lost as a result of past collecting.

5.1 Policy and legislation

5.1.1 No action proposed.

5.2 Site safeguard and management

5.2.1 At three sites threatened with extinction, experimentally implement practical recommendations, resulting from research in 5.5.3, in an effort to reverse declines. (ACTION: CCW, RBG Edinburgh, SNH)

5.3 Species management and protection

5.3.1 Establish *ex-situ* collections of spores and sporophytes ensuring that collections do not further reduce likelihood of recruitment. If stocks permit, make spores and/or plants available to specialist horticultural outlets and fern enthusiasts to reduce any temptation to collect from the wild. (ACTION: RBG Edinburgh)

5.3.2 Restore populations to three former sites (identified in 5.5.2 as suitable) by 2003. (ACTION: CCW, EN, RBG Edinburgh, SNH)

5.3.3 If methods of improving natural recruitment fail (see 5.2.1) or cannot be defined, carry out reinforcement of three populations threatened with imminent extinction, ensuring that any period of *ex-situ* cultivation does not lead to any reduction in the genetic variation of introduced material. (ACTION: CCW, EN, RBG Edinburgh, SNH)

5.4   Advisory

5.4.1 Ensure that landowners at all remaining sites are aware of the presence and significance of this species. (ACTION: CCW, EN, SNH)

5.5   Future research and monitoring

5.5.1 Ensure that the location of all individuals at known populations is recorded and monitor their fate at regular intervals to assess damage, patterns of survival, and viable spore production. Monitor suitable adjacent areas for recruitment. (ACTION: CCW, EN, SNH)

5.5.2 Survey all former sites to confirm that the species is absent and report on the suitability of sites for reintroduction. (ACTION: CCW, EN, SNH)

5.5.3 Complete research on the reproductive biology and ecology of oblong woodsia to identify causal agents of decline and propose practical measures to circumvent them. (ACTION: RBG Edinburgh)

5.5.4 Carry out investigations of genetic variation in existing populations of oblong woodsia (if this can be done without threatening them further) to determine if loss of genetic variation might be inhibiting recruitment, and to guide management and reintroduction policies. (ACTION: CCW, EN, RBG Edinburgh, SNH)

5.6   Communications and publicity

5.6.1 Incorporate oblong woodsia in education programmes on rare British plants. (ACTION: CCW, EN, RBG Edinburgh, RBG Kew, SNH)

5.7   Links with other action plans

5.7.1 None proposed.

Woodsia ilvensis

■	4	•	0
●	2		0
O	7		0
✕	0		0
+	0		0

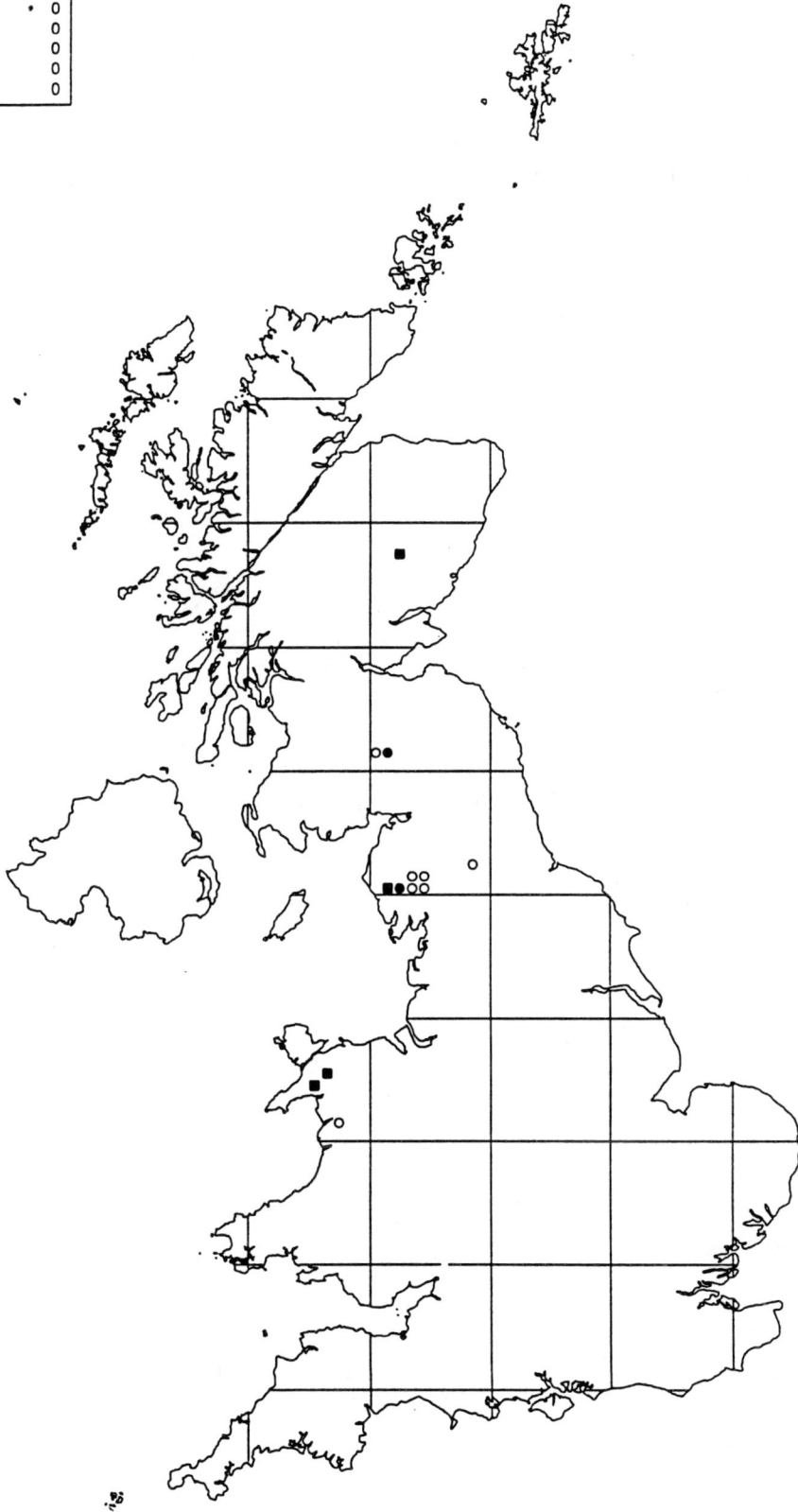

Distribution of Woodsia ilvensis - oblong woodsia in Britain & N.Ireland, (by 10km square). Source British Red Data Book - Vascular plants, 1998, 3rd edition.

■ - records post 1980
● - records 1970 - 1987
O - records pre 1970
✕ - introduced records post 1970
+ - introduced records pre 1970

Annex 5   Action plans costings

Summary table showing estimated additional costs in £K per year for the first and second five years of each Species Action Plan

Species Action Plan	1st five years	2nd five years
Mammals		
Barbastelle bat *Barbastella barbastellus*	27.8	26.7
Bechstein's bat *Myotis bechsteinii*	28.0	26.9
Lesser horseshoe bat *Rhinolophorus hipposideros*	33.3	26.7
Birds		
Marsh warbler *Acrocephalus palustris*	7.1	4.1
Nightjar *Caprimulgus europaeus*	29.5[1]	15.0[1]
Linnet *Carduelis cannabina*	89.0	77.0
Cirl bunting *Emberiza cirlus*	134.0	119.0
Reed bunting *Emberiza schoeniclus*	98.9	77.0
Wryneck *Jynx torquilla*	2.0[2]	10.0[2]
Red-backed shrike *Lanius collurio*	11.1	0.9
Woodlark *Lullula arborea*	15.4[1]	20.0[1]
Common scoter *Melanitta nigra*	80.5	69.3
Corn bunting *Miliaria calandra*	89.6	77.0
Spotted flycatcher *Muscicapa striata*	18.2	5.0
Tree sparrow *Passer montanus*	101.1	87.0
Red-necked phalarope *Phalaropus lobatus*	12.3[3]	3.0[3]
Bullfinch *Pyrrhula pyrrhula*	88.7	80.6
Roseate tern *Sterna dougallii*	2.5[4]	0.0[4]
Turtle dove *Streptopelia turtur*	92.1	75.0
Amphibian		
Pool frog *Rana lessonae*	18.3[5]	20.9[5]
Vascular plants		
an alchemilla *Alchemilla minima*	16.4	11.7
Tower mustard *Arabis glabra*	25.5	19.8

1 Many of the necessary actions (and costs) are covered by the lowland heathland HAP.
2 Many of the necessary actions (and costs) are covered by the native pinewood HAP.
3 These figures are in addition to current and projected costs of £25k/annum for existing programmes.
4 The SAP relies heavily on the continuation of current action.
5 Costings assume that reintroduction is attempted

Species Action Plan	1st five years	2nd five years
Wild asparagus *Asparagus officinalis* ssp *prostratus*	11.3	6.5
Interrupted brome *Bromus interruptus*	10.9	8.8
Scottish small-reed *Calamagrostis scotica*	3.7	0.9
Prickly sedge *Carex muricata* ssp *muricata*	9.2	3.4
True fox sedge *Carex vulpina*	15.2	5.0
Cornflower *Centaurea cyanus*	22.0	8.3
Shetland mouse-ear *Cerastium nigrescens*	3.1	1.3
Stinking hawk's-beard *Crepis foetida*	2.7[6]	2.1[6]
Deptford pink *Dianthus armeria*	15.5	4.3
Red-tipped cudweed *Filago lutescens*	20.9	14.2
Broad-leaved cudweed *Filago pyramidata*	16.9	12.1
Purple ramping-fumitory *Fumaria purpurea*	32.1	23.5
Red hemp-nettle *Galeopsis angustifolia*	43.0	45.1
Corn cleavers *Galium tricornutum*	18.5	11.8
Dune gentian *Gentianella uliginosa*	28.7	13.2
Hawkweeds *Hieraceum* sect *Alpestria*	19.9	8.8
Pigmy rush *Juncus pygmaeus*	19.9	12.4
Cut-grass *Leersia oryzoides*	9.6	1.3
Rock sea-lavenders *Limonium binervosum* agg	39.1	18.5
Marsh clubmoss *Lycopodiella inundata*	69.4	48.1
Pennyroyal *Mentha pulegium*	26.1	20.7
Pillwort *Pilularia globulifera*	51.1	47.1
Grass-wrack pondweed *Potamogeton compressus*	32.3	16.5
Woolly willow *Salix lanata*	19.4	8.4
Shepherd's needle *Scandix pecten-veneris*	20.9	10.3
Triangular club-rush *Schoenoplectus triqueter*	15.9	1.6
Perennial knawel *Scleranthus perennis* ssp *prostratus*	2.9[6]	0.9[6]
Small-flowered catchfly *Silene gallica*	55.8	44.9
Greater water-parsnip *Sium latifolium*	14.4	3.3
Ley's whitebeam *Sorbus leyana*	13.4	2.3
Cotswold pennycress *Thlaspi perfoliatum*	14.7	7.0
Spreading hedge-parsley *Torilis arvensis*	25.4	10.9
Broad-fruited corn-salad *Valerianella rimosa*	17.9	11.0
Oblong woodsia *Woodsia ilvensis*	36.0	12.2

6 Costings exclude work planned under existing species recovery project.

Annex 6. List of abbreviations and acronyms

ASSI	Area of Special Scientific Interest (Northern Ireland)
BBS	Breeding Bird Survey
BTO	British Trust for Ornithology
CAP	EC Common Agricultural Policy
CBC	Common Bird Census
CCW	Countryside Council for Wales
DANI	Department of Agriculture for Northern Ireland
DANI(FS)	Department of Agriculture for Northern Ireland Forest Service
DETR	Department of the Environment, Transport and the Regions
DTI	Department of Trade and Industry
EA	Environment Agency
EC	European Community
EH	English Heritage
EHS	Environment and Heritage Service (Northern Ireland)
EN	English Nature
ESA	Environmentally Sensitive Area
FA	Forestry Authority
FC	Forestry Commission
FE	Forest Enterprise
GCT	Game Conservancy Trust
HS	Historic Scotland
IDB	Internal Drainage Board
IUCN	International Union for the Conservation of Nature
JNCC	Joint Nature Conservation Committee
LA	Local Authority
MAFF	Ministry of Agriculture, Fisheries and Food
MCA	Maritime and Coastguard Agency (Scotland)
MoD	Ministry of Defence
NGO	Non-governmental organisation
NNR	National Nature Reserve
NoSWA	North of Scotland Water Authority
RBG Kew/Edinburgh	Royal Botanic Gardens
RSPB	Royal Society for the Protection of Birds
SAC	Special Area of Conservation
SEPA	Scottish Environmental Protection Agency
SNCO	Statutory Nature Conservation Organisation
SNH	Scottish Natural Heritage
SO	The Scottish Office
SOAEFD	Scottish Office Agriculture, Environment and Fisheries Department
SPA	Special Protection Area
SSSI	Site of Special Scientific Interest (Britain)
WGS	Woodland Grant Scheme
WOAD	Welsh Office Agriculture Department